China's New Creative Clusters

Recognising that creativity is a major driving force in the post-industrial economy, the Chinese government has recently established a range of 'creative clusters' – industrial parks devoted to media industries, and arts districts – in order to promote the development of the creative industries.

This book examines these new creative clusters, outlining their nature and purpose, and assessing their effectiveness. Drawing on case studies of a range of cluster models, and comparing them with international examples, the book demonstrates that creativity, both in China and internationally, is in fact a process of fitting new ideas to existing patterns, models and formats. It shows how large and exceptionally impressive creative clusters have been successfully established, but raises the important questions of whether profit or culture is the driving force, and of whether the bringing together of independent-minded, creative people, entrepreneurial businessmen, preferential policies and foreign investment may in time lead to unintended changes in social and political attitudes in China, including a weakening of state bureaucratic power. An important contribution to the existing literature on the subject, this book will be of great interest to scholars of urban studies, cultural geography, cultural economics and Asian studies.

Michael Keane is an ARC Centre Fellow at the Australian Research Council Centre of Excellence for Creative Industries and Innovation, Queensland University of Technology, Brisbane. His research interests include China's cultural and media policy, creative clusters in China and East Asia and East Asian cultural exports.

Media, Culture and Social Change in Asia
Series Editor: Stephanie Hemelryk Donald
RMIT University Melbourne

Editorial Board:
Devleena Ghosh, *University of Technology, Sydney*
Yingjie Guo, *University of Technology, Sydney*
K.P. Jayasankar, *Unit for Media and Communications, Tata Institute of Social Sciences, Bombay*
Vera Mackie, *University of Melbourne*
Anjali Monteiro, *Unit for Media and Communications, Tata Institute of Social Sciences, Bombay*
Laikwan Pang, *Chinese University of Hong Kong*
Gary Rawnsley, *University of Leeds*
Ming-yeh Rawnsley, *University of Leeds*
Adrian Vickers, *University of Sydney*
Jing Wang, *MIT*

The aim of this series is to publish original, high-quality work by both new and established scholars in the West and the East, on all aspects of media, culture and social change in Asia.

1 **Television Across Asia**
Television industries, programme formats and globalisation
Edited by Albert Moran and Michael Keane

2 **Journalism and Democracy in Asia**
Edited by Angela Romano and Michael Bromley

3 **Cultural Control and Globalization in Asia**
Copyright, piracy and cinema
Laikwan Pang

4 **Conflict, Terrorism and the Media in Asia**
Edited by Benjamin Cole

5 **Media and the Chinese Diaspora**
Community, communications and commerce
Edited by Wanning Sun

6 **Hong Kong Film, Hollywood and the New Global Cinema**
No film is an island
Edited by Gina Marchetti and Tan See Kam

7 **Media in Hong Kong**
Press freedom and political change 1967–2005
Carol P. Lai

8 **Chinese Documentaries**
From dogma to polyphony
Yingchi Chu

9 **Japanese Popular Music**
Culture, authenticity and power
Carolyn S. Stevens

10 **The Origins of the Modern Chinese Press**
The influence of the Protestant missionary press in late Qing China
Xiantao Zhang

11 **Created in China**
    The great new leap forward
    Michael Keane

12 **Political Regimes and the Media in Asia**
    Edited by Krishna Sen and Terence Lee

13 **Television in Post-Reform China**
    Serial dramas, Confucian leadership and the global television market
    Ying Zhu

14 **Tamil Cinema**
    The cultural politics of India's other film industry
    Edited by Selvaraj Velayutham

15 **Popular Culture in Indonesia**
    Fluid identities in post-authoritarian politics
    Edited by Ariel Heryanto

16 **Television in India**
    Satellites, politics and cultural change
    Edited by Nalin Mehta

17 **Media and Cultural Transformation in China**
    Haiqing Yu

18 **Global Chinese Cinema**
    The culture and politics of hero
    Edited by Gary D. Rawnsley and Ming-Yeh T. Rawnsley

19 **Youth, Society and Mobile Media in Asia**
    Edited by Stephanie Hemelryk Donald, Theresa Dirndorfer Anderson and Damien Spry

20 **The Media, Cultural Control and Government in Singapore**
    Terence Lee

21 **Politics and the Media in Twenty-First Century Indonesia**
    Edited by Krishna Sen and David T. Hill

22 **Media, Social Mobilization and Mass Protests in Post-colonial Hong Kong**
    The power of a critical event
    Francis L. F. Lee and Joseph M. Chan

23 **HIV/AIDS, Health and the Media in China**
    Imagined immunity through racialized disease
    Johanna Hood

24 **Islam and Popular Culture in Indonesia and Malaysia**
    Edited by Andrew N. Weintraub

25 **Online Society in China**
    Creating, celebrating, and instrumentalising the online carnival
    Edited by David Kurt Herold and Peter Marolt

26 **Rethinking Transnational Chinese Cinemas**
    The Amoy-dialect film industry in Cold War Asia
    Jeremy E. Taylor

27 **Film in Contemporary Southeast Asia**
    Cultural interpretation and social intervention
    Edited by David C. L. Lim and Hiroyuki Yamamoto

28 **China's New Creative Clusters**
    Governance, human capital, and investment
    Michael Keane

China's New Creative Clusters
Governance, human capital and investment

Michael Keane

LONDON AND NEW YORK

First published 2011 by Routledge
2 Park Square, Milton Park, Abingdon, Oxon OX14 4RN

Simultaneously published in the USA and Canada
by Routledge
711 Third Ave, New York, NY 10017

Routledge is an imprint of the Taylor & Francis Group, an informa business

© 2011 Michael Keane

The right of Michael Keane to be identified as author of this work has been asserted by him in accordance with sections 77 and 78 of the Copyright, Designs and Patents Act 1988.

All rights reserved. No part of this book may be reprinted or reproduced or utilised in any form or by any electronic, mechanical, or other means, now known or hereafter invented, including photocopying and recording, or in any information storage or retrieval system, without permission in writing from the publishers.

Trademark notice: Product or corporate names may be trademarks or registered trademarks, and are used only for identification and explanation without intent to infringe.

British Library Cataloguing in Publication Data
A catalogue record for this book is available from the British Library

Library of Congress Cataloging in Publication Data

China's new creative clusters: governance, human capital, and investment / Michael Keane.
p. cm. – (Media, culture and social change in Asia; 28)
Includes bibliographical references and index.
1. Cultural industries–China. 2. Creative ability–China. 3. Human capital–China. 4. Investments–China. 5. China–Politics and government–21st century. I. Title.
HD9999.C9473K4534 2011
338.8'7–dc23
2011038099

ISBN 978-0-415-60396-6 (hbk)
ISBN 978-0-203-12450-5 (ebk)

Typeset in Times New Roman by PDQ Typesetting Ltd

Printed and bound in Great Britain by
CPI Antony Rowe, Chippenham, Wiltshire

Contents

List of tables and plates	viii
Acknowledgements	ix
Introduction: China's new creative clusters	1
1 Harmonising creativity	14
2 Redesigning China's creative space	37
3 Clusters and regional development	57
4 Beijing: creative capital or state-managed openness?	78
5 Art districts: the pin-up child of the Chinese creative economy	98
6 Shanghai's cluster-led creative renaissance	118
7 Media districts, parks and bases	137
8 Culture, creativity, innovation, imagination	159
Appendix 1: Category confusion	180
Notes	183
References	185
Index	200

Tables and plates

Tables

1.1	The innovation ecology of the Chinese cultural economy	32
2.1	Typologies of cultural and creative clusters	52
7.1	Key moments in Chinese media reform	140
7.2	National animation bases accredited by SARFT	155

Plates

1.1	Innovation is the soul of a nation's progress, Nanjing Rd, Shanghai	18
3.1	Loft 49, Hangzhou	74
4.1	Fangjia 46, cluster certificate	93
4.2	Fangjia 46, Beijing	94
5.1	798 Art Zone, Beijing	109
6.1	Tianzifang, Shanghai	124
6.2	Xindanwei, Shanghai	131

Acknowledgements

The research was made possible by an Australian Research Council Discovery Grant, Governance, Human Capital and Regional Investment in China's New Creative Clusters (2008–2010). My partner investigator was Prof Zhang Xiaoming of the Chinese Academy of Social Sciences (CASS). I would like to thank Prof Zhang and his team at CASS, Hui Ming, Lhamo Yeshi and Zhou Jiangang for their support. However, I would like to emphasise at the outset that the opinions expressed in this monograph are mine unless otherwise attributed. Likewise, any mistakes or factual errors are my own responsibility. I would like to acknowledge the support provided by the Australian Research Council Centre of Excellence for Creative Industries and Innovation (CCI) at the Queensland University of Technology where I was employed as a research fellow for the duration of this project.

Personal acknowledgements

Many people helped me in this project. Some names I have forgotten and some name cards I have misplaced. However, many people can be identified, people who helped me directly with the research, in accessing documents, securing resources and in the translation of interview material. My special thanks go to my research assistant in the final year of the project Hui Li, always reliable, and a great asset to the project. Thanks go also to Weihong Zhang, who provided invaluable support in the first two years of the project. I engaged in lively discussion with my PhD students who each had their own journeys, often coinciding with my interests. Angela Huang assisted with my search for information in Beijing's Chaoyang District, while taking in the delicacies of the capital's restaurants. Wen Wen guided me through the streets of Hangzhou and accompanied me to LOFT 49, White Horse Lake and Xixi Wetlands. Henry Li was a wonderful sounding board for ideas. Bonnie Liu contributed much to the work on media and animation. I benefited from discussions of ideas (not always about clusters) with Elaine Zhao, Joy

Zhang, Dai Juncheng, Guo Yong, Tim Lindgren, Yang Yongzhong, Ding Jijun, Linda Watterson, Seiko Yasumoto, Falk Hartig, Siti Isa, Sen Lee, Tingting Song, Hui Richards and Vijay Anand. I have had many engaging conversations on China and creative clusters with Justin O'Connor and Xin Gu over the past three years. I learnt much from my colleagues: Stuart Cunningham, John Hartley, Jean Burgess, Jason Potts, John Banks, Lucy Montgomery, Greg Hearn, Jo Tacchi (now at RMIT), Brian Fitzgerald, Terry Flew, Christoph Antons, Anna Rooke, and Cynthia Macnee.

I met persons at international conferences who became interested in my field of endeavour. I would like to particularly thank Jane Zheng for reading the final draft and for correcting a few of my errors.

In Beijing I received support from a number of friends and colleagues. At the Communication University of China (CUC) I spent a great deal of time with Fan Zhou, Qi Yongfeng, Li Huailiang, Yang Jianfei and Liu Jianghong who patiently helped me to understand some of the subtle differences between culture and creativity in Beijing. Zhang Jingcheng and Zeng Fanying at the Beijing Academy of Science and Technology (BJAST) are great friends and were a source of information and specialist knowledge. At Renmin University JinYuanpu was always helpful and encouraging, pointing me in the right direction. I am especially indebted to Su Tong and his own band of brothers: Fu Jing, Ma Chenyu and Wang Bing for inspired brainstorming. In Shanghai I had fantastic support from Marina Guo, who spent time at QUT on an Endeavour Scholarship and who is now working at the Shanghai Theatre Academy. Liu Yan and Chen Xu at Xindanwei were great sources of inspiration and 'sharism'. I would also like to thank Li Wuwei, Wang Ruzhong (SASS), Chen Beibei, Qian Xia, Jin Weidong (M50), Carol Wang (Shangtex) and Pan Jin.

I would also like to acknowledge the following people (and interviewees) for their time and advice, whether virtual or face to face: Shaun Chang, Ranus Kwok, Bert de Muynck, Mónica Carriço, John Howkins, Simon Evans, Philip Dodd, Brendan Harkin, Megan Elliot, Ned Rossiter, Simon Roodhouse, David Liu (Dotman), Xu Shuan (Shiao), George Yu (Hong Yang Cartoons Co.), James Xia (Wuxi), Zhang Xixun and Michael Jiang (Suzhou Animation Park), Qiu Dailun, Peter Han and Glacier Chen (Foshan Creative Industries Park), Du Yubo (LOFT49 and thanks for the scenic tour); Arito Go, Wei Na, Christopher Mahoney, Roger Lee, Gao Yin, Da Li, Zhang Chengcheng (Great Wall), Song Bo, Wang Yudong, Ma Da, Freeman Lau, Tom and Jerry Wang, and Maggie Wang.

Thanks also to the Media, Culture and Social Change in Asia series editor Stephanie Hemelryk Donald for her support of this work from the very beginning. Thanks to the editorial and production team at Routledge: Peter Sowden, Jillian Morrison and James Rabson.

My deepest thanks as always go to my partner Leigh, who was uncomplaining as I struggled to get this book completed. Finally, this book is dedicated to my father William John Keane who passed away in March 2011 aged 91.

Introduction: China's new creative clusters

>   The eagle old on Liangshan Marsh
>   Receives new wings to help its flight;
>   At the mountain stronghold
>   A renovation will be in sight
>   *The Water Margin* (Shuihu Zhuan) Ch. 48[1]

This is a book about culture, innovation and creativity in the People's Republic of China. Culture is heavily informed by traditional values and is highly politicised, largely due to the legacy of state management of cultural activities over the past several decades. Innovation and creativity are latecomers; in effect they are 'gains of trade', forced into the service of government over the past two decades as China opened to the world. With China's leaders determining that the country will be an 'innovative nation' by 2020, the challenge is to determine what kind of innovation China will excel in. On a political level innovation has often been used to describe China's history of reform (*gaige*) and its great reformers, Sun Yat-Sen, Mao Zedong and Deng Xiaoping. As scholars of modern Chinese history will be aware, to reform and remake society has been the defining objective of government since the collapse of the Qing Dynasty in 1911.

Beginning in 2006 creativity joined innovation in government rhetoric. Internationally, creativity is associated with individualism, with freedom of expression and cultural diversity. Its introduction into the lexicon of government has not been without opposition. Chris Bilton writes: 'The challenge of managing and structuring creative processes and people centres on the management and tolerance of contradictions' (Bilton 2007: 20). Chinese Communist Party cultural officials in Beijing, those charged with the responsibility of resolving ideological contradictions, initially restricted the dissemination of this 'foreign' idea. However, the allure was too powerful. Local government authorities and entrepreneurs saw creativity as a way to attract investment, especially in infrastructure development and real estate. It had international prestige. It offered an alternative to socialist culture. In order for creativity to be rehabilitated in China, its advocates therefore had to render it functional. It had to be 'industrialised' and 'harmonised'. This required giving it a collective identity. The dominant symbol of creativity in China would become the 'creative cluster' (*chuangyi jijuqu*). The overriding logic for the clustering of media and cultural activities from a national perspective is enhancing soft power and identifying human capital. The fact that clusters might attract creative talent provides a solution to the conundrum of creativity: what is it and how can it be harnessed? From a regional and local government level the principal logic of clustering is generation of tax revenues and real estate development. In other words, the local state is revenue-oriented and exploits the expansion of cluster projects as a means to stimulate urban growth (Zheng 2010).

Three assumptions

My argument in this book is that culture, innovation and creativity are co-joined and co-dependent. Culture provides the symbolic resources for the evolution of ideas. Creative inspiration, invention and discovery offer up new variations of existing resources. While innovation is essentially a more practical economic concern, it is often used synonymously with creativity. Accordingly, the book challenges a number of assumptions about the role that creativity is intended to play in China's development.

The first assumption is that Western-style pluralism is not necessary for creativity to flourish; in other words, creativity is a pragmatic solution to economic issues more so than an essential component of civil society. People will be creative if they are given appropriate incentives and work conditions. Of course, this assumption makes sense depending on how creativity is defined and evaluated. However, recent studies have demonstrated that provision of incentives alone can lead to impoverished outputs (Amabile 1996; Amabile and Kramer 2010). Creative sparks are more likely to be enhanced when people are emotionally engaged with their work.

The second assumption is that China's national competitiveness will be enhanced by providing managed work spaces for artists, designers, media producers and related occupations. There are two problems with this assumption. First, in the current 'weightless' post-industrial era of digital technology and falling communication costs, co-location in physical space is less important than it was several years ago when the cluster model came on to the radar of policymakers in China. Second, without effective governance there is no guarantee that corralling people in managed spaces will encourage trust and sharing of ideas and therefore lead to innovations. The provision of cheap or subsidised facilities itself is not enough to guarantee productive interaction between participants; while these factors are important in seeding business start-ups, dependency on policy largesse may lead to lock-in effects; in other words, a reluctance to take risks or seek out new approaches.

The third assumption relates to what Florida (2002) calls 'the creative class': this is the thesis that creative people are highly mobile and will flock to places that are open and culturally diverse. While there is a great deal of evidence to support this proposition, most of is taken from studies of liberal democratic societies. In China people are far less mobile due to the need to have residency permits. Moreover, the kind of cultural diversity displayed in many so-called creative districts in China is compromised by people's awareness of political limits on expression.

In this study I use the term 'cluster' to describe a geographically defined space where cultural activities occur or where businesses assemble to produce products and services for domestic or international consumption. In order to gain an insight into how China's new creative clusters are managed and funded, I spent a considerable amount of time visiting sites over a period of three years. I was assisted by many colleagues in China who were interested in the goals of my research. Undoubtedly some were sceptical that an outsider might be able to understand the complicated arrangements pertaining to cultural management; others were keen to share insights and to learn from international experiences. I presented my findings at conferences and this led to invitations to inspect emerging developments. In total I visited more than 50 cluster projects over three years, ranging from art districts to media bases to science and technology incubators. Most of my information came from interviews although I conducted surveys at several of the sites. My primary points of contact were cluster managers and employees of businesses. I also spoke with artists, designers, new media practitioners, officials, academics, residents and other visitors to these sites.

Industrial clusters

Scholars have frequently invoked the industrial cluster to describe China's rapid economic development and its dominance in exports. Originating from British neoclassical economist Alfred Marshall's 'industrial districts' (Marshall 1920), clusters gained new significance following Michael Porter's influential account of *The Competitive Advantage of Nations* (Porter 1990). Porter expanded his advocacy on clusters, writing in 1998: 'Today's economic map of the world is dominated by what I call clusters: critical masses – in one place – of unusual competitive success in particular fields' (Porter 1998: 78).

Studies on clusters have absorbed ideas from a wide range of disciplines and sub-disciplines. Accordingly, terminologies vary according to geographical location and spheres of activity; e.g. innovative milieu, learning regions, regional innovation systems and creative clusters to name but a few. In China the cultural (and creative) cluster concept is applied liberally to precincts (*yuanqu*), theme parks (*zhuti gongyuan*), culture streets (*wenhua jie*), film, TV and animation bases (*yingshi jidi*) and multimedia corridors (*duo meiti zoulang*). Many of these projects proudly bear the names of industrial spaces, now given a new lease of life with the injection of creative human capital.

The industrial cluster model first came to attention in China during the early 1980s as the enforced communes of Mao Zedong's revolutionary socialism gave way to another form of collective organisation under Deng Xiaoping's stewardship. Town and Village Enterprises, or TVEs (*xiangzhen qiye*), were concentrations of light industrial activity, often producing household goods, usually located outside city cores. In some cases these TVEs were owned by the local governments; in other cases they were joint enterprises with private capital from local, national and international sources (Gu and Lundvall 2006). Their success spurred other economic experiments, including the start-up of private firms based on small family workshops.

From 1988 onwards, economic and technology zones appeared (ETZs), first in the southern coastal areas of China and later extending to a large number of 'open' cities (McGee *et al.* 2007). Many of the ETZs featured high-technology parks or innovation parks, which were meant to attract foreign investment often through diasporic networks. By the 1990s a consensus was achieved among economic reformers: agglomeration economies were the best way of utilising material resources and managing low-cost human capital. Industrial districts and clusters increased in number. Such clustering parks were particularly suited to low-end manufacturing: according to a leading Chinese scholar they took 'the low road' (Wang Jici 2007, 2007a). Whereas clusters in developed countries have tended to specialise in higher-value niches, those in developing countries such as China serve segments of the market where competitiveness is determined by price.

Notwithstanding the road chosen, the most noteworthy aspect of this economic model is that districts, towns and even cities opted to become specialised production centres, churning out socks, clocks, toys, ties, shoes, belts and a range of household appliances. Provinces such as Zhejiang and Guangdong took the lead in this 'small dog economy', Zhejiang with its so-called lump economies (*kuaizhuang jingji*) and Guangdong with its specialised towns (*zhuanye zhen*). The main characteristic of such industrial clusters was that they were locally born, locally rooted and locally embedded: they formed quickly, becoming suppliers of components for global production chains, and in doing so demonstrated a sophisticated understanding of markets (Wang and Mei 2009).

These emerging 'forces of production' appealed to the values of collectivism, nationalism and modernisation. China's cultural policy-makers dared to imagine the next step. Could Chinese cultural activities be made more competitive? How could Chinese culture modernise? In the late 1990s Chinese culture was facing a crisis as the nation moved closer to being admitted into the World Trade Organisation (WTO). Joining the global trade regime was essential for long-term economic security; China's workers and enterprises would stand to benefit from the efficiencies of trade competition and would learn from international markets. Joining the WTO also provided the opportunity for China to be at the centre of the world, albeit the world of trade, after many years of isolation. Reclaiming a 'centre mentality' had much to do with gaining international and regional respect. In the twentieth century China had gone from being a backward nation to a modern society. For many the next step was to gain international respect for innovation and creativity.

International evidence pointed to the success of places: New York's Soho and Greenwich Village, and London's West End. Could the industrial cluster model be extended to culture? Although these 'clusters' were in capitalist countries and their success was in the realm of entertainment and leisure, this did not dissuade China's cultural reformers. The economic reforms in China had put more money in people's pockets, cities were expanding and consumers were spending more on cultural products. Private enterprises were forming as the state moved away from direct management of culture. Media production companies, post-production companies, advertising firms, animation businesses, music labels and art suppliers, and private galleries represented the new face of China's culture.

Leading Chinese officials, noting the rise of cultural consumption, were convinced that industrialisation (*gongye hua*) was the way forward. Industrialisation had worked effectively in manufacturing clusters, in free trade zones and in town and villages enterprises (TVEs). China's media and cultural sectors would become industries; these industries would be grouped into conglomerates; they would be organised efficiently; this would allow them to generate revenue while serving their essential function of educating the population. Within a few years this momentum led to the unveiling of the 'cultural industries'.

The creative industries: a contradiction in terms?

In 1998, when this industrial momentum was building, the 'creative industries' were born in the UK. The creative industries were the key element of a strategy devised by the Blair Labour government to promote a new image, which pundits called 'cool Britannia'. In part, the creative industries were about breaking away from a traditional image of conservative Britain, a nation that rose to greatness from the Industrial Revolution. The plan was to rebrand Britain, not celebrate the past. In confirming things that were 'cool' and British, such as the Beatles, Andrew Lloyd Weber and Norman Foster, the creative industries were about the future; they were about intangibles such as design services, digital content and copyrights. They celebrated taking risk-takers and entrepreneurs – and small and medium businesses which came to be called 'the independents' (Leadbeater and Oakley 1999).

The relationship between the creative industries and creativity would become a divisive issue. Much earlier Raymond Williams had written:

> no word in English carries a more consistently positive reference than creative... yet clearly the very width of the reference involves not only a difficulty of meaning, but also through habit a kind of unthinking repetition which at times makes the word seem useless.
>
> (Williams 1988: 19)

Almost all current definitions of creativity and innovation agree on the importance of three attributes: *newness, value* and *usefulness* (Rehn and de Cock 2009; Boden 2004). Of these three most attention goes to the first, which is often expressed in legal texts, in the economics of innovation, and in cognitive psychology as 'novelty'. The widely held assumption that originality and novelty are fundamental to the creative process is to some extent ideological. Creativity is not a neutral idea. This assumption predisposes us to think that what is old world/ old economy is in need of change and creativity is the means to deliver a better world – for instance manufacturing and processing industries are polluting while design is clean.

Despite the general celebration of novelty, the creative industries, as defined globally, are made up of practices, occupations and commodities that are more often routine, frequently standardised and generally derivative. The fashion industry identifies its outputs as creative but its success comes from recycling trends and picking the right time to introduce these into the media. Television is endlessly repetitive: reality TV is frequently concerned with the mundane and the familiar. Formats dominate schedules. Creative occupations are also problematic. Are pastry chefs and hairdressers creative? What about scientists; shouldn't we consider their outputs as creative even if they spend a great deal of time in labs?

The discourse of the 'creative economy', which has had a positive reception globally, beginning with the 2001 book of the same name by John Howkins (2001), and extending more recently with the *Global Creative Economy Report 2008* (UNCTAD 2008), has produced a massive endeavour to categorise creative occupations and creative goods and services, and then to associate credible value to their outputs. The inclusion of non-creative activities in the UNCTAD report has provided a licence for countries and regions to expand their repertoire of creative activities, which has in turn led to inflated data and the inclusion of dubious categories such as photographic plates, carpet manufacturing, antiques, toys and tourism. A more helpful term is the 'cultural economy', which allows for the inclusion of symbolic goods and services that are standardised and non-changing, which currently constitute so much value in China and developing countries. The cultural economy permits the inclusion of traditional craft items, whether authentic handmade goods or mass-produced copies for tourists.

Moreover, in showing how the creative industries idea penetrated China, I will challenge the idea of creativity, how it has been used in the West in the past and how it is applied in China today. The interest in creativity and innovation in China has generated tensions between new and old, between foreign and indigenous, between values and practice (Baark 2007: 338). My intention in this book is to shed more light on what is a very grey area: where creativity actually begins and ends. This leads me to propose an alternative definition of creativity as:

> The fitting of new ideas and imagined possibilities to perceived realities, norms, values and patterns; encompassing imitation, differentiation, adaptation, learning, and social diffusion.

In stepping away from the standard definition of creativity as 'new, valuable and useful' I will show how the idea has been appropriated in China. There are great expectations: creativity offers a new key to open the door to international pre-eminence. It is believed that the forces of creativity can be managed by policy. In the programmes that are built around the creative industries, particularly in China, we notice the rhetoric of value adding, social and industrial upgrading and a happy workforce (Li Wuwei 2009).

Perhaps unsurprisingly considering the success of the 'Made in China' development model, the applications of creativity are associated with economic development. The 'creative industries' and 'creative economy' reflect ambitions of policymakers, reformers, local government officials and a new breed of cultural scholar. Within these globally fashionable terms there are three fields of emergent creativity in China: *economic*, *cultural* and *technological* and two organisational forms: *social* and *individual*.

Economic creativity

Economic creativity encapsulates a range of aspirations in China today. At Songzhuang Capital Arts District and the 798 Art Zone in Beijing (see Chapter 5) it illustrates aspirations of the local government to generate profit from the labour of artists and to raise land values; in Hangzhou it represents ambitions to construct China's leading animation hub and be the leading 'creative province' in China; in Shenzhen it is enfolded into plans to be a 'international city of design'; in Shanghai it includes all of these; in addition it embraces business culture. Economic creativity in

China brings with it an assumption that imagination, skill and technique can be directed in certain ways. Certainly this social engineering model has been the guiding template for cultural policy in China during the past six decades. Cultural policy is now closely aligned with economic data, urban regeneration and local entrepreneurship. The strategy of economic creativity is to bring together ideas, talent and capital in innovative ways.

Cultural creativity

Cultural creativity describes the traditional, and some would say most appropriate, mode of understanding the expressive responsibility of the artist within society. For many the word 'creativity' conjures up an image of the iconoclast. In China we can identify an eclectic list: writers Lu Xun, Cao Yu, poets Dufu and Li Bai, the artists Qi Baishi, Chen Yifei and Cai Guoqiang. Yet cultural creativity is something we all engage in; we all tinker with words, ideas, melodies and construct our representations of forms and genres. Of course, from an economic perspective, such works need to be evaluated by connoisseurs and consumers. More significantly, perhaps, the expressive mode of cultural creativity is central to civil society in liberal democracies. The artistic temperament should according to this view be encouraged. Whereas the artist is one who identifies problems and raises awareness in the West, in China the artist is one who must necessarily avoid stepping over the line.

Technological creativity

Technological creativity is conventionally associated with innovation, and is often subsumed under the umbrella of 'science and technology' in China. The term R&D reflects the goals of China to become an innovative country by developing novel technologies, what the government likes to call 'endogenous innovation' (*zizhu chuangxin*). According to Breznitz and Murphree (2011), however, China's technological innovation operates best on the level of 'second generation, production and process innovation'. They say: 'although other countries may be advancing the technological cutting edge, China continues to grow in importance as a critical location for innovation built upon these discoveries' (2011:3). In turn, the preoccupation with exploitation rather than exploration of new knowledge favours diffusion over innovation (Baark 2007).

Social creativity

Social creativity offers a way to think about the situated nature of art, design and media production. The creative process extends to the issue of resources, as well as political and organisational constraints. Constraints include censorship, peer communities and the role of social networks. Mihaly Csikszentmihályi has proposed a complex dynamic systems model of creativity, in which creativity is not an attribute of individuals but the social systems making judgements about individuals (Csikszentmihályi 1990; Mockros and Csikszentmihályi 1999). The issue of social or situated creativity raises a conundrum of intellectual property. How are ideas generated in project-based activities? How can they be shared, for the purpose of generating innovation, and protected in order to maintain competitive advantage? In China the profusion of creative clusters, bases, zones and precincts are places where originality and intellectual property are duly celebrated. Impressive slogans adorn hallways and entrances. The reality however is that many of these parks function simply as outsourcing zones; they produce a high proportion of work designed and created outside China. In many such parks there is widespread disregard for intellectual property. As I will argue, business problems result from a bureaucratic, highly regulated cultural market, one in which there is a low recognition of the value of authorship, and one in which imitation provides a better business model than innovation.

Individual creativity

Individual creativity is the wellspring of most academic literature and underpins popular perception of the role of art and artists in liberal democracies. The issue of providing more leeway for individual creativity is less conspicuous in the minds of Chinese policymakers and reformers. This is unsurprising, taking into account China's recent political history, symbolised in the consciousness of international audiences by the image of a lone protester attempting to halt a tank in Tiananmen Square in June 1989. The inordinate attention recently accorded to the dissident artist-curator Ai Weiwei by the Chinese state, which seeks to defuse his reputation, and by the international community, which champions him up as a symbol of free speech, is testimony to the problematic nature of individual creativity in China.

However, the question of whether or not individual consciousness is in fact the locus of creative activity has been cast into doubt by recent research. If creativity, like knowledge acquisition, is understood as essentially a collective endeavour, maybe there is alternative way of thinking through China's emergence. Creating, exchanging and sharing of ideas are primary social activities for the generation of people born since 1980, an 'individualised' generation born without the affective connections of siblings (Hansen and Svarverud 2010).

The challenges, as well as opportunities for democratisation, come from the way that Chinese government chooses to navigate the tensions inherent in these modalities of creativity. Prior to the discovery that artist communities 'attract' business (*zhao shang*) – and in doing so raise land values – many local government officials regarded the 'creative economy' as problematic: a waste of resources and contributing little to job creation (Zheng 2010). In practice however, the refitting of industrial space is relatively cheap and provides an expedient solution to management of creativity: the participants are visible. Is the term 'creativity industries' popular therefore because of what it promises to deliver as a percentage of GDP and for its contribution to local tax revenue? Is this just lip-service to openness or is there a greater social transformation in progress? Is creativity transforming China?

Chapter outline

In the following chapters I investigate how China's creative clusters function and how they are governed. In Chapter 1 I describe the background to the development of the cultural and creative industries in China. In doing this I take two historical detours, the first to the period when China geared up to join the World Trade Organisation in the late 1990s, the second to the period following the Opium Wars in the mid-nineteenth century. I describe how the creative industries are categorised in Chinese policy language and propose a cultural economy innovation ecology model to explain the rationale for clustering. In the final section of this chapter I sketch out four scenarios that impact on governance, human capital and investment in China's new creative clusters.

Chapter 2 addresses relevant literature on the topic of cultural and creative clusters, specifically the concept of localised external economies, initially developed in Alfred Marshall's account of industrial districts in the UK over a century ago (Marshall 1920). I begin by suggesting that the cluster is a sub-species of the region and the city; to put it another way, regions and cities cluster people and businesses. The best ideas have traditionally come from concentrations of people living and working in supportive networks or environments. Many locales are recognised for their innovative environments and capacity to attract human capital and investment. However, just as some environments breed new ideas, others disenfranchise them. In China the cluster takes two main generic forms: the cultural quarter and the industrial park; in between these we find five variations: specialist agglomerations (usually one sector), artists' zones often spontaneously formed, related variety models (a mix of sectors), media parks, and incubators.

Chapter 3 begins with an overall appraisal of the rationales for creative parks, zone, bases and clusters in China. In assessing the relative success of creative industries clusters and cultural quarters in China I examine how the policy landscape compares with international best practice. I look at the mechanics of cluster governance and investment from the

Introduction: China's new creative clusters   11

perspective of 'growth coalitions', epistemic communities and local government actors. I discuss the rationale for local government interest in clustering and the role of informal economies. Following this I identify three stages of cluster development in China. I investigate a successful 'stage three' cluster project in Guangdong Province, the Foshan Creative Industries Park. I then examine developments in Hangzhou, a city which aspires to be the 'National Cultural and Creative Industries centre' of China. The examples from Hangzhou are LOFT49 and the White Horse Lake Creative Eco-City.

In Chapter 4 my attention turns to Beijing. I look at how Beijing has repositioned itself as a creative city, rather than a historical, cultural or political city. Politics permeates daily life in Beijing more so than in any other Chinese city. Political change is incremental, highly compromised and often convoluted: innovations in the management of media and cultural activities, including clusters, are therefore more likely to happen elsewhere. Accordingly, I examine contradictions that come with the popularisation of 'creative industries' within local growth coalitions. In particular, the chapter demonstrates the role of epistemic communities in cluster development. The case studies in this chapter are Nanluoguxiang and Fangjia 46, both *hutong* (alleyway) clusters in central Dongcheng District. In the main these examples demonstrate an ideal type of creative industries cluster environment, one in which participants are not driven solely by economic concerns but have a deep interest in maintaining a conducive innovative milieu.

The focus of Chapter 5 is art clusters. Art districts zones are a visible expression of China's culture-led economic renaissance. Considering the many troubled relationships between the state and artists in recent Chinese history, these projects appear to vindicate the government's commitment to ongoing social reform. In this chapter I look at the historical development of art districts since the late 1990s, focusing on 798, Songzhuang and Caochangdi in Beijing and Dafen Art Village (*Dafen cun*) near the southern city of Shenzhen. 798 is frequently referred to as an Art Zone; more specifically, it is a group of galleries, bars, design studios and cafes which developed in the late 1990s; by 2007 it had become a commercial venture with the full support of the local government. The second case, Songzhuang Capital Arts District, is a state-administered contemporary art commune further to the east of Beijing. Caochangdi is an art village not far from 798 on Beijing's northeastern fringe; its status remains unclear despite attracting an international reputation as a creative milieu. Dafen's success tells a much different story: how the industrial organisation of art can regenerate a rural community. The Dafen model is supported by cultural entrepreneurs from Hong Kong, who have set up production studios there, assembling teams of workers to 'reproduce' well known art works. Many artists in Songzhuang and Caochangdi have distanced themselves philosophically from the overt commercialisation of 798 and the 'copy culture' of Dafen.

Shanghai is the focus of Chapter 6. In this chapter I look at the city's prominent role in establishing and renovating creative clusters. Some bear descriptive titles like Creative Warehouse, Creative Garden, Creative Shanghai Riverside River and Media and Culture Park; others like Bridge 8, New Ten Steel and M50 retain a link with the industrial heritage of the past. I argue that local government's concern with designation and management of creative parks (there are now more than eighty) in Shanghai may be having the unintended effect of diminishing the city's status as China's preeminent creative city. In effect, municipal and local governments' deep involvement in cluster parks points to the fact that Shanghai may not be as innovative as government publicists proclaim, a point also made by Huang (2008) in relation to the city's microeconomic environment. I look at four of Shanghai's many creative parks; these are KIC, Tianzifang, 1933 Old Millfun District and M50. KIC or the Knowledge Innovation Community is an ambitious aspirational project in Yangpu district that is attempting to attract international digital content investment; Tianzifang is a consumer-focused milieu in the French Concession District on Taikang Road; the 1933 project is a high-profile architectural conversion of a disused abattoir built by British engineers in 1933 in Hongkou District; M50 is located in the Suzhou Creek precinct in the Putuo District; it is owned and operated by Shanghai Textile Group, a Chinese Fortune 500 listed enterprise with a stake in Shanghai's fashionable 'makeover'. In the final section of the chapter I look at a much different model of creative clustering called Xindanwei, literally the New Work Unit. Xindanwei is a co-working space located in the French Concession area.

The penultimate chapter concerns media clusters. The first study is the Beijing CBD International Media Industry Cluster, sometimes called the Central Media District, other times referred to as the Capital Media District, a mega-cluster of production, post-production and ancillary services in commercial Chaoyang District. The second example is the Suzhou National Animation Base located in the Suzhou Industrial Park, 100 kilometres west of Shanghai. Media clusters are a common model of organisation in many countries. Film and television clusters can be found in Europe, Canada, Australia, New Zealand, Romania, South Africa and many developing countries. Obviously the most well known media cluster is in Los Angeles. Media industries in China illustrate a particularly salient point about governance, namely acts of government by the state. Media industries globally are subject to a range of regulatory policies designed to both limit concentration of ownership, to regulate public taste and to provide opportunities for independents. In examining the relevance of clusters to media content innovation, I question the proposition that the Chinese state's desire to expand its soft power might lead to liberalisation of media policy.

In the final chapter I offer some further thoughts about the relationship between culture, creativity and innovation. My concern is to reflect in a different way on the outbreak of creative clusters and *inter alia* the unprecedented interest in creativity in China and East Asia. Several key questions remain unanswered. Is creativity, however construed, an answer to China's economic development problems? Does the focus on economic creativity override individual creativity, the touchstone of Western pluralism? Is commercial culture lessening the ideological straightjacket that many say has suppressed creative imagination? Is recombination a better description of the creative process than originality and if so is China defining a new paradigm? In attempting to answer these questions I want to emphasise the elasticity of the idea of creativity: there is no gold standard; likewise in creativity there is no east or west, just different ways of seeing.

1 Harmonising creativity

Great anticipations

At 8 pm on 8 August 2008, members of the Chinese Communist Party's politburo joined a national and global television audience to witness the opening ceremony of the Beijing Olympics. For the organisers, it was a moment of great anticipation. Following months of restrictions on people's movements, the stage was prepared. Factories had been closed in the weeks leading up to the great event and potentially troublesome migrant workers were moved away from Olympic venues. Taxi drivers, trained in rudimentary English, French, German and Japanese, were expected to deal in a civilised and harmonious manner with the many foreign visitors.

Despite international criticism of a carefully stage-managed media event, people of Chinese heritage throughout the world were generous in praise. The opening and closing ceremonies exceeded expectations. Compared with stereotypical extravaganzas like the Chinese New Year party broadcast annually on the national TV network, this was a spectacle, both in terms of the sheer numbers of moving performers and inventive use of technology: 2,008 drummers pounded a thunderous overture, digital images unfurled on a large scroll illustrating the path of Chinese civilisation, and fireworks exploded in the skies above. As the cauldron was lit, former Olympic gymnast Li Ning ran along the upper wall of the stadium suspended by wires.

The opening ceremony conveyed a 'harmonious' message. Although patriotic Chinese flag-waving took place, it was vindication of achievement against the odds as much as expressive nationalism. For China's leaders 'the high-tech, green, "people's Games"' symbolised the success of social and economic reforms which had generated double-digit growth for a decade. In anticipating international criticisms of China's human rights record, the event diverted attention to China's glorious history, to times when the description 'middle kingdom' reflected China's influence over vast territories.

The practice of shifting attention away from contemporary political pressure points is familiar to China's film and television directors. Choreographed primarily by the renowned film director Zhang Yimou, who over time has developed a feel for international perceptions of China, the opening and closing ceremonies were a makeover of China's international image. The theme of 'soft power' featured heavily in planning meetings. According to reports, Zhang had been advised by China's leaders to make his choreography 'softer', to make the army of 2008 drummers seem less threatening (Callaghan 2010).

The nation's publicity apparatus was effusive in praising China's 'creativity' (*chuangyi*), an idea that had been brewing for several years in academic and business communities and government think-tanks. The 'creative China' theme was also picked up by international media reports. Predictably, many international journalists chose to downgrade the creativity on display by drawing attention to a pretty little girl in the opening musical sequence, a last-minute substitute. The replacement performer had lip-synched. Despite criticisms, it was evident that the Games symbolised a coming of age, what cultural reformers imagined as 'the Chinese creative project' (Liu 2004; Li 2011)

In this chapter I have three main aims. The first is to set out the economic and social context that led to the flowering of hundreds of cultural zones, creative parks and media bases from the early years of the first decade of the twenty-first century. To do this it is necessary to take two historical detours: the first takes us back to the mid-1990s as China prepared to join the World Trade Organisation; the second detour returns to the period of empire, the years following the Opium Wars in the mid-nineteenth century when China's leaders were confronted by superior Western technologies. During both these periods questions arose in relation to the inability of Chinese culture to adapt to modern times.

My second objective is to demonstrate why the term 'creative industries' captured the policy high ground in China's cities and provinces after 2005 and to show how creative clusters became the default setting for the revitalisation of China's cultural economy. In doing this I outline six levels of the innovation ecology of China's cultural economy. In the final section I look at four scenarios that impact upon governance, human capital and investment in China's creative clusters. I conclude by asking if the discourse of creativity has been effectively 'harmonised' in the interests of economic development. Harmonisation usually refers to the sense of bringing rules systems in different countries into concordance. However, the term 'harmonisation' in China is frequently used by critics of the Chinese Party-state to imply the neutralising of troublesome ideas and concepts. In effect, creativity is now in harmony with a number of key party slogans.

The Made in China conundrum

The 2008 Beijing Olympics symbolised China's emerging 'soft power' (*ruan shili*). Notwithstanding the dissonance between the ideal of spontaneity and stage-managed performance rituals, a deep and lingering question was not far from the surface. Why had it taken so long for China to display its creative credentials? Could this be a script for a more progressive China?

While the Beijing games were taking place the economy was moving faster, higher and stronger. Chinese culture received unprecedented exposure. The year 2008 was devoid of the kind of political anniversaries that require re-enactments of military campaigns – those anniversaries so beloved by hardliner Chinese Communist Party members which translate into large production slates of propaganda movies and TV serials. In the relative absence of 'red culture', traditional culture, contemporary art and tourism had impressive sales. Public and private funds were siphoned into high-profile cultural development projects (*xingxiang gongcheng*). As China looked forward to the celebration of the thirtieth anniversary of its economic reforms (*jingji gaige*) in December 2008, these were heady times for cultural reformers.

Within six months the euphoria of the Beijing Games was dampened by the global financial crisis. China, with its heavy dependence on exports to the US, was facing new uncertainties. Economic data sheets, tied to low-cost and low-value-added production models, were rapidly losing ground. By mid-December 2008, China's exports had fallen 2.2 per cent, the biggest drop in seven years. Economists expressed alarm that the Chinese economy was going down 'at the speed of diving' (Diao 2008). The Chinese real estate construction bubble had cooled, factories were closing, and thousands of migrant workers were out of work. Unsurprisingly, given the origins of the financial crisis, the blame was shifted to US-style capitalism. Experts were in demand on TV talk shows, offering Confucian-style ethical remedies. Looking to stabilise the impending crisis of confidence, the central government moved to pump-prime infrastructure development in order to absorb displaced labourers.

The limits to growth were spelt out as the nation assessed its losses. Significantly, it was a report from the Development Research Centre of the State Council in December 2008 that suggested a long-term remedy (Diao 2008). The report proposed that China needed to adjust its product structure; it needed to encourage enterprises to make more high-value-added products rather than continue to rely on cheap labour reserves and what economists call 'unbundling', the global shift that has seen time-consuming processes and tasks outsourced to low-cost regions (Baldwin 2006; Dicken 2003). The economic crisis was a call to arms and an opportunity for cultural reformers to spell out a new vision for China, one that would contribute to soft power and in doing so erase some of the humiliation of the past. In 2011, Li Wuwei, a leading industrial economist who also happened to be a vice-chair of the Revolutionary Kuomingtang Party wrote:

> GDP by itself means neither wealth nor happiness; nor does it mean ecological sustainability. China's economic growth has relied largely on investment and export, giving rise to problems such as exhaustion of natural resources, environmental pollution and lack of innovation. Behind the apparent dynamism of 'Made in China' is a huge loss of profits for Chinese enterprises. A transition from 'Made in China' to 'Created in China' is the future strategy for China's economy.
>
> (Li 2011:8)

The creative economy and the creative industries

The discourse of creative China gained momentum in the period following the Olympics, leading into the 2010 Shanghai World Expo. It featured not only in policy reports, official speeches but also on talk radio and in newspapers. In his keynote speech to the seventeenth National Congress of the Communist Party of China in 2007, President Hu Jintao (2007) stressed the need to enhance the nation's 'soft power':

> [We must] enhance China's capacity for independent innovation and make China an innovative country. This is the core of our national development strategy and a crucial link in enhancing the overall national strength

and:

> Culture has become a more and more important source of national cohesion and creativity and a factor of growing significance in the competition in overall national strength...[We must] enhance culture as part of the soft power of our country to better guarantee the people's basic cultural rights and interests.

The question I therefore want to consider is: How did this idea find its way into Chinese political discourse alongside lofty themes of harmonious society, national strength and economic development? Under Chairman Mao Zedong creativity was associated with individualism and capitalism. While there are a number of factors contingent on the rehabilitation of creativity into China, there are two important geo-political factors. The first is the influence of East Asian popular culture; the second, and ultimately more powerful, is the globalising discourse of the creative economy.

18 *China's New Creative Clusters*

Plate 1.1 Innovation is the soul of a nation's progress, Nanjing Rd, Shanghai

Long before Chinese Communist Party strategists had developed national soft-power slogans (Ding 2008; Keane 2010), China's East Asian neighbours had disseminated their versions of cultural soft power. For more than a decade Japanese and Korean popular culture had won over the hearts and minds of China's youth. Japanese *manga* (cartoons) and *anime* (animation) epitomised the idea of 'cool' in East Asia (Oyama 2009; McGray 2002; Iwabuchi 2002; Black *et al.* 2010; Chua and Iwabuchi 2008). While China's strict official restrictions on importation and broadcast of Japanese content had reduced their impact on China's domestic media industries, a worrying trend was the amount of Japanese *anime* available in pirated DVDs. Adding to this black-market activity was the emergence of fan communities who not only consumed but also reformatted and redistributed Japanese *anime* and *manga* (Pang 2009). At a time when China's cultural ministers were urging producers to make better local content, Chinese animation (*dongman*) and cartoons (*manhua*) had acquired a distinctively Japanese look.

In Korea soft power had activated cultural nationalism. By 2004, exports of Korean TV programmes were double the value of imports (Lee 2008). Korean pop culture products made initial forays into China in 1997 with the popularity of the television serial drama *What is Love All About?*

(Shim, 2006, 2008). The term 'Korean wave' (*hanliu* in Chinese, *hallyu* in Korean) symbolised the way that Korean popular culture was flooding into the mainland, enrapturing not only mainstream Chinese TV drama audiences but creating a buzz about Korean fashion, food, lifestyle and celebrities. Korean pop music, video games and movies quickly gained popularity with Chinese youth (Pease 2009). Adding to the concern was the fact that in 2005 China's exports of TV serials to Taiwan and Hong Kong had depreciated in value due to competition from Korea (Keane 2008). Both Japan and Korea had highly developed commercial content industries. In Japan Sony's background in electronic entertainment technologies gave it a competitive edge. In the early 1990s massive investment from state-linked conglomerates such as Daewoo and Samsung had stimulated Korea's cultural ascendency. Known as *chaebol*, these conglomerates brought professional management practices into the film and TV industries (Shim 2008). In the late 1990s the government set up the Korean Culture and Content Agency (KOCCA) with the aim of expediting the export of Korean culture. In 2009, this agency was subsumed under a larger umbrella organisation, the Korean Creative Content Agency.

China's proximity to East Asia explains much about the cultural insecurity of its producers and cultural officials. The second factor impacting on China's take-up of creativity is more noteworthy. Over several decades developed countries had transformed their economic foundations, recognising the limits of growth in manufacturing and the need to become service economies. Fragmentation of production activities and outsourcing of trade in tasks to low-cost destinations had changed the physical appearance of many Western cities (Baldwin 2006; Breznitz and Murphree 2011; Kenney and Florida 2004; Storper 1997; Dicken 2003). The post-industrial era had arrived.

Policymakers in regions, cities and districts became aware of the capacity for culture to generate new income streams. This awareness was generated by a number of changes in the global economy (Dunning 2000). The first was the increased role of 'intellectual capital', illustrated by the rising contribution of services in GDP. As service-led growth impacted upon production, knowledge was combined in different ways to produce more goods and services. For firms to increase, or deploy their intellectual capital effectively, it became necessary to complement knowledge with that of other firms, often by way of collaborative agreements. This increase in co-operative ventures along with levels of integration among the main wealth-creating nations led to alliances in knowledge-intensive sectors such as IT, media and communications and internet services. A third change concerns market liberalisation. Market liberalisation increased with protected economies trading sovereignty for free-trade concessions. Fourth, and most importantly, new major economic players emerged. The rise of the new industrialising economies of East Asia created a shift in the locus of development in high-technology and communications industries.

Governance and culture

As I will discuss in the following section the terms 'cultural' and 'creative economy' joined the stable of 'new economies' such as the information economy, the knowledge-based economy and the experience economy. According to George Yúdice (2003) culture had become a resource. Yúdice saw an extended role for culture. Culture's resourcefulness – its expediency – was enhanced by rapid globalisation. If nature provides resources, Yúdice argued, culture is resource rich: it can be invested in, not so much from the perspective of residual value – for instance, the preservation of cultural traditions and relics – but for its usefulness in assuring the governability of populations.

The governability of cultural workers assumed importance as neoliberal policies were adopted by governments eager to minimise costs. Could cultural workers be made more entrepreneurial, less reliant on government? In the UK the term 'creative industries' had captured the cultural policy high ground. Kate Oakley (2011) describes how the decline of manufacturing and growth in service sectors, and the ascent of the 'knowledge economy', precipitated the genesis of this idea. Oakley notes how New Labour thinkers such as Charles Leadbeater promoted a view that the rise of small independent creative firms, together with more post-Fordist workplaces, would generate a more innovative culture, something perhaps even emulating the spirit of Silicon Valley. In this account of economic development a raft of social problems could be tackled. Oakley's description of the evolution of creative industries policy in the UK suggests an underlying and often misguided belief in a model of benign development, a theme that would emerge a decade later in China's own 'harmonious' development of the cultural sector.

The creative industries were a product of the times. The genesis of the idea had much to do with the revitalisation of the British Labour Party during the late 1990s, culminating in New Labour's electoral triumph under the leadership of Tony Blair. Whereas 'old' Labour has been traditionally associated with the working class, New Labour's strategy was to connect with a demographic of swinging voters in traditional conservative electorates, mostly in the south of Britain, by appealing to the values of creative entrepreneurship; in effect the strategy was about giving small business owners recognition for their work ethic rather than earmarking public funds for flagship cultural institutions as the Tories had done. The shift from culture to creativity entailed a radical policy makeover together with economic justifications, which the incoming government was able to do by mustering an array of industry sectors and sub-sectors under the banner of 'creative', despite misgivings as to their fitness for purpose; for instance, IT and software industries were expediently tossed into the creative industries stew. The Department for Culture Media and Sport (DCMS) defined the creative industries as follows: 'those industries which have their origin in individual creativity, skill and talent and which have a potential for wealth and job creation through the generation and exploitation of intellectual property' (DCMS 2001: 4).

In a short period of policy renovation the cultural industries, so beloved of Old Labour and endorsed by the Greater London City Council in the mid-1980s, became the creative industries. Banks and O'Connor (2009: 336) are among a number of critics of the DCMS' 'contradiction-free marriage of culture and economics' and the unresolved problems of how to measure sectors defined in mapping documents. Even though many activities aggregated in the mix were technical, mundane and repetitive, the idea had political traction in a nation that lagged behind the US in global entertainment markets. John Howkins captured the essence of the *zeitgeist* in his book *Creative Economy: How People Make Money from Ideas*: 'People with ideas – people who *own* ideas – have become more powerful than people who work machines, in many cases, more powerful than people who *own* machines' (Howkins 2001: ix).

Within a decade, municipalities in China had fitted the creative industries idea into cultural and urban policy initiatives. Howkins' propositions made sense to Chinese municipal governments who cared about their bottom lines. The global financial crisis of 2008–2009 provided a way to sell creativity as an input into productivity – but less so into innovation as was the intention in the UK and elsewhere where the idea took root (Kong *et al.* 2006). The fall in China's earnings from manufacturing exports was used to argue the case for expansion of investment in creative industries projects, specifically clusters, precincts and industrial parks. Commentators wrote about people's needs for entertainment in times of crisis, citing references to the positive effects of Charlie Chaplin, Buster Keaton and Steamboat Willie on people's minds in the Great Depression, and to the sudden rise of Japanese anime during the oil crisis of the 1970s (Li 2011; Zhang 2009). As the enthusiasm mounted among growth coalitions the momentum for projects moved from the centre of cities to city fringes, from central business districts (CBDs) to other 'business districts'.

As one might expect from the past history of Chinese cultural policy (see Kraus 2004), the idea of creativity evokes a distinctly ideological agenda in China. Its rehabilitation was not without controversy. The central government in Beijing resisted the incursion of this foreign idea, finally accommodating the creative industries under the sovereignty of the 'cultural industries'. The accommodation sees 'new' industries such as design, animation, gaming, digital content and advertising working to liberate 'productive forces'. Once socialist, these forces are now capitalist, once collective they are now entrepreneurial. This is the *expediency of creativity*, promising powerful effects and almost magical properties.

Unlike the UK there are no votes to be gained in China. The creative industries were effectively 'harmonised' within a few years of their emergence. The liberation of the new productive forces came at a surprising speed. Creativity was embedded in government slogans: 'soft power' (*ruan shili*), 'innovative nation' (*chuangxin xing guojia*) and 'independent innovation (*zizhu chuangxin*) (Li 2011). The rehabilitation of creativity is evoked in utopian language. According to Li Wuwei, a senior national policy advisor, and former director of the Industrial Economics Institute at the Shanghai Academy of Social Sciences:

> Creative industries advocate the release of human potential and the realization of self worth to make people feel happy about their efforts and bring about a return to 'people-oriented' values... This development concept has not only changed the value orientation of economic development but also created a new lifestyle combining work with entertainment.
>
> (Li 2011: 55)

The term 'creativity' quickly became an article of faith among business and policymakers in China. Widespread benefits would accrue – benefits that were individual, collective, technological and organisational. It was a green idea in a country where industrial pollution had turned skies a brownish grey. A short list of its benefits for China included wealth creation, re-conversion of traditional resources, enhanced productivity combined with cleaner greener production, talent renewal and the ever-present theme of industrial catch-up.

The power of the creative industries is validated in data-heavy reports that echo a global perception perpetuated by UNCTAD (2010) that these 'new industries' are outperforming old polluting economies and increasing in value yearly. In 2007, the GDP growth of Beijing, Shanghai and Shenzhen was 12.3 per cent, 13.3 per cent and 15 per cent respectively while their creative industries growth was 19.4 per cent, 22.8 per cent and 25.9 per cent respectively. In China's second-tier cities the story is similar. In 2008 value added by creative industries in Hangzhou and Qingdao reached RMB 57.986 billion and RMB 31.9 billion respectively, up by 17.6 per cent and 22.6 per cent. In China's middle and western areas the story continues in the same vein. The value added of creative industries in 2008 in Chongqing, reached RMB 24 billion while Changsha had RMB 27 billion, an annual growth of 30 per cent and 17 per cent respectively (Zhang 2009).

However, the benefits of the intangible creative economy in China are difficult to measure, not just because of the rubbery nature of Chinese statistics. Definitional and categorical problems persist that are not evident in the manufacturing sector, on which China has based its development model. This is a problem that faces those who advocate the creative industries as a growth model. What is in? What is out? What is the core and what is non-core? Are they just another industry or do they deserve special attention? Where is the evidence base? While 'creative industries' appears to break down the foundations of rigid notions of culture, some regard the term as oxymoronic. How can creativity, essentially something emanating from the individual, be an industry?

Culture as resource, creativity as essence

Despite incongruities, contradictions and oxymorons the 'creative industries' captured the attention of China's leaders. However, this is a story with political roots that date back a decade and deeper psychological scars that go back more than 100 years. The insecurity of the past humiliations suffered at the hands of the 'great Western powers' surfaced at the tail end of the 1990s as China's leaders confronted yet another challenge to cultural sovereignty. With entry into the World Trade Organisation pending, China was committed to gradually open its media, cultural and communications sectors to international competition, a political compromise that produced anxiety in senior political ranks. Would Chinese people be seduced by sophisticated Western ideas, by foreign fashions, by Hollywood's popular culture? Alarmed by such a scenario, conservative thinkers initiated the concept of cultural security (*wenhua anquan*) to highlight the crisis as China faced off against the rest of the world (Hu 2002). The foreign 'wolves' were waiting, they said, coveting the spoils of the huge Chinese consumer market. Cultural security entailed strengthening media and cultural institutions, making them large, efficient and profitable.

Much conjecture ensued about how to tap into the resources of China's past (see Knight 2006). The Tenth Five Year Plan for Economic and Social Development announced that China would address the problem of 'cultural commercialisation' by focusing on how to increase the volume of culture-related products for the domestic and overseas market (Xinhua 2000). Ye Lang, the director of a newly established Cultural Commercialisation Research Institute at Peking University, weighed into the debate, commenting that cultural commercialisation had allowed developed countries to 'dump their products' in developing counties. A senior literary scholar, Ye believed this dumping had 'unpredictable impacts' on economic values and social patterns (Xinhua 2000). In the same year the Chinese Academy of Social Sciences initiated a research centre attached to its Philosophy Institute. The centre subsequently initiated a series of annual *Blue Book Reports on China's Cultural Industries* that would provide the theoretical and evidence-based justification for cultural development policies (Zhang *et al.* 2006).

The term 'cultural industries' (*wenhua chanye*) began to feature regularly in government study groups and in internal 'reference documents' but knowledge of how cultural markets functioned was lacking. The challenge was to integrate international market experience into China's sensitive media and cultural sectors. Market knowledge was well developed in capitalist systems; it was a foreign commodity, something that could be brought in and tailored to Chinese environments. In a re-versioning of the *tiyong* formula that had surfaced more than 100 years previously when the Qing Dynasty imploded in the face of Western technology, China began to look for technical expertise outside its borders. In the discourse of *tiyong*, Chinese civilisation was substance (*ti*); Western technology was the means (*yong*). The iron gunboats that brushed aside China's defences in the first Opium War of 1839 were technologically superior to China's wooden junks. At that time many reformers believed China could simply borrow technology.

As Ci Jiwei (1994) explains, the *tiyong* reformers of the nineteenth century regarded technology as practical knowledge, at a lower level than culture. In time it became clear that the technology that defeated China was more than just practical knowledge. The gunboats were the end product of foreign ideology, the rewards of an outward-looking mentality. Ci writes about China's attempts to transform its institutions: 'Technological modernization (yong) proceeded slowly because it was constantly reined in by traditional values and institutions (ti)' (Ci 1994: 32). Reformist intellectuals like Zeng Guofan and Li Hongzhang argued that Western ideas were superior to the inward-looking culture of the Manchu empire (Teng and Fairbank 1979). After the fall of the Qing Dynasty in 1911 the old feudal culture founded on neo-Confucian principles was called into question. A period of looking abroad for solutions ensued. During the first two decades of the twentieth century, in the New Culture Movement Chinese intellectuals experimented with many Western cultural ideas. The eminent Chinese writer Lu Xun advocated the principle of 'taking' (*nalai zhuyi*), a way of cherry-picking the best ideas from outside in order to refresh China's culture (Wang 2008). In 1922, China's new reformers 'took' a Western 'substance', the idea of Marxism, to invigorate its own *ti* (Ci 1994).

Contemporary comparisons with the fall of empire and the spread of Western technologies in China and Japan provide an interesting footnote to contemporary insecurities. A century after the collapse of the Qing Dynasty, China discovered that the key problem it faced was management. In his memoirs of the Open Door Period from 1978 to the mid-1980s the former vice-premier Li Lanqing writes that many enterprises did not know how to run their imported production lines: 'As a result many imported installations could not perform efficiently, and some enterprises even became laughing stocks because they could not operate the foreign things properly' (Li 2009: 411).

Within a decade China's leaders were facing the reality that the institutional system of cultural supervision developed according to

Marxist-Leninist principles was locking Chinese culture into an innovation trap. In following the requirements of producing pedagogy for the socialist masses, China was playing into the hands of its competitors who were providing entertainment for capitalist mass audiences and in the process successfully disseminating capitalist ideology. The acceleration of globalisation and information technology in the 1990s meant that China had to compete more effectively in the realm of ideas. Cultural market consciousness was weak. The Marxist-Leninist *ti* was unfit to equip Chinese culture for its new challenge. Culture needed revitalisation, but how could this be achieved? It was not only reform-minded intellectuals and those with Western education who yearned for a new way, but many ordinary Chinese. Many younger Chinese, while essentially patriotic, were critical of Chinese culture: they expressed their criticism by consuming overseas movies, television and fashion, especially from China's East Asian neighbours, Korea and Japan.

Among the fundamental problems China faced in coming to terms with commercial cultural production was a lack of institutionalisation. Cultural production under the socialist planned system from the 1940s onwards was subject to a high level of monitoring by officials. Cultural and media units were fragmented and dispersed under a system that delegated authority to local government officials and propaganda officials. This model persisted into the 1990s when significant changes occurred as a result of Deng Xiaoping's wide-ranging reforms. The state continued to employ workers in what Zhang Xiaoming (2006) calls public cultural service units or public institutions (*shiye*). This system discouraged autonomy and encouraged vigilance. Economies of scale achieved by large capitalist media organisations were unachievable. Work units would be given a task of producing what was required; for instance a local television channel received a production quota or specific direction regarding content themes from the local branch of the State Administration of Radio Film and Television, which in turn responded to directives from the Central Propaganda Department and the Ministry of Culture.

The economic reforms that took place in the early 1990s following Deng Xiaoping's tour of southern China impacted on media and cultural units, which were directed to find new ways of financing while still adhering to the lofty principles of socialist culture. The idea of making capital from culture was attractive to people who had been employed in state-owned cultural enterprises (see Zha 1995; Schell 1995). With the cultural market legitimised independent enterprises began to form, seeking out ways to make profits. Many enterprises were underground or quasi-legal; for instance illegal book-publishing studios acquired publishing numbers (*shuhao*) from official state-owned enterprises (Schell 1995). Independent television and film companies formed, although they operated in a fragile and uncertain relationship with authorities (Keane and Liu 2009). In effect, due to censorship, the legacy of fragmentation and a lack of intellectual property consciousness the Chinese cultural market evolved in a way that was unique. Distribution was difficult, copyright violation was high, and with the exception of large television broadcasters and publishers profits were mostly hard to come by.

In spite of bottlenecks, people increasingly moved into cultural production. The state responded by emphasising policies of transforming institutions (*shiye*) into industries (*chanye*) and provided tax sweeteners and other incentives to encourage this transformation (see below). As I discussed in the previous chapter, the evolution of the market took a characteristic form; in many ways it followed the industrial logic of the export-led manufacturing and processing sector. Aside from the 'independent' practices of quasi-legal operators, many operators sought out outsourcing and service work opportunities in animation, fashion, design and software sectors. Others found market opportunities by imitation of successful products which could be distributed in local markets, thereby avoiding intellectual property litigation. In due course, companies began to cluster, to seek out partnerships and aim for wider markets. By the time China joined the WTO the term 'cultural industry' was an appropriate description of what was occurring across many parts of China.

In 2006, the topic of China's cultural trade deficit made news. While the cultural market followed the lead of the manufacturing economy, Chinese culture was not internationalising. Much was made of the fact that China's East Asian neighbours were selling their TV dramas, movies and animation into the mainland, but China was struggling to tell its own stories to the world. Strategists sought to restrict Chinese people from accessing imported television programs and animation in prime time by establishing quotas. More worryingly, the trade imbalance extended into other areas of cultural production including publishing and performing arts. Zhao Qizheng, a member of the Chinese People's Political Consultative Conference (CPPCC), was damning in his assessment of China's performance saying, 'The country's weakness in culture should be blamed' (China Daily 2006). In April, Ding Wei, the assistant Minister of Culture, announced the nation's deficit in international cultural trade, revealing that the ratio of imports of cultural products to exports stood at 10.3 to 1. The general manager of China's Arts and Entertainment Group, Zhang Yu, added soberly, 'China's foreign trade in culture is very weak.' In the television industry the picture was especially depressing. According to Zhang Xinjian, the deputy director of the cultural market department with the Ministry of Culture, 'Most exported Chinese TV dramas are old fashioned and poorly packaged by international standards, which doom them to fail' (People's Daily 2006).

By the Eleventh Five Year Development Plan (2006–2010) China's leaders had begun to address the longevity of the Made in China economic development model. The eleventh Five Year Plan proposed efforts to strengthen service industries, recognising that China's weak tertiary industry sector was having a negative impact on competitiveness. In the terminology of Marxism, the strengthening of service industries indicates a concerted shift of emphasis from the material base to the intangible superstructure: or as one popular slogan put it, from Made in China to Created in China. While Chinese policymakers and advisors recognised the need to join the 'international track' to prosperity, they were unwilling to discount the centrality of the term 'industry'. The cultural sector was tailor made to fit the new industrial policy. According to Zhang Xiaoming:

> Over the past 30 years the government has used industrial policy to advance the economy; the government believes this industrial model plays a strong role; in the 80s and the 90s, they used parks including industrial parks, international parks. The current cultural industry park continues this practice: we have to ask: why does cultural industry need this kind of clustering treatment?
> (Interview with author March 2011)

According to many commentators in China most cultural industries are small, weak and unco-ordinated. Zhang says that one key reason for this weakness is that the cultural sector is in an initial development stage due to China's relatively low average annual income, approximately USD 3,000. In developed Western economies cultural industries have accounted for more than 60–70 per cent of service sectors for a considerable period of time.

Trojan horses and Rorschach blots

The creative industries came to Shanghai in 2004. Long regarded as China's most business-friendly metropolis, Shanghai maintains a close association with developments in the Special Administrative Region of Hong Kong. In 2003, a *Hong Kong Creative Industries Baseline Study* was published by the University of Hong Kong Cultural Policy Unit (CCPR 2003). This influential report in turn seeded an emerging discourse of cultural development in the mainland, a discourse that faced away from the national preoccupation with tradition. The form that these modern industries would take in China was influenced by debates in Hong Kong. A report published by the Hong Kong Chamber of Commerce in 2003 noted the potential economic benefits of revitalising the city. A flagship project called the West Kowloon Cultural District was earmarked for construction in the late 1990s. While the West Kowloon project was being debated, Hong Kong's policymakers identified an alternative cheaper strategy of using artists to broker a connection with the broader community. The Cattle Depot Art Village in Kowloon was a place where artists were clustering spontaneously. The unused slaughterhouse had a heritage value and the cheap costs of location had attracted artists. One report noted:

> The Cattle Depot should establish itself as an anchor supported by branches elsewhere in the territory. A good prospective resource is the impending redevelopment of the tenement blocks opposite the Cattle Depot by the Urban Renewal Authority. Besides residential and commercial development, there will be opportunities for communal and social activities.
> (Hong Kong General Chamber of Commerce 2003).

The migration of the creative industries idea occurred with the assistance of the British Council and a creative industries consultancy firm, Burns Owen Partnership (now BOP Consulting). In 2004, a delegation from the Shanghai municipal government and the Shanghai Academy of Social Sciences visited the UK, then the global centre of the creative industries.

The Shanghai Academy of Social Sciences would become a focal point for definitional clarity in respect to creative industries in China. In time, just as Hong Kong had done, Shanghai would reconvert a heritage-listed cattle slaughterhouse into a hub for designers, artists and fashion entrepreneurs. In spite of the enthusiasm brewing in Shanghai in 2004-5, however, the advocates of the new development model had to convince a political community in the nation's capital, namely the incumbent power brokers within the central Ministry of Culture (MoC). For conservatives the creative industries were a 'cargo cult', even a Trojan horse; it was incompatible, alien and suspicious; furthermore it had not made its way through Chinese Communist Party work groups, the complicated system that adjudicates on sensitive policy reform. Its appeal to city planners, officials and entrepreneurs, many of whom were clandestinely dismissive of Beijing's cultural ministers, had short-circuited this process.

Understandably, in the light of the contestation of wills between conservative propaganda officials and progressive cultural reformers, the UK Department for Culture, Media and Sport's definition of creative industries provoked consternation. As the creative industries gained support, officials and cultural scholars in Beijing's universities were duly informed to maintain the party line and to resist the tendency to ape international concepts.

Perhaps fearing the erosion of 60 years of Chinese cultural policy under socialism, an influential article by a Ministry of Culture spokesperson appeared in the *Blue Book of Chinese Cultural Industries* in 2007. The writer, Wang Yongzhang, argued that whereas the Chinese cultural industries integrated economics and ideology, the UK creative industries were lacking ideology. As evidence, Wang noted that core creative industries in the UK included industrial design, which 'had no ideological character' (Wang 2007). In contrast, the core cultural industries in China have ideological elements which are necessarily managed by the state.

Whichever way the cultural sector is sliced, packaged and rearranged, one theme is consistent. The business of culture in China is expanding, as is the business of providing reports stating that the cultural economy is expanding. Much of the content of *Blue Book* reports on China's cultural and creative industries are dedicated to counting the numbers. Moreover, whereas the UK model of the creative industries could not find a place for tourism, the sector was welcome in Beijing. The inclusion of tourism is logical as a cultural industry; after all, China has thousands of cultural parks, and more seem to be added each day. Moreover, the fact that Beijing is a historical cultural capital boosts its cultural and creative industries GDP significantly (Keane 2007). Competition between Shanghai and Beijing is one explanation for the retention of tourism in Beijing as the latter claims ownership of many cultural 'crown jewels' in China's history. However, tourism data are derived from national statistics and show no differentiation between cultural tourism, recreational tourism and national holiday tourism. As I have argued elsewhere (Keane 2009), an overabundance of traditional resources in China inflates data: from this perspective it might be pertinent to ask: what is *not* cultural, or indeed, how much of China's cultural industries resources have creative elements?

Definitional imbroglios are likely to remain. International experts arrive in China and provide their own interpretations depending on their background and familiarity with such concepts. Stuart Cunningham (2009) describes the creative industries concept as a Rorschach blot: that is, the concept is invested in for different reasons and with different outcomes. In 2009, when the World Design Forum was held in Beijing, the same cultural official that had two years earlier castigated the creative industries for its 'lack of ideology' opened the forum proclaiming that Beijing would soon be China's 'international city of design' and that the creative industries were integral to this goal. Notwithstanding the necessity of getting the tone right when addressing a room full of design practitioners, the compromise 'cultural and creative industries' is likely to win the day in the long term.

Debates about the relative importance of culture, creativity and innovation have taken place against a background of insecurity about the impacts of globalisation and the relevance of Chinese culture. Anxiety prevails within government circles about the trade deficit of China's cultural economy, in direct contrast with the apparent endless boom in manufacturing and exports. However, apprehension also exists about the long-term future of manufacturing and the negative image of China as the 'factory of the world' (Keane 2007). The idea that industrial models can be applied to cultural production recalls the kind of thinking that prevailed in the *tiyong* era of the nineteenth century. The transformation of science parks into creative incubators and the gentrification of disused industrial space is evidence of this mentality. There is a tendency on the part of many officials, supported by developers, to argue that the construction of cultural parks will attract 'talent'. In a nation where talent was traditionally identified from above: through the imperial examination process prior to 1911 and by the ability to integrate Marxist principles into artwork under revolutionary socialism, the idea that creativity emerges from the grassroots is somewhat foreign.

The innovation ecology of the cultural industries

In 2001, when the cultural industries received the imprimatur of China's State Council, policymakers in the Ministry of Culture in Beijing identified 'things' they wanted to see produced and marketed; apart from media content such as cinema and television, these were tangibles: landscape paintings, calligraphy, traditional artefacts, antiques, relics and curios, souvenirs and CDs. The cultural industries sought to protect and preserve traditional culture, to build better museums and cultural theme parks.

As the creative industries idea made its way through Anglophone countries its pathway towards Asia was observed by Chinese scholars. For some, including business communities, the distinction was already clear: the creative industries were the future; the cultural industries were ideological, they looked towards the past. This represented a dilemma for Chinese thinkers. How could these two ideas co-exist? Could you have creative industries without abandoning the cultural industries?

In 2004, when the creative industries were introduced, Jing Wang expressed doubt that such an idea would be accepted under a system so guided by central planning, particularly when the 'cultural industries' were state policy. She wrote, 'The thorniest question triggered by the paradigm of creative industries is that of "creativity" – the least problematic in the western context. How do we begin to envision a parallel discussion in a country where creative imagination is subjugated to active state surveillance?' (Wang 2004: 13). Indeed the idea of creativity and its association with individualism and iconoclasm would seem to render it redundant in a cultural system that privileges stability and unity.

The cultural industries represented the hegemony of Chinese culture: in the minds of cultural officials this was an ideological domain; in the minds of many consumers culture, even popular culture, had the feel of an endless history lesson; stories about role models, patriotic soldiers, selfless women and obligatory villains, often Japanese or Guomindang military. Making Chinese culture more marketable to Chinese people, or profitable, had seldom exercised the minds of cultural officials prior to the 1980s. The Open Door Policy was the first indication of cultural competition from afar: the decade saw the importation of television drama serials from Latin America, Japan, Hong Kong and the US. The domestic cultural market began to show signs of emergence during the late 1980s and early 1990s. A number of breakout TV dramas, novels and pop renditions of revolutionary songs, which were stimulated by a period of relative liberalisation of content, provided a sense that China would make its own idiosyncratic way forward. However, these were generally exceptions to the rule. Although encouraged to seek out sponsorship, Chinese culture and media production was heavily tied to a propaganda model, which rewarded conformity. Production was invariably organised around state-owned cultural institutions (*shiye*) in which there was little risk taking. It was difficult for Chinese cultural producers to take initates in proposing new genres.

In short, when China first opened its cultural sector to private investors in the mid-1980s, there was little knowledge of how to proceed, of how to organise commercial production, of how to turn culture into a commodity. Opportunities gradually arose for people to move from state-owned cultural troupes and broadcasters into private cultural activities. The problem was how to start up a cultural business. On the other hand, what China lacked in management knowledge, it made up for in willing labour, available at low cost.

In order to understand the role played by creative clusters in China we therefore need to step back and look at where they fit in the Chinese cultural innovation ecology (see Table 1.1). In my previous work I introduced this ecology. There are six layers in the ecology. These layers overlap.

In the initial commercial stage (1990s) many participants opted to produce whatever the market (or the state) wanted; that is, they waited for others to determine the form and prescribe the content. Work was outsourced from international companies. In effect, the cultural sector learnt from the industrial sector, which at that time was organising itself into small and medium clusters, or larger industrial factories, financed from outside China. Time-consuming work in animation, design, software programming and TV and film production moved to China to take advantage of labour costs. This paralleled the trend in IT and manufacturing industries, where considerable 'trade in tasks' activity migrated from Hong Kong and Taiwan to the mainland, particularly Guangdong Province in southern China. Companies, including animation companies, set up in locations such as Suzhou Industrial Park (see Chapter 7). Taking on such work allowed Chinese entrepreneurs and workers to understand elements of the value chain but in most cases they were effectively denied access to the 'sweet spot' of economic growth; that is, real insights into the creative process.

As the cultural market began to demand more ideas, media industries began to look for local versions of international successes. The second stage in the innovation ecology, derogatively referred to by critics as 'cloning' (*kelong*), saw producers directly imitating. A 'follow the leader' pattern ensued: this occurred in TV, animation and video games. Little

Table 1.1 The innovation ecology of the Chinese cultural economy

Form	Strategic form
Low-cost off-shoring	Trade in tasks. Production work moves from higher-cost centres and economies; mostly fee-for service work denying local intellectual property development. Minimal spillovers: animation, design, fashion production: off shore international film and television production
Isomorphism and imitation	Local actors and producers duplicate global and regional products without committing to intellectual property regimes. Most evident in replication of television formats; also evident in design sectors; includes shanzhai products (low-cost unbranded replicas)
Co-production and formatting	Local actors seek international partners through joint ventures, co-productions, or through licensing content and formats. Film TV and animation sectors: rise of independent production
East Asian creative economy	Capacity building occurs as opportunity comes from exploiting cultural proximity and co-productions within East Asia. Recognition of China's 'true' markets
Industrial cluster	Strategies to achieve agglomeration economies and deliver distinctive branded content and economies of scale have resulted in a proliferation of clusters, parks and bases: seen as a means of identifying creativity but is mostly based around real estate speculation
Peer communities	Post-collective models of user-led innovation in new media challenge the producer/supply model. Offline creativity is both creation and recreation. Challenge for government is how to manage scale-free creativity

risk-taking was to be found during the 1990s and there was little recognition of IP.

The third and fourth stages saw Chinese producers entering into co-production and knowledge-sharing arrangements with foreign players. This occurred more rapidly in non-sensitive media such as advertising and video games as China entered the World Trade Organisation. The rapid rise of the Korean wave soon alerted Chinese media players and policymakers that their true markets were in Asia, not the West. If the fourth stage was recognition of Asian markets, the final move was the formation of numerous media bases and clusters, often co-opting investors and personnel from East Asia.

The need to understand the creative process is most apparent in the fifth level, the industrial cluster. Hundreds of designated clusters – art centres, animation bases, cultural zones and incubators have sprung into life from disused urban industrial sites, echoing the post-industrial transformation seen in the developed countries in the 1980s and 1990s. With names such as the Cyber Recreation District (Beijing), Creative 100 (Qingdao),

Creative Island (Dalian) and Creative Warehouse (Shanghai), many are in the early stages of operation; some are already conspicuous by the lack of output. Like many so-called innovation parks in China, most are driven by real estate speculation. There is a tendency to follow the model of low-cost production and high volume of sales, in effect a result of a lack of incentives to target high-value niches (IP, etc.) (Wang Jici 2007).

The innovation ecology of the cultural industries is fundamentally industrial, echoing the success of industrial clusters and paying lip service to the rhetoric of 'industrialisation' (*gongyehua*). The question is: how effective is this ecology? The move up the value chain (levels 3–5) involves processes of learning, which combined with market facilitation – clustering, industrial policy, protection and regulatory quotas – aspire to unlock the door to success. In these upper stages of the ecology knowledge transfer mechanisms, such as inter-firm collaborations, professional networks and labour mobility are crucial. Co-operation entails learning, while trade reflects the desire to integrate into markets, particularly profitable East Asian markets where there is the advantage of cultural proximity. Differentiation is the key value-add often overlooked, the capacity to make products that are high in quality, utilise new technologies and attract intellectual property rents (Caves 2000).

It is believed that the clustering strategy is a way to upgrade creativity (the term 'upgrade' is frequently found in policy reform blueprints). However, the clustering phenomenon has inevitably generated an innovation trap. Participants are locked into cultural 'parks' where they are closely 'managed' instead of being free to think outside of the box. It seems the only way to spring the trap is to bring in new ideas from outside the mainland or to commit to substantive IP reform; that is, to change the environment of uncertainty and rent seeking to an environment in which innovation is rewarded and where creativity is acknowledged.

In comparison with commercial fields of production, the sixth stage of the ecology considers the impact of unofficial culture: how online social networks act as incubators for ideas that are subsequently taken up commercially (Montgomery 2010; Keane 2007). The non-official or amateur world of production is a sphere of creation and re-creation, where ideas collide and are disseminated virally. These scale-free networks might be called China's creative clusters 3.0. I will return to this question in the final chapter. Much of the invention currently occurring in online communities is not aimed directly at profiteering, but rather functions as informal and amateur incubation. On this level we see a proliferation of cultural adaptations known collectively as *shanzhai*. Many find niches and efficacious uses in the market; these include communication appliances: mobile phones, fashions, food and beverages, etc. that are often 'passed off' as being international luxury brands (Chew 2010).

Harmonising creativity

In concluding I want to set out four possible scenarios for the longevity of the creative industries idea in China, particularly the potential of the discourse of creativity to effect social change. The first scenario says that while creativity and innovation are currently fashionable, these ideas remain in the realm of policy-speak and have no real capacity to effect any substantial social change. This leads into the question: is there a disjuncture between the Western idea of creativity, with its roots in European Enlightenment and democracy, and traditional Chinese understandings on the harmony of nature and culture? Indeed, these are debates that have occurred in the past. Hegel believed that 'the Orient' never experienced a rupture with nature, such as had occurred in Greek tradition, which ultimately led to discontinuity, together with a propensity to separate nature and culture (Hegel 1975, cited in Puett 2001; see also Makeham 2003). Voltaire (1828) argued that continuity between nature and culture – as expressed in Chinese cultural artefacts and writings – had allowed China a period of early advancement, which was followed by stasis. While there is a danger of equating the mindsets of today's cultural officials with a longing for an idealised harmonious past, nevertheless the ghosts of the past are never completely laid to rest. The creative process is sometimes understood in Confucian societies as a process of recombination rather than invention. For this reason, the propensity of Chinese academics to generate models as a means of finding solutions to political, economic and social problems might be seen as a pragmatic and harmonious form of creativity.

The second scenario is that the concept of the creative industries is fundamentally misunderstood in China; that is they are more appropriately construed as cultural industries; and because cultural tradition exerts so much influence in national policymaking the creative industries offer little hope of change. In this respect, the relationship between culture (*wenhua*), innovation (*chuangxin*) and creativity (*chuangyi*) remains unclear. The Ministry of Culture official mentioned above, Wang Yongzhang, is one of many Beijing-based officials who adhere to the need to steer public institutions (*shiye*) gradually towards industries (*chanye*) (see Zhang 2006). The key point here is that the gradual transition from the former state-owned and managed institution model to the more autonomous industry model is a process guided by enlightened officials who have the best interests of the population at heart. For some state-owned companies, however, the shift to becoming entrepreneurial is not so easy; it means adopting changes in management style and accepting risk. In addition to demonstrating the fit between guided development and markets, The official points to the fact that the emphasis on wealth creation and employment in the DCMS is different from China's core intention 'to cultivate autonomous innovation capacity', which he says entails producing famous brands and nurturing competitive cultural enterprises, as well as enterprise groups that generate their own intellectual property (Wang Yongzhong 2007). In this reading, the Chinese government should avoid international trends and maintain its right to define 'soft power' (*ruan shili*) in terms that reflect national sovereignty.

One senses that while this is the course set by cultural officials in Beijing, the initial reluctance to admit the new international discourse into national policy paradoxically led to the strengthening of the idea of creativity in epistemic communities and think-tanks further from the centre. It is common to hear the term 'creative industries' used in cities throughout China.

The third scenario suggests that the creative industries are here to stay in China although they will always be managed by party officials, thus negating the positive externalities associated with artistic freedoms in the West. In effect, this 'harmonisation' steers the discourse of creativity into the service of cultural bureaucrats. As this study will show, the pace of development has increased with the establishment of more spaces for the exhibition, sale and production of cultural artefacts, together with provision of restaurants, bars and coffee shops. The expansion of venue spaces has meant more exchange of ideas between local and international artists. The propaganda and local government officials who manage creative clusters and cultural zones can see opportunities in such exchange, even if their own venues are not producing creative output. The labelling of districts as creative may be enough in many cases to attract investment, to generate real estate and land use value, and to attract tourists to buy artefacts. The creative clusters that dot the countryside now are more real estate than real innovation; they allow cultural officials to identify 'talent' and in some instances provide support; they function as new enclaves for China's creative classes; they redistribute wealth accordingly as the value of creativity rubs off on the industrial remnants of the old society.

The fourth scenario is that the creative industries are changing China. Indeed, this is the title of a recent book by Li Wuwei in which he writes:

> The creative economy will undergo a long development process for the formation of the creative economy, ranging from talent cultivation to urban transformation. It requires vision. It requires adaptation to developments in the global economy. It requires confidence in our own developmental advantages. It requires us to put a high priority on those industries that will make important contributions to China's economic growth and coordinated social development in the future. Backed up by 5,000 years of Chinese civilization and increasingly dynamic creative potential, China is determined to develop into a creative nation with global influence.
> (Li 2011: 6)

The extent to which the proliferation of creative clusters has changed, or will change China's cultural and media sectors, is the subject of the following chapters.

2 Redesigning China's creative space

The elasticity of the term 'cluster' is both useful and confounding when applied to the economics of cultural and media industries. Usually a cluster implies a spatial co-location of activity; from the perspective of innovation and regional studies literature co-location exploits shared resources and indicates a desire for innovation effects (see Mommaas 2009, 2004). However, not all forms of cultural production benefit from proximity. Alternatively creative clusters may be aspatial; for instance in Singapore, policy advisors have designated three 'industrial grouping clusters': arts and culture, design, and media (Kong 2009: 64). Mommaas says that creative clusters can be differentiated according to their form of organisation; for instance those organised around the autonomous arts (the artistic professions), those that are more applied and entrepreneurial (design, fashion, media) and those that pertain more directly to technological, scientific or economic notions of creativity (Mommaas 2009: 53).

Writing from the standpoint of economic geography, Martin and Sunley argue that the cluster concept: 'is being applied so widely that its explanation of causality and determination becomes overly stretched, thin and fractured' (Martin and Sunley 2003: 28–29). In short, the terminology of cluster promises a great deal but the evidence of how clustering generates innovation remains speculative. This caveat hold true in the People's Republic of China where the cluster has become an umbrella term for a wide range of industrial concentrations.

The cluster is a recent addition to scholarship on culture. Michael Porter's work on *The Competitive Advantage of Nations* (Porter 1990) introduced the business cluster concept into the policy mainstream. Porter (1998) defined a cluster as a geographically proximate group of interconnected companies and associated institutions in a specific field based on commonalities and complementarities. Prior to Porter's intervention economic geographers had promoted a number of terms including industrial districts, new industrial spaces, territorial production complexes, regional innovation milieu, network regions and learning regions, without winning the support of policymakers. In making the 'cluster' popular, Porter's work allowed the terminology to make its way into the cultural economy, paving a way for a new generation of scholar-consultants to offer their services to urban planners.

From the perspective of regional economics and economic geography a cluster is a concentration of business activity in a specific region: these agglomerations may be large in scale, similar in focus and significant in output; for instance Hollywood is the global leader in film financing production; Silicon Valley is the acknowledged global centre of high-technology business; whereas Zhongguancun in Beijing aspires to be 'China's Silicon Valley'. Clusters may be small or medium-sized agglomerations with a mix of local and international linkages such as we shall see in the following chapters; alternatively they may be concentrations of similar businesses – communities of practice brought into existence by favourable policies but which for various reasons struggle to make significant impressions on the market. Clusters can form organically and they can be initiated by policymakers and entrepreneurs. In spite of the variation in types of clusters, there is a great deal of optimism that they are a means to gain economic advantage.

This chapter has three sections. I begin by suggesting that the cluster is a sub-species of the region and the city; to put it another way, regions and cities cluster people and businesses. Before moving on to the topic of what a creative cluster looks like in China, I want to discuss the relationship between international creative cities discourses and the envisioning of cultural infrastructure projects such as performing arts centres, mixed-use cultural regeneration projects, iconic buildings, stadiums, theme parks and museums. This is a global phenomenon. In China the momentum has increased to the point where questions are now being raised about sustainability of grand cultural projects, and where, and to whom the benefits flow.

In short, the current academic fascination with clusters is a reflection of the competitive advantages of regions. The concept of a 'learning economy' draws attention to the importance of human capital. Lundvall describes the learning economy as a development context where agents are exposed to frequent and rapid change (Lundvall *et al.*, 2007: 214; Hodgson, 1999). The best ideas have traditionally come from concentrations of people living and working in supportive networks or environments. Many environments are recognised for their innovative capacity and attract human capital and investment. However, just as some environments breed new ideas, others inhibit them. The extent that a creative cluster functions as a learning economy will depend on a number of factors including the design, location, management and output of the locale.

Moreover, competition in the era of increasing regional specificity is problematic. Global evidence points to the importance of sustained first-mover advantages. Economic success stories reveal that some places develop learning capabilities in an organic sense, while others rely heavily on policy intervention.

In examining the interplay between tangible and intangible resources, Andersson and Anderrson (2006) employ the concept of 'cultural infrastructure'. The tangible infrastructure includes facilities such as churches, temples, museums, theatres and amusement parks. These primarily represent slow-changing goods. Other facilities (concerts, exhibitions, festivals and sporting events) support faster-changing cultural activities. Intangible resources, what Landry (2000) calls 'soft infrastructure', are the recipes of culture, namely cultural ideas. In many instances, the intangible infrastructure is a precondition for the tangible: for instance, modernism and its effect on architecture and industrial design in the nineteenth and twentieth centuries. Intangible ideas, expressed as creativity or innovations, facilitate the transformation of infrastructure and therefore the broader economy.

One of the most striking aspects of China's urban transformation in the past decade is the perceived success of creative cities, districts, zones and clusters. Accordingly, international creativity experts and innovation gurus are feted at annual expos and prevailed upon to reveal the ingredients for harnessing economic creativity in China. As one might expect, the results have been mixed; expectations are often raised in such events, suggesting that China has moved from a benign authoritarian model of governance to the kind of liberal environment that encourages free association of ideas. In short, advocacy of the benefits of civil society in international artistic and creative communities is not what local authorities necessarily want to hear.

In the second section, I discuss relevant literature on the topic of cultural and creative clusters, specifically the concept of localised external economies, initially developed in Alfred Marshall's account of industrial districts in the UK over a century ago (Marshall 1920/1990) The link between Marshallian industrial districts and art districts might appear on the surface to be problematic. However, collectively organised production of cultural artefacts occurred in pre-industrial times, most notably in craft-based communities and guilds. Collective organisation and systematic division of labour took place in traditional China in silk and ceramic production. In the twentieth century the recognition of the concept of cultural quarters provided a theoretical means to link Marshallian industrial districts to contemporary cultural regeneration projects. The cluster, from this perspective, is a generic term to describe mutual co-operation through informal and formal economies of scale by which information is shared in socio-economic networks.

In China, the post-industrial 'turn' is most evident in large cities, which are striving to renew, to be modern, fashionable and international. While the term 'creative cluster' is popular with policymakers and cultural academics in China, it enfolds into two variations: the first is *cultural quarters*, where the focus is on retail, small-scale business activity, lifestyle and consumption; the second is *industry bases*, where the main concern is to stimulate productivity, but where one finds little original creation. What is common, however, is the propensity to promote growth in the number of clusters for purposes of stimulating regional urban growth rather than regulating these projects to maximize efficiencies (Zheng 2010). In effect, I will argue that most of China's successful clusters fall somewhere in between these two categories: the uncertainty of being 'in-between' generates a hybrid production-consumption mentality.

However, the uncertainty between culture and creativity, between consumption and production, and between innovation and outsourcing allows sufficient opportunities for entrepreneurs and intermediaries to convince local government officials that such projects are sustainable. At least, this has been the story to date. In effect, a reshaped field of cultural production has formed. Ultimately, however, the benefits flow to government officials in terms of tax revenue and increased land value under the pretext of providing the infrastructural conditions for innovation.

Following the discussion of relevant literature I note stages of creative cluster development in China. I identify five categories: (i) locales specialising in similar products, often located in reconverted factories; (ii) organic creative milieu; (iii) 'related variety' developments; (iv) media production bases; and (v) incubators and science and innovation parks. I explain various rationales for clustering. The examples in this study show how cluster developments in China are heavily integrated in urban planning and contingent on local government support through preferential policies, assisted loans, rent relief and tax holidays. In many cases the cluster management partners with local government, private investors and developers to construct amenity infrastructure. This often includes the provision of transport and communications infrastructure, the addition of apartments and work spaces, and the planting of trees and parks. The influence of real estate speculation is therefore significant; aside from the obvious success of consumption-based cultural clusters like 798 Artzone in Beijing (see Chapter 5), increases in land values and rent provide the only viable business model.

Furthermore I argue that the emphasis in China today is mostly directed to material infrastructure: that is, 'stuff' that can be seen – hundreds of cultural and creative parks, more outsourcing enterprises, more channels for content and more cultural real estate. A driver of such initiatives is the fear of being left behind in the context of intense competition among regions and cities. It is economics more than politics that is driving the planning of creative space.

Creative cities: history and location

The relationship between environment and innovation, or indeed between milieu and creativity, has come to the fore in the current era of ever-increasing regional competition. The search for innovation captures the attention of bureaucrats, planners and research centres. The quest has also moved beyond the high-value and high-technology sectors. There is now a widespread perception that the seeding of cultural and creative industries projects is a necessary element in the competitiveness of regions (Florida 2002; Roodhouse 2006; Landry 2000; Martin and Sunley 2003; Wu 2005).

This is not a new story. If we look at significant creative centres from history, we note the 'ethos' of cities, the distinctiveness of a culture or a period, 'the background network of worldviews, styles and inspirations found in a society, or a framework for cultural interpretation' (Cowen 2003: 48). Certainly this was the case in Chinese dynastical capitals: Chang'an (now Xian) during the Tang Dynasty, in Bianjing (now Kaifeng) during the northern Song Dynasty and in Hangzhou during the Southern Song. Dieter Kuhn writes of the affluence of Lin'an (now Hangzhou), a city visited by the Venetian traveller Marco Polo. Around the Imperial Boulevard: 'the proliferation of workshops, markets, and family businesses was without parallel elsewhere' (Kuhn 2009).

During the Renaissance, European cultural capitals drew artists and thinkers together, spawning new networks of exchange. Venice was a meeting place of international trade. Luxury goods from the Orient infused enthusiasm for the arts and diffusion of knowledge about art. By the sixteenth century Venice had become a centre of publishing, producing well over half of all books in Italy (Zimmermann 2008). The success of Venice was due to specialisation, a deliberate business strategy of cultural entrepreneurs to harness the resources and human capital of the city.

In scientific endeavours certain places generated intellectual fruition. In Galileo's Italy a new community of scientific enquiry emerged. The centre of discovery later moved to Austria, both in the human sciences and the social sciences. Howard Gardner (1993) tells of Vienna in the early twentieth century and how a diverse community developed around the intellectual leadership of Sigmund Freud. Within the same German-speaking intellectual milieu, although operating in different disciplinary registers, were the economist Joseph Schumpeter, and the sociologists Max Weber, Emile Durkheim and Georg Simmel.

By the late twentieth century science cities and technology hubs had became a matter of policy intervention. Compared with the cities like Vienna and Berlin, which developed organically, a list of modern science cities would include Los Alamos (USA), Cartuga (Spain) and Tsukuku (Japan). Technological infrastructure has fed the clustering of human capital. Silicon Valley's proximity to Stanford University provided research collaboration and synergies with the Valley's highly internationalised human capital (Kenney 2000). Margaret O'Mara (2005) argues that the success of Silicon Valley and Boston's Route 128 did not simply result from fortuitous combinations of capital and entrepreneurship (2005: 1). The role of policy was instrumental in making and shaping these locations, and in providing the ideal environment for science to grow and prosper. Such science and knowledge cities grew away from 'the distractions and disorders of the changing industrial city' (2005: 2). Elsewhere the term 'knowledge city' is applied with less focus on science (Ergazakis et al. 2004; Carillo 2006). Ergazakis et al. (2006: 4) describe the knowledge city as one that encourages the continuous creation, sharing, evaluation, renewal and update of knowledge. Examples of knowledge cities in this definition include Barcelona, Stockholm, Munich, Montreal and Dublin.

In Asia similar development possibilities have captured the attention of planners. Government-initiated techno-poles include the Multimedia Super Corridor in Cyberjaya Malaysia and the Cyberport in Hong Kong, the former a large-scale government-primed project which has struggled in times of economic crisis, the latter a digital content hub financially supported by the SAR Hong Kong government. As I will discuss later, many technology and creative cluster projects in China have followed the model of the free trade zone in attempting to lure businesses with promises of low tax and free rent in the hope that technological and knowledge spillovers will pass from stronger to weaker firms. The rationale is that technology gaps between developed and developing countries can easily be reduced. In the main research suggests that foreign companies in such clusters have limited impact on local production and diffusion of technology (Zhou 2008: 17; Lemoine and Unal-Kesenci 2004).

Creative cities movements: creative cities discourse

Cities have always attracted talent. In modern times avant-garde arts movements have clustered in 'quarters': among the most famous are the Latin Quarter of Paris, as well as Montmartre and Montparnasse. Bohemians spawned alternative cultural movements, culminating in underground and counter-culture movements. The Paris fashion scene developed in the royal court as *haute couture* in the nineteenth century and since then has been located around the Rue de Honoré (Zimmerman 2008: 42). These fashionable areas are renowned for luxury brands and bourgeois lifestyles. The fashion industries of Paris and Milan are characterised by proximity of related sub-sectors: photography, exhibitions and fashion shows, as well as suppliers of garments.

Working-class agglomerations have been important in the transformation of cities although in Europe during the nineteenth and twentieth centuries working classes lacked the purchasing power of elites. State intervention into urban cultural development projects sought to ameliorate social disadvantage (Bennett 2003). Culture-led regeneration was a key to fostering the arts and culture, often building on popular pastimes; for instance, Manchester's renaissance from working-class city to cosmopolitan centre had its roots in the emergence of nightlife and a 'cultural quarter' in the late years of the nineteenth century. Simon Gunn notes that Manchester's cultural economy was based on the development of a 'traditional' working-class culture 'closely aligned with the growth of a capitalist leisure industry' (Gunn 2008: 115).

Charles Landry, author of *The Creative City* (Landry 2000), the first publication to capture the spirit of creative place competition, describes an idea he calls the Creative City Movement. Landry says that whereas the contemporary obsession with creativity – what he calls 'a creativity rash' – pre-existed in the 1980s, at that time it was encompassed in terms such as ingenuity, skill and inventiveness (Landry 2006: 388). Alternatively, Stuart Cunningham (2012) speaks of 'creative cities discourse' (CCD). Cunningham says that such discourse represents a rapidly growing literature across the discipline fields of urban studies, urban planning, architecture, design, media communication, and cultural and economic geography. Furthermore, writings on creative cities are usually strongly policy-oriented and often highly technical; for instance dealing with urban zoning regulations, land use regulations, and architectural design standards. Adding to such complexity are the well known problems of statistical dissonance that make meaningful creative city comparisons difficult, although this has not reduced the propensity for scholars to construct indexes (Florida and Tinagli 2004).

In effect, the international idea of creative cities is seductive but much of the evidence remains speculative and rhetorical. Graeme Evans (2009, 2005) describes the global 'movement' driving creative cities and creative spaces as interventions based on evidence-based policy. However, despite various types of published evidence and performance indicators, much policy formulation is fast (Peck 2005), takes a cookie-cutter approach (Oakley 2004) and is often reckless. Joel Kotkin (2005) is a strident critic of the tendency to see hip culture as a means of rejuvenating cities and districts. He cites examples of Cleveland, Detroit, Baltimore, New Orleans and Newark in the US as cities that have continued to deteriorate despite attention to cultural programmes. Cunningham (2012) believes that place competitiveness provokes 'what many academics might regard as egregious and tendentious displays by civic officials as they jostle to put their city on the map'.

Creative city discourse lends itself to arguments for more public investment in arts. The economist David Throsby (2010: 139) writes:

> The concept of the creative city describes an urban complex where cultural activities of various sorts are an integral component of the city's economic and social functioning. Such cities tend to be built

upon a strong social and cultural infrastructure; to have relatively high concentrations of creative employment; and to be attractive to inward investment because of their well-established arts and cultural facilities.

Throsby's approach is unapologetically supportive of the human capital attributes of the trained artist as the core factor in creative industries policy interventions. The economic contribution of the arts, and artists, to national and regional economies was recognised by the late 1970s in North America and from the mid-1980s in Europe (Evans 2001: 140). Culture-led rejuvenation discourses focused on city-regions (Toronto, Ontario; Liverpool, Merseyside; Port of New York/New Jersey; and Greater London).

Creative city branding gained momentum following the work of Landry (2000, 2006), Montgomery (2003) and Florida (2002, 2008). Landry estimates there are more than 60 cities in the world that make some claim to 'creative city' status, either self-conferred or designated by international agencies: 20 of these alone are in Britain. Following the Lord Mayor's Creative London campaign in 2004, a bandwagon effect ensued: the list includes Creative Manchester, Sheffield, Bristol, Plymouth and Norwich in the UK; Creative New York, Cincinnati, Tampa Bay in the US; Creative Amsterdam, Create Berlin in Europe; Creative Toronto, Vancouver, Ottawa in Canada; in Greater China there have been Creative City branding campaigns in Hong Kong, Hangzhou, Singapore and Taipei. In addition, cities jostle for nomination in UNESCO's Creative Cities Network: a list of designated creative cities includes Seoul and Incheon (Korea); Shanghai, Chengdu, Shenzhen (China); Edinburgh, Glasgow (Scotland); Kobe, Nagoya (Japan); Sydney, Melbourne (Australia); Saint-Etienne, Lyon (France); Berlin; and Buenos Aires.

Cunningham (2012) notes structural tensions in creative cities discourse between consumption-centricity and production-centricity. This duality draws from Florida's work on the creative class. Prior to identifying this uber-concept, Florida's work on 'learning regions' had defined a new age of capitalism, one in which human capital had become the primary source of value. In 1995, Florida wrote that learning regions:

> function as collectors and repositories of knowledge and ideas, and provide an underlying environment or infrastructure which facilitates the flow of knowledge, ideas and learning. Learning regions are increasingly important sources of innovation and economic growth, and are vehicles for globalisation.
>
> (Florida 1995: 528)

In 2002 Florida published the highly influential *The Rise of the Creative Class*, which moved the focus from regions to cities, and expanded the concept of creative human capital to include bohemians, scientists and broad white-collar demographics such as engineers, computer programmers and education professionals. The essential point Florida made, and has continued to make in his highly productive lecture tours of aspirant global cities is that lifestyle-based choices drive city renewal and growth. While the great scholars of the city such as Lewis Mumford, Jane Jacobs and Peter Hall observed and analysed the success and failures of cities, Florida provides specific policy interventions that promise the discovery of hitherto hidden or neglected resources (Cunningham 2012).

In subsequent work Florida has returned to the importance of the region, referring to the 'underlying economic power of the *clustering force*' (Florida 2008: 61; italics in original). In placing the emphasis on human capital, Florida writes:

> When people – especially talented and creative ones – come together, ideas flow more freely, and as a result individual and aggregate talents increase exponentially: the end result adds to more than the sum of the parts...this in a nutshell *is* the clustering force.
> (Florida 2008: 66)

Florida's work has been the subject of much criticism and he has spent a great deal of time attempting to clarify his assertions and to justify his indexes. In trying to show how places have measurable advantages and disadvantages in human capital and technology, Florida speaks of 'spikes' and 'valleys'. The point he makes is that the world is not flat: the global spikes are cities where there a great deal of diversity and agglomeration, for instance, Tokyo and New York. Places tend to retain such competitive advantages. Elsewhere work on industrial districts has referred to 'sticky knowledge'. Stickiness refers to how knowledge is imperfectly accessible and does not flow easily; much knowledge is tacit, exchanged through direct experience, collective support systems, common languages, conventions and habits (Storper 1997; Belussi and Sedita 2010).

Finally, it is worth noting Durkheim's notion of 'collective effervescence'. Durkheim recognised that dynamism and change occurred in societies when people regularly came together and associated with each other. Societies and communities were subsequently reinvigorated and regenerated (Swedberg 2006). Another way of explaining effervescence is the idea of related variety, which draws on Jane Jacobs' (1961) work on twentieth-century American cities. Related variety explains why innovation occurs, often organically, in places where there is a mix of specialist and diverse skills. In *The Death and Life of Great American Cities*, Jacobs noted that cities are:

> the natural homes of supermarkets and standard movie houses plus delicatessens, Viennese bakeries, foreign groceries, art movies and so

on, all of which can be found co-existing, the standard with the strange, the large with the small. Wherever lively and popular parts of cities are found, the small outnumber the large.

(Jacobs 1961: 146–7)

Cultural and creative clusters

Advocates of cluster-led growth in China often cite secondary evidence; they speak earnestly about the success of the 'global creativity economy' (UNCTAD 2008, 2010). When invited to international conferences in Asia international experts are quick to foster the image of developing countries fast-tracking to environmentally sustainable growth and knowledge-based futures. Such arguments, coming from so-called international 'experts', are persuasive in China where the national government has established an agenda to be an innovative nation (*chuangxin xing guojia*) by 2020. 'International' cultural and creative industries conferences, forum, expos and symposiums are held annually in most large Chinese cities. In particular demand are experts who have demonstrable economic credentials. For example, John Howkins, the author of *The Creative Economy*, has established himself as 'the father of the creative industries' in China where he has worked closely with the Shanghai and Wuxi municipal governments.

Unfortunately there is little hard evidence to assess the performance of clusters. There is a reluctance to admit that the clustering model is flawed in many respects. However, before looking at China's engagement with cluster models it is useful to examine key approaches. As mentioned earlier, two broad categories that inform developments in Chinese cities are cultural quarters and industrial parks. Cultural quarters are usually linked to the regeneration of inner-city regions whereas industrial parks, at least in urban China, are located on the fringes of cities, often in industrial zones. Globally regeneration strategies fall into two divides: cultural and economic regeneration. The former is more concerned with community self-development and self-expression while economic regeneration is about property development and place marketing (Bassett 1993; Evans 2005).

Cultural quarters

According to John Montgomery, cultural quarters tend to combine increased consumption of the arts and culture with cultural production and urban place-making (Montgomery 2003). Building on the insights of the US urban scholar Jane Jacobs, planners have become aware of four essential preconditions that promote diversity: a mixture of primary uses, intensity of built form, permeability and a mixture of building types, ages, sizes and conditions (Jacobs 1961). Jacobs' prescriptions for diversity allow planners in China a degree of latitude as many selected regeneration sites are already inner-city, have a mixture of built form, and are often old buildings with relatively narrow streetscapes.

Culturally led urban development began to emerge in the UK from the 1980s, the most well-known instances being the Sheffield Cultural Industries Quarter (the late 1980s) and the Manchester Northern Quarter (from 1993). The policy question that emerges for aspiring local governments is: do successful cultural quarters emerge spontaneously or can they be planned? Furthermore, at what stage should government intervene and what kind of policy intervention is appropriate? Certainly in China, where the government has a long record of planning cultural activities there is a belief that once established, they can be successfully managed. As I will discuss in the following chapters, the governance of China's creative clusters adopts a different approach to what we might find in most international projects.

The success of cultural quarters is a contentious topic. From the perspective of urban regeneration, they have the potential to increase the flow of business, provide employment opportunities, and transform the identities of locales that have suffered from processes of deindustrialisation, poverty and crime. More specifically, increased production and consumption of goods and services generates tax revenues and increases land values. There may be significant new investment in infrastructure, both public and private. Echoing Florida's 'creative class', the success of cultural quarters and districts may encourage businesses to relocate, in turn adding new economic and social ingredients to the milieu.

Industrial clusters

The industrial park or district is well established in the literature on economic geography: its articulation into the creative economy is an interesting story. According to Alberto Guenzi (2009), the precursor to modern industrial parks was the ancient guild system, a workshop model that allowed the transmission of tacit knowledge and skills with the purpose of eventually allowing the novice to become a craftsman or entrepreneur. Richard Sennett takes up the story at the time of the Italian Renaissance:

> The craft workshop continued as the artist's studio, filled with assistants and apprentices, but the masters of these studios did indeed put a new value on the originality of the work done in them... this contrast still seems to inform our thinking: art seems to draws attention to work that is unique or at least distinctive, whereas craft names a more anonymous, collective and continued practice.
>
> (Sennett 2008: 66)

The passing of the guild model gave way to the regulation of production systems based on craftsmanship. A similar industrial model existed in traditional China. According to Lothar Ledderose (2000), in the year 1577 pottery makers in the city of Jingdezhen received an imperial order to supply 174,700 pieces of porcelain. The delivery was made possible because of the sophisticated division of labour that existed in the pottery kilns. Likewise whereas Chinese silk making in the Ming and Qing Dynasties was organised in large factories, the actual work was subcontracted out to teams (Faure 2006: 19). Ledderose claims that Europe learnt about standardisation of production, division of labour and factory management from China.

We can look back even further to the construction of the famous terracotta warriors that guarded the tomb of the first emperor. Produced by massive teams of indentured labour, each porcelain warrior was assembled in modular from and final embellishments were added. The point about such production was recombination. Likewise, in thinking of the industrial production facilities that arose in fashion and shoemaking industries in Italy, we find a combination of craft skills and know how. These techniques are accrued by observing and learning.

External economies

More than just the application of technique, the industrial cluster has been successful because of its capacity to attract skilled workers. From an economic perspective the key idea is *localised external economies*; in other words, the benefits to co-location of businesses competing in similar markets but cooperating in the development of similar knowledge. Storper (1997: 27) argues that external economies 'are complex outcomes of interaction between scale, specialization, and flexibility in the context of proximity'.

The value of external economies is well known (Porter 1998). Businesses in similar markets gain from spatial co-location in several ways. Potts (2011: 152–5) provides a good summary of the attractiveness of clusters. First, because there are both greater and more diverse opportunities for specialised work, clusters attract a pool of skilled workers. This lowers the cost to firms of finding and employing specialised skilled workers. This effect also extends to other input resources, which may be directed to the cluster in greater quantity and thus, via scale economies, at lower price. Second, the presence of many similar firms creates incentive for other business to establish specialist services to these firms that would not be viable if there were only one or two businesses, but do become so in a cluster. This enables firms to concentrate on their core capabilities, thus improving the average productivity and refining the competitive advantage of all firms within the cluster. Third, infrastructure, utilities, transport and other business requirements and institutions can be more efficiently supplied to a cluster, again lowering average costs and reinforcing the global competitiveness of firms within the cluster. Fourth, a cluster provides a physical focus for consumers of the cluster output. By lowering the costs of search, consumers benefit from the existence of the cluster as a market. These four factors all interact to generate the increasing returns common to cluster formation (Krugman 1991; Belleflamme *et al.* 2000).

Creative clusters and innovation

The relationship between creative clusters and innovation is less clear than between the cluster model and division of labour. Inevitably, how spaces are planned, used and governed impacts on dynamism. Duxbury and Murray (2010) identify three creative 'models': incubators, creative habitats and multi-sector convergence projects. The first category, incubators, captures the idea of creative networking. It includes artists' co-operatives, media arts centres and new media artist-run centres. Duxbury and Murray say that while many incubator spaces are multidisciplinary, many others are defined by their specialities, 'usually serving in a "hub" role for particular communities, operating as an extension of them, and evolving over time' (2010: 204). In contrast, the 'creative habitat' model refers to an ecology of production, and usually entails a combination of space and place enjoined with a sense of community, neighbourhood, networks and entrepreneurial support. The third category, multi-sector convergence projects, describes physical spaces designed 'to maximize socialisation, networking and random collisions within them' (ibid.).

Indeed, the dynamic logic of clusters requires movement of people to act as a conduit for new ideas and knowledge. In terms of innovation effects, there is ideally some sense of competition within the cluster and the ability of participants (e.g. firms, individual entrepreneurs) to learn from each other, or be spurred by other's developments, experiments and ideas. Jason Potts (2011) notes that in clusters with relatively mature technology or stable markets, this effect may be less important. In fact, in the industrial cluster model that has been so successful in many parts of China the role of interactive learning is less important than efficiencies and cost competition (Wang Jici 2007). Creative industries, however, are characterised by novelty and experimentation. The dynamics of interactive learning are therefore likely to be the most important economic rationale (Potts 2011). Creative clusters are important not because of external economies in production, nor external economies in demand – although both remain important – but because of external economies in innovation.

Potts (2011: 154) writes:

> External economies of innovation provide the central rationale for why creative industries need to cluster. This is particularly so for new,

small and start-up creative industries businesses that derive much of their 'R&D' not from in-house production but from learning from other firms (through invited or tacit observation), and by tapping into and exploiting the social networks that grow and develop within a cluster context.

This extends to learning associated with new ideas and innovation, which is often highly tacit and requires face-to-face interaction, feedback and observation.

While clusters do form organically, from the regional perspective there is a strong competitive rationale for public intervention to create the initial developmental conditions. The surge of interest in media, cultural and creative clusters in China is therefore not surprising considering a legacy of collective organisation, which includes the Peoples' Communes movement, which began in the late 1950s and concluded at the end of the Cultural Revolution in 1976; the subsequent breakout of town and village enterprises (TVEs) around city fringes in the early 1980s; the establishment of science and technology parks in the late 1990s and early 1990s, mostly in Economic and Technology Zones; the establishment of media conglomerates (*jituan*) in the late 1990s and early 2000s. In differing ways these collectivist models responded to, and in some instances anticipated reform policies. However, while the latest stage, creative clustering, is hailed for its 'cultural economy' benefits and a capacity to change the international perception of China from a 'world factory' to 'world studio', many questions still remain about whether such projects can actually generate innovation.

The rationale for clustering in China, aside from the obvious perceived economic advantages and place marketing, is to find and harness creative human capital (*rencai*). In comparison, industrial clusters in the manufacturing sectors in China are more concerned with harnessing compliant labour. Many of my respondents expressed the opinion that the government is unsure of the best way to manage creativity. According to Zhang Xiaoming from the Chinese Academy of Social Sciences, the Chinese government is predisposed towards the cluster model because:

> The most convenient way is to provide a space and then establish a government *institution* to manage the space. This is called a cultural industries cluster management committee. It is hard to identify creative companies without clusters in China. Even with clusters, the government still can't manage to find out who is qualified for the preferential policies. Therefore, the most convenient and low-cost way is clusters. Companies can enjoy policies as long as they qualify and government can implement such policies at a relatively low cost.
> (Interview with author May 2011)

In effect, the current fascination with cultural and creative industries in China places a great deal of weight on the term 'industry' but underplays the importance of creativity. In short, the strategic challenge for China's business leaders and policymakers is to better understand the process of creative agglomeration.

A hundred clusters bloom

Chinese cities are currently undergoing extraordinary transformation. Central business districts have received makeovers, SOHO apartments have emerged in the vicinity of artist lofts and galleries, while iconic architectural developments have sprung up in the space of razed living spaces. A great deal of land, particularly on the fringes of cities, has undergone re-zoning. The accelerated urbanisation process is driven by multiple forces, but in particular by local bureaucratic entrepreneurs who are embedded within 'urban regimes' or 'growth coalitions' (McGee et al. 2007). These bureaucratic entrepreneurs have established relationships with government officials, developers and investors.

As mentioned earlier, China's current wave of clusters reflects a legacy dating back to the 1950s which saw the establishment of industrial estates. During the Second Five Year Plan (1958–1962) China began its long love affair with the factory. Soviet experts were available to provide managerial assistance. Factories with related functions were co-located in large cities. A well known example in Beijing was the 731 Switching Factory in Dashanzi (see Chapter 4).

The development of cultural and creative clusters in China has advanced through several distinct, although overlapping stages (see Table 2.1), informed initially by the perceived success of industrial clusters in Guangdong and Zhejiang provinces. As mentioned previously, the idea of industry connoted increased productivity more so than novelty.

The first cluster phase, most evident in Shanghai in the years 2004–2006, saw an outbreak of specialist agglomerations, for instance spaces dedicated to industrial design, graphic design, fashion, antiques, animation and sculpture. Many designated 'industry clusters' were situated in disused industrial space which had become available as a result of the relocation of industry away from city centres. The rationales for the instigation of these clusters included efficiency, ease of management, their proximity to art and design faculties at nearby universities and academies and ultimately the capacity to establish brand and place recognition. The co-location of artisans with similar interests presupposes sharing of knowledge and standards from a restricted field; for instance jewellery fabrication.

Meanwhile, a second iteration of clustering projects saw the evolution of artist zones and cultural districts; many began as organic communities, later converting to gentrified districts and zones, combining strong tourist

Table 2.1 Typologies of cultural and creative clusters

Form	Function	Examples
Specialist agglomerations	Spaces dedicated to one sector or sub-sector of the creative industries, e.g. jewellery, graphic design	Shanghai Sculpture Space; Songzhuang Capital Arts District
Cultural quarters and artist zones	Consumption-oriented, often in popular urban locales serving tourist markets; usually with an international profile, galleries, coffee shops, restaurants and bars; sometimes with theme-park function	Nanluoguxiang (Beijing); Tianzifang (Shanghai); 798 Art Zone Beijing
Related variety	High presence of small businesses and start-ups; a mixture of related businesses especially design, new media, media consulting, fashion, often favouring loft-style occupancy	Fangjia 46 Beijing; Foshan Creative Industries Park (Guangdong); Creative 100 (Qingdao); Xinghai Creative Island (Dalian); LOFT 49 Hangzhou
Media clusters	Parks ratified by SARFT or Ministry of Culture, usually administered by provincial and municipal governments, often located in outer-city industrial estates	Suzhou Industrial Park Animation base; Hengdian World Studios, Zhejiang
Incubators, science and technology parks	Aspiring to bring technology parks into the creative policy remit; elsewhere refers to occupation of old industrial sites by university departments	Tsinghua Science and Technology park (Beijing); Zhongguancun Creative Industries Pioneer base; KIC in Yangpu District Shanghai; The Design Factory, Shanghai

pull with consumer services. The story here follows a familiar global trend. Depending on one's perspective these developments are an indictment of the ethos of financial gain, upscale growth and the economic power of capital (Zukin 2010), or opportunities for social and urban renewal. Critics argue that neighbourhood life is sucked out and replaced by the presence of 'bourgeois bohemians' ('bobos'), who 'don't mind a little dirt on the streets as long as they feel safe' (Zukin 2010: 7). In urban China the 'management handover' of organic communities to government officials and private real estate companies is justified by the claim that cities, locales and districts have an image crisis, that they must compete for international and regional investment and they must consider tourism earnings. The most notable project to illustrate this trend is the 798 Arts Zone at Dashanzi in inner northeast Beijing (see Chapter 5). Significantly, it is the demonstration effect of high-profile international cases such as London's Soho, New York's Greenwich Village, and Tokyo's Roppongi Hills that drives officials, developers, academics, artist-entrepreneurs and financiers together in growth coalitions.

The 'third model' encourages the co-location of similar enterprises and actors. A greater element of planning is evident from the outset. Many such locations in urban China make use of reconverted factory space to provide space for selected 'related variety' sectors. Such places house a mix of small enterprises specialising in design, media production, fashion, painting, photography and sculpture, as well as marketing and branding. This third phase is both about upgrading existing natural clusters with add-ons such as bars, restaurants, galleries and bookshops and the deliberate planning, design and construction of new clusters, often a hybrid of the cultural quarter and the industrial district. The impetus here is municipal policy, which encourages the designation of these projects subject to their feasibility. In the north Chinese city of Dalian in Liaoning Province, the Xinghai Creative Island claims to be Dalian's own 798. Inside the reconverted factory situated next to a 'thinker's park' (*sixiang gongyuan*), the walls are emblazoned with the UK definition of creative industries, listing the various sectors. The chosen few – the space is relatively small compared with the expanse of 798 – occupy pristine new workspaces. Offerings include producing oil painting, graphic design, media content, animation, porcelain and reproductions of traditional artefacts from the Shang Dynasty. As well, there is even a space specialising in nude photography. Not to be outdone, nearby Qingdao in Shandong Province offers the aptly termed Creative 100 precinct, a mixed-use facility.

A fourth model is represented by media content clusters, often within existing industrial zones throughout China, notably in the field of animation. China now has more than 20 'national animation bases': the term 'national' can be conferred either by the central government or by the municipal government. I discuss this model more in Chapter 7. Elsewhere on a larger industrial scale we see stand-alone cinema, television and animation production centres, servicing the domestic audio-visual market and providing production sets and low-cost facilities for producers from Taiwan, Korea and the US.

The industrial park model is an important dimension of China's soft-power push. Creative industries parks are intended to provide greater productivity to help fill Chinese broadcast channels with 'good content'. The main animation production centres, often situated within an existing industrial area, are in Beijing, Shanghai, Hangzhou, Suzhou, Shenzhen, Dalian, Suzhou, Changzhou and Wuxi. The problem with the industrial park model for some is location. Often located outside the CBD in the fringe industrial zones, the centres are not able to tap into the dynamism of the very consumers they are targeting. As one digital content executive interviewed comments: 'Such parks are for nerds' (author interview). Another successful animation company CEO suggested to the author that it was fine to be in an industrial park as far as the business incentives were concerned, but it was not a place to be creative (author interview).

Much of the activity in industrial parks is routine fee-for-service work. The transfer of knowledge from international companies is limited. Foreign studios outsourcing in such locations continue to resist handing over control of creative work (e.g. conceptualisation and pre-production). The same applies to large film lots such as Hengdian World Studios, situated inland in central Zhejiang Province. Branded as China's Hollywood, the land-locked nature of Hengdian puts it at a disadvantage to the large urban centres of Shanghai and Beijing. To offset this disadvantage Hengdian absorbs a great deal of low-cost television drama production, particularly dynastical costume dramas. However, it compensates for the cyclical nature of audio-visual production by running a profitable theme park which cashes in on the success of its cinematic and TV drama output.

Finally, the most ambitious element in the creative development scenario is the re-conversion of science and technological space into (ersatz) creative space. The proximity of many science and technology parks – also called innovation parks – to prestigious universities and development zones reflects a national desire to incubate something above and beyond standard products. The problem with this vision is that many existing S&T parks are hardly innovative. Critics like Wang Jici (2007) contend that industrial parks are regarded by government as infrastructural, a means to attract enterprises from outside.

There is more than a degree of optimism in the genesis of such hybrid projects considering the fact that most creative cluster projects internationally are found in disused industrial spaces. Among the first 'wave' of cultural and creative clusters in Beijing was the Zhongguancun Creative Industry Pioneer Base. The rationale for the 'base' was to broker an interaction between innovation and creativity, bringing together the multitude of talent working in high-tech start-ups with the potentially profitable creative sectors. Proclaimed 'creative incubators' are now to be found in Chongqing (the Ideas Industry Centre); Tianjin (the Heping District Creative Animation Park; the Taida Science and Technology Park); Dalian (the Creative Incubator Garden); Hangzhou (The Hangzhou Innovation and Creative Industry New Base); Beijing's Zhongguancun Creative Industries Pioneer Base; and Shanghai's Zhangjiang Hi-tech Zone in Pudong and the KIC (Knowledge Innovation Community) in Yangpu District.

Proximity to high-tech districts, however, does not guarantee transfer of innovation capabilities and knowledge spillovers. Zhongguancun is a district in Beijing's Haidian that developed from a district earmarked for scientific research and higher education into a thriving hub of hi-tech businesses and R&D centres, Zhongguancun owes its success to a constellation of factors, a 'quadrangular system of innovation' which includes central and local government policies, the proximity of public universities and research institutions, the presence of multinational corporations and the activities of local technology firms. Zhou (2008) contends that it is necessary to view Zhongguancun's development not as a result of inexpensive labour, but demand from the domestic market. However, because of the strong domestic demand for cheap technology the success of Zhongguancun subsequently entails a predominance of 'second generation innovation', which is defined by Bresnitz and Murphree (2011: 4) as the ability to exploit the demand for the mixing of established technologies in order to come up with new solutions – 'the science of organizational, incremental, and process innovation'.

The wave continues

Initial enthusiasm for creative clusters came from Shanghai. On 8 January 2005, the Shanghai Creative Industry Centre (SCIC) began its operation. A month later the Shanghai Economic Commission published a glossy promotion called *Shanghai Creative Industry Clustering Parks*. The 14 clusters in this 'first wave' were mostly disused industrial spaces in high-value commercial districts. Some were already operational. Significantly, most of these initial cluster developments were dedicated to the manufacture of specific cultural or creative products.

In December 2006, the Beijing city government formally established its first wave of 'cultural and creative clusters'. The hybrid term 'cultural creative industries' responded to reservations among national Ministry of Culture officials in Beijing, who had invested resources in fostering 'cultural industries' (*wenhua chanye*). Beijing's first wave of ten cultural creative clusters included the resolutely uncreative Panjiayuan 'flea market' (a market for antiques and replica antiques), the already commercial 798 art district at Dashanzi, and potential 'big picture' developments such as the Zhongguancun Creative Industries Pioneer Base, the Songzhuang Art and Cartoon Zone, the Huairou Film and TV Base and the Beijing Cyber-recreation District in Shijingshan. While Shanghai had listed some 70 creative cluster sites on its books by 2007, Beijing's aimed to emphasise key projects.

By 2008, the number of projects in Beijing claiming, or at least aspiring to be clusters, zones and cultural creative parks had suddenly risen. These included theme parks, folk-custom streets, a fashion business district, Olympic Games constructions and sports culture centres. In particular, the economic prosperity of the cultural cluster model was boosted by the success of the Songzhuang artists' collective in east Beijing, which by 2007 had become the focal point of China's contemporary art scene. The cluster allowed artists a 'natural' environment to work, albeit under the gaze of local party officials, a supervision that has ensured output is unlikely to challenge the political establishment (Keane 2009).

Outside Beijing the creative space momentum was building. To the southeast, the city of Tianjin had undergone massive infrastructural development since 2005. In the shadow of Beijing, as far as the benefits of the international tourist industry were concerned, Tianjin's planners believed the city could share Beijing's resources. Tianjin was competitive in the sense of having lower business and living costs. These might be attractive elements for wooing creative enterprises and talents. In the northeast, Dalian was positioning itself in the creative industries opting to becoming the new Bangalore of East Asia. In the south, Shenzhen was aiming to exploit Hong Kong money, utilising its lower production costs and its migrant workforce. In the southwestern centre of China, Chengdu and Chongqing were busy with their own creative city and creative industry plans, leveraging on the national policy of revitalising the western regions.

For city planners in these huge cities, the creative industries were a new development template on which they could inscribe regional characteristics. In more coastal regions of Hangzhou, Suzhou and Nanjing the focus was animation, software, as well as the reuse of industrial space for housing a new wave of artists, designers and related professional services. Hangzhou, in particular, has set its aspirations to become the 'Silicon Valley in Paradise' – obviously a brand strategy to compete with China's other Silicon Valley wannabes Zhongguancun (Beijing) and the Zhangjiang Hi-tech Zone in Pudong (Shanghai).

In general, creative industries projects have been led by real estate developers. Gentrification together with consumer service functions provides the bottom line. In all, hundreds of reconverted factories throughout China have incorporated assorted design, painting, media, fashion and advertising services, which are made more commercially viable by recreational add-ons – bars, restaurants, massage, book and souvenir shops. In a sense, it is not the creativity or the networks of interaction that fund this wave of construction: it is the production and sale of tourist commodities. While one could argue that this mix of design-related activities does constitute 'related variety', the commercial focus has conspired to produce competition for markets rather than co-operation in learning. As a result many have bemoaned a loss of authenticity and crass commercialisation. The end result has been a manifest increase in land value and rents, but with often little 'innovation spillover'.

3 Clusters and regional development

How do culture, creativity and innovation align in clusters of industrial space, human capital and local investment in China? Is policy-driven clustering really identifying and assisting creative human capital or are benefits flowing to privileged groups, including those that manage the spaces, to developers and to local officials?

This chapter begins with an overall appraisal of the rationales for creative parks, zone, bases and clusters in China. In assessing the relative success of creative industries clusters and cultural quarters in China it is worth noting how the policy landscape compares with international best practice. I then look at the mechanics of cluster governance and investment from the perspective of 'growth coalitions', epistemic communities and local government actors.

Following this I identify three stages of cluster development in China. I investigate a successful 'stage three' cluster project in Guangdong Province, the Foshan Creative Industries Park. This project has adopted an entrepreneurial approach to cluster management, one that its charismatic proprietor Qiu Dailun hopes to franchise. I then examine developments in Hangzhou, a city which aspires to be the 'National Cultural and Creative Industries centre' of China. The examples from Hangzhou are LOFT49 and the White Horse Lake Creative Eco-City.

Benchmarks and challenges

Culture-led urban development takes many forms internationally. Creative clusters and cultural quarters have garnered most attention in the past decade. The rationales for such projects include neighbourhood regeneration, the provision of public cultural services, the construction of hubs for cultural, social and economic development, and attractions for tourists (Montgomery 2003; Evans 2001, 2009; Roodhouse 2006; Sugden et al. 2006; Belussi and Sedita 2010; Potts 2011). The thinking behind many cluster projects is to 'pick winners': in this sense the growth of clusters in China since 2005 is not so very different from the early 1990s, a period that saw an outbreak of innovation parks, most of which inevitably failed to deliver measurable innovation and ultimately served as revenue-generating sources for district governments via real estate speculation. Are today's cultural quarters and creative clusters so different then?

The enthusiasm for cultural and infrastructure projects which began in earnest in 2006 is now diminishing. In the main, clusters have not succeeded in raising the quality of Chinese cultural output. Most of the 'evidence' for cluster failure is however anecdotal. Performance, or lack of it, is hard to quantify. Few studies have been conducted to measure success or failure. One of the main problems is that government officials preside over urban developments in China and such actors are averse to open scrutiny of projects. In particular, government officials are not well placed to understand how flows of tacit knowledge lead to innovation effects. In most successful clusters and quarters internationally, participants self-select; that is, participants are drawn to a locale by the cultural atmosphere, opportunities for interaction and the suitability of work and exhibition spaces; hence the term 'cluster'. Creative clusters therefore require creative space: these may be creative workshops and studios or market spaces (e.g. 798 in Beijing). However, this also implies a mental space and an entrepreneurial space – willingness to experiment with new ideas. In addition, creative space entails competitive co-operation across networks of businesses, some degree of interactive learning and sharing of successful ideas.

How do these ideals play out in China? First, the selection of clusters and the leasing of space for enterprises have been *ad hoc* in many regions. Policy sweeteners and cheap rent, not the opportunity to be innovative, attract enterprises to locations. While the success of cluster projects is unproven in China the publicity that surrounds them, or more specifically a few benchmark projects like 798 Art Zone and the Shenzhen City of Design, is seemingly enough to persuade other Asian regions to jump on the bandwagon. The cluster movement has spread to Hong Kong and Taiwan in the past few years. In Hong Kong disused industrial spaces and public buildings such as the old Police Barracks Married Quarters, the Cattle Depot and Mallory Street in Wanchai have been turned over to artists. Significantly however, the rationale for projects in Hong Kong is informed by artists' contribution to civil society, not just economic benefits. In Taiwan clusters are on the development agenda following the perceived success of Huashan 1914 Creative Park in Taipei, now promoted heavily as a tourist venue.

The economic, social and cultural background of the locality is integral to creative space making. For those charged with the implementation and planning of such projects in China there is the temptation of duplicate construction (*chongfu jianshe*), the tendency to replicate projects from one city to another or from district to district with minor variations.

Unfortunately, the national policy directive of developing the cultural industries (and sometimes the creative industries) has precipitated a 'herd effect' among policy advisors. Very few projects take into account the mix and impact of actors – that is, firms, enterprises and officials – within the cluster. Many projects fail to acknowledge and retain characteristics of the locality; in many projects gentrification changes the dynamics of local culture. In some instances regional cultural dynamics are restructured: locals become service workers and cleaners for the new creative classes. In other examples, as in Beijing's Nanluoguxiang (Chapter 4) locals have assumed the role of landlords and small business operators. But this phenomenon is rare.

Governance extends to inclusion: in the past inclusion was accomplished by means of the neighbourhood committee although this was primarily intended as a form of surveillance. In contemporary cluster governance, a Communist Party official is never far from the decision-making action. Local actors (e.g. citizens) are rarely found in decision-making networks. The proxy for local residents is inevitably the local party secretary of the Chinese Communist Party. In the case of Songzhuang Capital Arts District (see Chapter 5) it would appear from statements by the local officials that interests of locals are central to all decisions. Alternatively, in many urban cluster developments there are other governance groups involved, including district street offices (*jiedao banshi chu*). Nonetheless there are clearly powerful economic forces at play behind the scenes as cities and districts seek to raise their economic profiles.

The motives of outside actors and financiers are crucial in how the cluster maintains its identity. Policies that encourage investment and human capital operate under constraints of place competition. Districts compete for investment and capital and the cluster is viewed as a good way to facilitate this. Many clusters, particularly those in large urban centres, actively seek out foreign participants. The introduction of foreign enterprises can have a positive impact on human capital development; in many cases enterprises, particular those in animation bases (see Chapter 7) acknowledge that non-Chinese companies bring different styles of management as well as new skills sets.

The challenge of generating a learning economy within the cluster and the locality is often secondary to the necessity of making projects viable. Ideally a cluster should have elements of 'hot spots' (Gratton 2007); that is, it should have an open innovation structure that encourages the kind of networks that deepen the learning processes. Many successful clusters internationally have training institutions built into the environment but this is not common in China. Knowledge is an important ingredient, particularly new knowledge, but there are inevitably issues about sharing and dissemination. In the absence of public management and direction, learning effects occur organically simply because of the collective benefits that accrue to various 'stakeholders'. However, the extent of interactive learning effects is conditional upon the ability of the stakeholders to co-ordinate resources and actions. There is thus a clear role for local and regional policy actors to facilitate this process. Yet the co-ordination of resources and actions is not well developed in many Chinese cultural/creative clusters. In effect this lack of effective co-ordination is a result of a lack of incentives to target high-value niches and intellectual property returns. The cheap and non-creative outputs and the add-ons such as services tend to win the day: a focus on quantity not quality. Such clusters may lead to such efficiencies and cost savings, but not necessarily to innovation.

Ideally the impact of clusters extends beyond increased rents for councils and landowners. A successful creative cluster will have significant spillover effects into the regional economy. These benefits are difficult to quantify precisely because they lead to structural changes in the workforces, the composition of businesses and markets and so on. These are more than simply cultural spillovers, but improvements in the competitive advantages of not just the cultural and creative sector, but potentially many other industries (e.g. through improved access to design services, architecture, media and communications, and so on). While often diffuse, it is these 'dynamic benefits' of clusters that have the greatest impact on growth and development (Potts 2011: 158).

As mentioned in the previous chapter, despite several variations the Chinese approach to clustering sits between the cultural quarter model and the industrial district. Transitioning from these models to a creative cluster requires a more competitive and regulated market for high-value content, which is currently lacking in China. The actual output of clusters, aside from servicing the tourist demand for souvenirs and artwork, is mostly devoted to low-end domestic consumption. In spite of the fact that many developments are labelled as creative clusters, they are fundamentally consumption oriented (cultural quarters) or production oriented (industrial parks). The missing ingredients are experimentation and risk-taking. From this perspective if they are not contributing to innovation, they are not creative clusters.

There is a tendency to be one or the other: a cultural quarter directed towards consumption (art zones, theme parks) or production clusters (animation and film bases, design centres). Alternatively there is a compromise strategy of being both: cultural creative clusters. As I show in the examples that follow, finer distinctions emerge when we identify business models and the strategic responses associated with these. Both cultural quarter and industrial district models present opportunities for gains though asset holdings associated with the cluster, if successful. This, in essence, is no different to land speculation. Most rents accrue to consumers, developers and landowners.

What then does the evidence tell us? First, as I have mentioned previously, it is important to see most of these projects as an extension of industrial development models, a necessary stage within the innovation ecology of China's cultural economy. The cluster is a collective form of production in China. Because of this it has received the blessing of the central government. From a competitive advantage perspective it is imperative that many of these clusters fail. Unfortunately, the failure of clusters is not a future that local officials countenance; the result is that all efforts will be made to give the impression that projects are delivering economic and social benefits.

Growth coalitions and government

China's experience with cultural and creative clusters needs to be understood within the framework of urban and regional development policy and national reform. Urbanisation has increased dramatically, absorbing people from rural regions, resulting in the transformation of land use, from agricultural to industrial and from industrial to commercial. The reform of land use regulations plays into the hands of, and is often motivated by developers who are key players in 'growth coalitions'. From a broad perspective a growth coalition includes national economic policy bureaus and relevant policy advisory committees, national and international business interests and communities. Moreover, growth coalitions comprise representatives of local and district governments who engage with developers, financiers and entrepreneurs.

The principal driving force behind cluster projects is national and regional reform policy. Whereas reform is ultimately conducted by party officials, the role of thinking about reform is increasingly delegated to epistemic communities. Intense competition occurs among local networks of developers, entrepreneurs, investors, artist-entrepreneurs, officials, intellectuals and residents who offer various development models. Many of these communities are embedded in the growth coalitions that have emerged to exploit the current interest in creativity. In creative cluster projects, these coalitions are augmented by cultural academics and think-tanks. Academics with credentials in the cultural or creative industries can make a good side income from consulting on local projects. Foreign experts are often co-opted into this process as well as into the process of influencing government thinking.

Ideas require translation into the lexicon of government discourse. All provinces and municipal governments promulgate policy and experiment with development models but for the idea to become national policy it has to be fed into the national propaganda machine. This process occurs via a number of avenues, one of which is the National Committee of the Chinese People's Consultative Conference (NCCPCC), a political advisory group made up of delegates from a range of political parties and organisations. This organisation includes independent scholars and persons of renown in various occupational domains. The NCCPCC meets annually, generally at the same time as the National People's Congress, and allows a broad canvas of opinions to be tabled. It has 25 vice-chair persons: currently these include Sun Jiazheng, the Minister of Culture, and Li Wuwei, a vice-chair of the Central Committee of the Revolutionary Kuomingtang Party and author of *How Creativity is Changing China* (Li 2011). The political rank of these vice-chairs is equivalent to premier, which means they can be powerful conduits for new ideas.

Within the Chinese Communist Party apparatus regular study sessions are prescribed on important reform topics. These study groups pass on advice to Politburo members; they sometimes include Politburo members. The study sessions take place around every 40 days. The Chinese government's series of Five Year Economic Plans are the master template in which discursive variations can be advanced. The National Eleventh Five Year Plan (2005–2010) introduced new reform ideas which were taken up in the media; in particular the Eleventh Five Year Plan signalled a change in direction, a desire to modify China's economic development model and its self-identity by looking outward. Terms such as 'soft power' (*ruanshili*), 'going out' (*zou chuqu*), 'autonomous innovation' (*zizhu chuangxin*) and 'innovative nation' (*chuangxin guojia*) gradually superseded the rhetoric of modernisation in Chinese media reports. Even the very Confucian slogan of 'harmonious society' (*hexie shehui*), entails recognition that the nation is becoming a global power. The construction of a harmonious society is a socio-economic vision that serves as the ultimate goal for the ruling CCP, which aims for a 'basically well-off' middle-class oriented society and a 'new socialist countryside'.

The key player in the development of urban cultural projects is invariably local government. McGee *et al.* (2007) note that in China local governments usually function 'not only as the chief decision-maker but also the largest investor directly responsible for investment, development and operation of key industrial, transport and urban projects' (McGee *et al.* 114). In particular, local governments compete to position their locality to capture the benefits of development. Iconic projects (*xingxiang gongcheng*) are one way to attract attention to a locality and to 'upgrade' their cities in the international order; for instance to become world cities or 'international cities'. There are four ways to attract investment for projects in China: state budgetary allocation, foreign investment, bank loans and local fund raising. With devolution of power to provinces and municipalities over the past decade, the main sources of capital for projects are local fundraising and bank loans; this may entail strategies to set up 'seemingly independent' companies or institutions aligned with government that can receive bank loans (McGee *et al.* 2007: 19).

The strategy employed by local governments is captured in the phrase 'attracting business and investment' (*zhaoshang yinzi*). As Philip Huang (2011) notes, local governments have the resources and wherewithal to provide land and infrastructural support below cost; they can provide special subsidies and tax privileges, and they can circumvent formal rules and regulations on labour use and environmental protection. Huang says that these practices taken together represent an 'informal economy'. Local governments are willing to absorb losses to attract investment: 'most important are the chain reactions to follow: services and smaller businesses that will emerge to support the new enterprises and generate new sales and income tax revenues (*yingyeshui* and *suodeshui*), which go 100 percent to local government' (Huang 2011: 18). This development strategy is illustrated by Wu *et al.* (2007) who describe the expediency of land use regulations, particularly in respect to rural land. Land can be transformed from 'collective use' to 'state owned', and from 'agricultural use' to 'non-agricultural use'. Wu *et al.* argue that while such proposals are generally initiated by municipal governments, land transactions require approval by central or municipal governments. As I describe below, the local government invests in upgrading the infrastructure and then makes it available for users.

Whereas Chinese national policy impacting on cultural development is inherently conservative, municipal and district policymaking is generally more flexible (*biantong*) and forward looking. However, this does not imply that local clusters are better managed than central ones. I have already suggested that creative clusters are a one-dimensional solution to the complex problem of China's competing in the global cultural market. Rather than legislating for effective market and social institutions to nurture and reward creativity, the policy momentum is directed towards constructing physical spaces that can be carefully managed, and which hopefully will produce economic value. A key problem, however, is that management is more concerned with the bottom line than with creativity.

The bottom line brings with it a degree of liberalisation. The current governance of creative space is relatively tolerant compared with previous regimes in which cultural workers were closely monitored. Prior to the 1990s cultural workers had very little autonomy. Richard Kraus writes: 'From the 1950s the Party set a high priority on controlling the cultural market, however weak it may have been. It regarded commercialised culture as a source of decadent values, soft on imperialism, and often ignoring class virtue' (Kraus 2004: 10). Today's cultural and media enterprises, and workers, have greater mobility and independence. Commercial culture is the prime driver of most activities and is recognised as a positive influence on people's lives as long as boundaries of expression are not transgressed.

Attracting businesses and investment (*zhaoshang yinzi*)

Although registration costs vary from city to city, district to district, it is relatively easy to establish a private media or cultural enterprise in China.

The closer to the central business district, the higher the premium. Set-up costs for private enterprises in Beijing's central Chaoyang district are among the highest in the country. Likewise the cost of space in downtown centres in Shanghai has attracted criticism from advocates of artists' welfare (see Chapter 6). Cheaper spaces are available out of town or in prescribed industrial zones. Many regions, municipalities and districts officials and cluster managers actively seek out enterprises and individuals engaged in new media, design and animation to populate their premises. Policy 'sweeteners' are common. Once established, businesses might be prevailed upon to purchase professional services; if businesses are unsuccessful or dissatisfied they will often relocate to a different cluster expecting more concessions.

For the government the payoff of clustering is being able to identify and aggregate creative companies, or at least companies that self-identify as creative. Much is made of the task of identifying human capital (*rencai*). Governments can provide space, even if this means displacing or relocating local residents. In many cities clusters often emerge on the fringes of cities; agricultural land use regulations and relevant zoning by-laws are changed to allow commercial operations. Examples below of this model are the White Horse Lake Eco-Village on the fringe of Hangzhou and the Qujiang New District project in Xi'an. In urban centres the conversion is often simpler. State-owned enterprises with factory assets are keen to turn these over to new forms of knowledge-based labour. Transferring land use, and the consequent fees, are not necessary and the enterprise can claim to be transforming and diversifying its business model while at the same time preserving heritage sites. In comparison with other models of economic development such as new technology centres, the cultural economy does not require massive investments from government. In this sense, clustering is convenient, low-cost and is generally seen as low risk.

According to Zhang Xiaoming from the Chinese Academy of Social Sciences, there have been three development stages in the clustering of cultural production in China. The first is the simple strategy whereby a growth coalition (e.g. local entrepreneurs, officials) proposes a cluster plan or responds to a government initiative, with the hope the local authorities will assist in making it sustainable. In most cases a municipal or district government 'promotion office' or 'leading group' will designate a certain area for development, often a disused industrial space. Following this a budget will be allocated and policies devised to attract cultural enterprises or culture-related enterprises. The government often provides land and infrastructural support at low cost anticipating higher returns as the cluster generates momentum. Moreover, as the key value proposition resides in real estate, the land can be resold to developers at a considerable profit.

The next step is to establish a cultural industries cluster management committee. Because a budget is allocated, the local government is able to waive rent for enterprises. Normally enterprises are exempt from tax and rent, or at least would have considerable reductions in taxes and rent. Incentive policies such as these usually extend for between three years and five years: in many instances, three years of no tax and free rent, then two years low tax and rent. In this stage, the core business model of the cluster management is to secure a building or space from government and funds from local government every year to operate the infrastructure. Both the government and the cluster management want to see full occupancy. The objective of the cluster management company is to have companies coming in so that they can apply for funding from the government. The outcome is realised as long as the clusters have enough registered companies and the government has allocated its budget. However, these policies are designed to attract enterprises: they are not industry promotion initiatives.

In the second stage the cluster management committee might set up a development company (*kaifa gongsi*). If the management committee has obtained land from the government rather than premises, they have to build the cluster from the ground up. The development company in this instance will most probably be a land developer. If the building already exists, then the development company is a commercial operations institution (*shangye yunying jigou*). By this stage, the government is likely to reduce financial support; the development company compensates by providing professional services in the cluster, such as human resource training, information service or marketing, even brand promotion. Because most of the companies in a cluster are SMEs, and because there is limited knowledge of cultural markets, most need help in relation to commercialisation. The cluster management committee develops services and charges accordingly. If the services are appropriate, the service fee earned compensates for the money that might have been collected through rent. According to Zhang Xiaoming, if the service provided is not good enough or if they are unable to provide such a service, then the cluster might be forced to seek more financial support from government. In effect, the business model is to use business services income to offset the cost of running the cluster, thereby keeping the rents relatively low.

Zhang believes most clusters remain in the first stage and are dependent on government funding. The problem here is that admitting failure is likely to be a blot on the record of local officials. But there are a few success stories. Zhang mentions a cluster in Shenzhen, called the Shenzhen City of Design, managed by the Sphinx Cultural Industry Investment Company. This cluster has been operational for five years and is now doing well: being a design cluster it has the advantage of being surrounded by clients and manufacturing factories. In turn the profit gained by professional business services is enough to be sustainable, turn a reasonable profit and attract an international reputation.

The third stage, one that is fast approaching according to Zhang, is where there are many companies specialising in the development of clusters. Such professional companies or entrepreneurs acquire funds including bank loans or investment from listing on the stock market. The aim is to attract enough investment to form a network of clusters. In this regard running a cluster is effectively property management except it requires specialised services. There are only two real outcomes of this model: success and failure. While money from rent and services is some compensation under this professional franchising model the cluster will most likely die if enterprises are unsuccessful; at the same time if the management doesn't provide good services the enterprises will find it hard to grow. The cluster will then ask for government funding to continue. The problem is that the government's tax revenue is not increasing because the businesses are not successful.

The success scenario plays out when companies in the cluster are robust. In turn, the services provided by the cluster improve. The end result is that the cluster, companies, as well as central and local government all win. In a version of creative destruction Chinese-style best practice wins the day and the weak drop-off. Zhang believes that the third stage is inevitable: more operators will emerge as cluster development companies. However the basic business model will be similar to real estate.

Local governments learn from each other very quickly. As soon as a new model appears it is copied. In practice clustering has become a way of urban expansion. An example is the Qujiang district of Xi'an, a large city in northwest China famous as the imperial capital of the First Emperor, Qinshi Huangdi. Situated outside the city centre, Qujiang was a decaying district with a long history but few remaining historical sites. With land prices low, the Qujiang New District government realised an opportunity that aligned with the Eleventh Five Year National Economic Development Plan. It rezoned land and designated a large area as a cultural cluster. In August 2007, the Xi'an Qujiang New District was awarded the title National Cultural Industry Model Park by the National Ministry of Culture. Cultural facilities were built in the middle of the district and artists were invited to set up lofts and studios. The development was then publicised as Xi'an's exemplary creative cluster. When the land price doubled the government sold the cluster.

Such strategies are common in many urban-fringe clusters. Affluent Chinese with apartments in inner-city locations are keen to acquire a country 'retreat' in less crowded, more open areas. Local governments oblige by planting trees and building new roads. However, for many of the locals the conversion of their land to a cluster means that they have no clear means of subsistence; they have to learn new skills. Alternatively they might provide low-cost services to the new creative classes or move somewhere else. With the resettlement of artists and white-collar workers, the land values rise and the tax benefits to the local district bureau (*dishuiju*) increase. Because local tax revenue derives from registration of businesses, the cluster management prefers to seek out small local companies rather than businesses registered in other jurisdictions. This localism policy, however, inevitably constrains the injection of new life and cross-province linkages.

Although pure real estate, the Qujiang model has been hailed as a success and copied by other places. Despite a lack of noticeable business innovation, governments still like to use the term 'creative cluster'. Two other prominent examples of real estate-driven clusters are Qipanshan district in Shenyang and the city of Qufu in Shandong. The Qipanshan 'cultural creative industries model district' in Shenyang is a new district in which government increased land values by building and branding cultural infrastructure. While investors have made profits by selling villas, few of the cultural projects in the district have been successful. Qufu, the hometown of Confucius, is in northeastern Shandong Province; again this is fundamentally real estate branded as 'creative industries' with a focus on cultural tourism. Zhang admits that while very few cultural clusters in China have viable business models this does not stop the government from broadening the concept. The Chaoyang District government in Beijing recognises Sanlitun, a bar district frequented by foreigners, as a cluster. Elsewhere shopping zones, fashion zones and places that have one or more museums and theatres are given the accolade of creative clusters.

In an ideal scenario the benefits of a creative cluster might be expected to extend beyond increased rents for councils and landowners, or consumption earnings from tourists. Truly creative clusters are few on the ground in China, primarily because a short-term approach to development prevails. The success of a project means a great deal for local officials and for this reason the cultural quarter model based on 798 and the real estate model based on Qujiang are most popular. In effect, these are far from creative places. Nevertheless, the economic success of these projects provides a stimulus for other districts to imitate 'the Qujiang Model' or 'the 798 Model' respectively. Depending on one's perspective on what constitutes a creative industry, these are viable templates for development. The Dafen Painter's Village in Shenzhen, which I discuss in Chapter 5, provides an illustration of the herd effect. This oil painting cluster, which has provided employment in the visual arts for thousands of untrained migrant workers and farm labourers, is extolled as an economic success story. The business model of the village is to produce replicas of famous artwork and sell these into international markets, assisted by Hong Kong business entrepreneurs. In nearby Xiamen, the Wushipu Oil Painting Village has followed this 'model'. In effect, the term 'industry' is an appropriate description for these activities. The term 'creative' is probably redundant, unless we are referring to the marketing and distribution.

Foshan Creative Industries Park, Guangdong

Most parks in China are built on co-operative relationships with local governments who invest a great deal of resources in return for tax and real estate revenues. Private companies and state-owned enterprises do provide resources but these are often infrastructural: for instance, the use of SOE premises for conversion to a cultural cluster. There are very few examples of significant stand-alone private investment. Foshan is an industrial centre near Guangzhou known in recent times for manufacturing household appliances, furniture, plastic and stainless steel products, and in the past for its porcelain. In comparison with Dongguan, the other large regional manufacturing centre east of Guangzhou, which attracts a high level of Hong Kong investment in industrial clusters, Foshan is noted for its local entrepreneurship.

During the research for this book I visited Foshan Creative Industries Park (FCIP) on three occasions from 2008 to 2010 as the global financial crisis was impacting on many areas of China's boom economy. The FCIP is adjacent to the Nanfeng Ancient Kiln International Creative Industry Park. Both are situated about 30 minutes by road southwest from Guangzhou. As far back as the Tang Dynasty Foshan artisans were making porcelain by heating local clays in open kilns at high temperatures. The atmosphere reflects the industrial landscape. In 2008, local officials named the seven sins of Foshan's development as 'severe pollution, energy waste and high emissions, shortage of resources, weakness in innovation, limited scale, poor self-discipline and a restricted international market' (Jiang 2008).

The 'Foshan Model', as it is called, reflects both the second and third stage of cluster development described above. The two parks in Foshan are the vision of Qiu Dailun, a former lawyer who has become a charismatic 'creative park entrepreneur'. Qiu Dailun is small in stature but gives the appearance of constant movement and answers questions as a series of numbered statements. The Foshan Creative Industry Park is a related variety park incorporating ceramics, software and animation. It covers 16 hectares; 30 per cent of this development is garden space embellished with Qiu's design ideas. Outside the FCIP is a sign that says: 'we turn triteness into novelty'. Qiu makes a point of talking about the soft infrastructure of Foshan rather than the material embellishments. His philosophy is that the physical infrastructure is interpenetrated by what he calls 'cultural, creative and commercial cells'.

Qiu is quick to point out his own aspirations to promote his 'experimental model': he believes he can replicate his business and management structure throughout the country enabling the national transformation from 'Made in China to Created in China'. His idea is to radiate the innovations of FCIP into a special creative zone model. As an entrepreneur he is aware of the intentions of Guangdong Province's government officials to shake off the image of the province as a low cost production and copy centre. His future intention is to travel the world and pick out the best ideas globally to introduce into his model. Qiu says: 'Maybe I cannot change the world but I will do the best to improve my park.'

As well as franchising his model, Qiu wants to encourage businesses that can extend their operations across the country rather than just focus on local markets. In this respect the Foshan Park is demonstrating the attributes of a creative industries cluster. Qiu is aware of the problem plaguing other parks and the creative industries in China, in particular a lack of trust and co-operation. In Foshan he believes this problem is mitigated by developing social capital, a community of trust. He expects people to work in co-operative projects and develop a 'moral community' where they respect the rules of co-operation. He says that when people don't observe the obligations of mutual trust their contracts will not be renewed.

The FCIP is equipped with high-speed wireless internet access. It features business, exhibition and conference centres. According to Qiu, the park has formalised partnerships with over 100 enterprises, many of which are tenants in the park. While ultimate decision-making is obviously deferred to Mr Qiu, governance adopts a more democratic model. There is a deliberate effort to be inclusive, allowing businesses to pitch their ideas to a selected list of 8–10 park consultants. Brainstorming sessions are conducted among participating members, at least those with an interest in innovation and 'making a better park'. Participants are encouraged to modify and improve their working routines and to aim for innovation above efficiency. Recruiting sessions are conducted monthly, inviting outside businesses and artists to experience the culture and learn about the benefits of moving to Foshan. The park operates a culture of co-operation and competition through its service support mechanisms, including procurement and business development assistance, recruitment programmes, intellectual property rights protections and business licensing services. In addition, Qiu has established a RMB 1 million intellectual property protection fund to assist any of the businesses or artists take action against copyists. He wryly notes, 'this is my area of speciality'.

Qiu talks about his development model: he says, 'culture is the soul, industry is the root but the platform is essential. In facilitating culture, you facilitate industry and this attracts the talent'. Qiu has made internationalisation and innovation conjoined priorities, in contrast to many other park developments, which have merely looked to international companies for service work. The idea of the learning economy is evident. Qiu has attracted Italian, French and Singaporean businesses and artists. He says that is it necessary to combine local elements with global culture. International artists are able to take advantage of flexible residencies in the Nanfeng Ancient Kiln International Creative Industries Park and to undertake courses in Chinese language, martial arts, cuisine and culture.

Businesses are also able to negotiate flexible leases. Transfer of ideas occurs within a local–global nexus, which Qiu believes provides a stimulus for the best 'talent' to move to Foshan. This impressive development includes an extensive museum complex, artist studios, spacious galleries and the world's largest DIY pottery workshop. The park provides opportunities for schoolchildren to learn about the history of Chinese ceramics as well as display their own creation on a special wall.

As for the question of the global financial crisis and its impact, Qiu was optimistic the first time I met him in late 2008. The first positive, at least in the short term, he said was the falling price of commodities such as steel, which will allow him to move quickly into the next stage of construction. As for the falling value of Chinese art, he believed this would not affect his model, which is not about selling products as providing a 'selling point' for innovation; in other words, it is the reputation of the artists and business that will grow the innovation ecology. Qiu says the only salvation for China in the current crisis is to innovate. In relation to international involvement in his projects, he believed the financial crisis would facilitate more international experts and artists to consider locating in Foshan in order to take advantage of the low-cost resources, but at the same time tapping into what he hopes will become the ceramics capital of the world. When I next met Qiu in October 2009, he was still optimistic about the creative industries, acknowledging that human capital was becoming easier to find and recruitment was therefore easier. Furthermore, he believed the global financial crisis had redirected many Chinese consumers back to the domestic market.

In effect, the Foshan project is a unique model of a cultural quarters combined with creative entrepreneurship. In contrast to the 'models' mentioned previously it facilitates a learning economy in which the benefits are disseminated both with and beyond the region.

Hangzhou: LOFT 49 and White Horse Lake Eco-City

A city situated on the southern wing of the Yangzi River Delta in central Zhejiang Province, Hangzhou is well known throughout history for commerce and trade. Hangzhou was one of the seven capitals of imperial China. In the thirteenth century the legendary Venetian traveller Marco Polo called Hangzhou the most magnificent city in the world. Past representatives of Hangzhou culture include Bai Juyi (772–846), a renowned poet of the Tang Dynasty who was appointed as the governor of Hangzhou; Shen Kuo (1031–1095), a polymath scientist and statesman of the Song Dynasty who penned the *Dream Pool Essays*; Su Dongpo (1037–1101), a writer, poet, artist, calligrapher and pharmacologist, and Gong Zizhen (1792–1841), a reform-minded writer and poet whose works foreshadowed the modernisation movements of the late Qing Dynasty.

Today Hangzhou remains famous for lush hills, scenic lakes and the affluent and relaxing lifestyle enjoyed by many of its residents. Tourism, recreation and exhibition industries have supported the city's goal of being a 'City of Quality Life'. In 2004, the State Administration of Radio, Film and Television (SARFT) designated a National Animation Base. The intention here was to facilitate a 'City of Animation' campaign. Following the directives of the national Eleventh Five Year Plan (2006–2010), and Zhejiang's initiative of 'building a Cultural Province' (2005), the Hangzhou municipal government established a Cultural and Creative Industries Office in 2007. The Office identified eight sectors: information service, animation and gaming, design, media, crafts, education and training, cultural recreation and tourism and cultural exhibition. In 2008, the Office announced that Hangzhou would aspire to be the National Cultural and Creative Industries Centre, an initiative which is now included in the Regional Plan of the Yangzi River Delta, ratified by the State Council in May 2010.

Much effort goes into justifying these development plans. Accordingly a range of data is utilised to produce positive stories. According to the Municipal Bureau of Statistics, the added value of cultural and creative industries in 2010 reached RMB 70.2 billion, or 11.8 per cent of the GDP of the city (Hangzhou Municipal Bureau of Statistics 2011). In the same year six creative cluster projects were accredited, taking the total to 16. In the draft document of Hangzhou's Twelfth Five Year Plan, development projects such as these are described as 'optimizing and upgrading the industrial structure'.

Hangzhou's relationship with cultural and creative clusters development can be traced back to a gathering of several designers and artists at an unused fibre factory in Gongshu District in 2003. Originally called 49 Warehouse, it was later rebranded as LOFT 49 Creative Industries Park. When the momentum for cultural and creative clusters broke out after 2007, local government recognised the site as a model for future developments, although its potential has been hampered by its positioning in between a senior middle school.

The reputation of LOFT 49 as one of the leading prototypes of 'related variety' creative clusters in China is well established. In 2003, a documentary called *49 Warehouses* was broadcast on China Central Television's international channels: CCTV Channel 4 and Channel 9 and on the culture channel. At the time the 798 Art Zone in Beijing was in a state of limbo with Chaoyang officials unsure of how to deal with the bohemian lifestyles of artists. According to Du Yubo, director of the Design Idea Company and the instigator of LOFT 49, the publicity was beneficial to 798. Yet the development of LOFT 49 is modest compared with 798 Art Zone and with many large-scale clusters that have since been instigated in Hangzhou. Situated 500 metres from the Beijing-Hangzhou Grand Canal in a northern district of Hangzhou, LOFT 49 is far removed from the tourism-focused West Lake district. Accordingly the atmosphere is relatively quiet.

Du Yubo had spent time working in the US prior to returning to Hangzhou in the 1990s. While in New York he had noticed the impact of downtown art districts. He became more interested in the possibility of creative clusters following the trailblazing initiatives of a Taiwanese architect in Shanghai. Deng Kunyan was responsible for converting an abandoned warehouse on the banks of Suzhou Creek in Shanghai into a contemporary art space incorporating features of traditional Chinese design. Deng's renovation generated media publicity in 2001, activating a connection between heritage protection and contemporary cultural production. Deng's personal investment in the idea of cultural reconversion eventually led to UNECSO recognition in 2004 in the form of the UNESCO Asia-Pacific heritage Award for Culture Heritage Conservation (Liu and Chen 2008). The precinct was called Creative Shanghai Riverside. In 2001, Du visited Xintiandi, an upscale development by a Hong Kong-based property developer, Shuion Land, which had successfully converted old tenement buildings into fashionable lofts surrounded by boutiques. Du began to look for suitable spaces in Hangzhou.

The site at Gongshu was identified in 2002. Despite the problem of severe air pollution from surrounding factories, the decision was made to push ahead and a lease contact was signed the following year. Du says:

> In 2003, we finished all the work. We renovated the place within one year. Six small companies moved in. By the end of 2003, we had a small scene with 20 companies – they came by word of mouth. The land owner evicted some of the manufacturing businesses and made clear intention to rent the place to higher value companies.

The cost of rent has been crucial to the operations of the cluster. Compared with the 5 yuan per square metre of Shanghai's M50, LOFT 49's residents pay only 0.4 yuan per square metre. By 2009, there were 30 enterprises occupying space employing approximately 400 workers. The enterprises focus primarily on design including graphic design, interior design, garden and landscape design, package design, arts and crafts design as well as web design and development, photography, sculpture and painting. While the relatively cheap costs have been important, the evolution of the 'LOFT 49 model' was timely in a political sense. In 2005, the Chinese Communist Party Committee of Zhejiang Province decided to brand Zhejiang as a cultural province. Du tells the story. One of the leading officials pointed out 'we have a loft here.' Others asked: 'What is a loft?' Suddenly this idea became a good fit for government policy as the central government was calling for more endogenous innovation (*zizhu chuangxin*). Hangzhou had a ready-made model.

Delegations came from Ningbo and Wenzhou to investigate LOFT 49. Gongshu District was an old industrial district and nobody had paid attention. Suddenly, the creative stuff attracted so much attention. The district government was really flattered and excited.... For us, we feel lucky and we know we are not going to be demolished.

Despite the attention from government the project has not achieved the fashionable status enjoyed by 798, nor has it received favourable tax and free rent policies enjoyed by many newer cluster initiatives. Du believes that LOFT 49's low key nature has much to do with the difference between Beijing and Hangzhou as well as the location of LOFT 49. In his opinion talented people would go to Shanghai and Beijing where there are rock and roll and avant-garde scenes. He says that while Hangzhou's night club scene is busy, it caters to business people not youth. He said they had hoped the cluster and the district could contribute more to the lifestyle of the city by adding coffee shops, creative restaurants, art studios, galleries, designer hotels and shops and to integrate more with the local community. The problem is that the businesses in LOFT 49 are only tenants. Du says: 'The owner of the old factory does not know what and how to do this; the city doesn't have enough manpower to manage this – they have bigger projects. This project is too small to be on the agenda.'

It is the larger and more recent projects that have captured the interest of investors and developers. Hangzhou's new clusters – ten have been officially endorsed by the Hangzhou municipal government – reflect the ambition of the municipality and its planners to claim a leading position in the nation's move towards 'Creative China'. Recent projects to consolidate under the umbrella of cultural and creative industries policy include Tangshang 433, a project located in old factory buildings. Leased in 2005 by an architectural services entrepreneur, the site currently has 30 design companies with more than 300 designers. The core business is interior design for shopping malls, hotels, exhibition space and large real estate projects. Another project, Kaiyuan 198, was jointly established by Shangcheng District and the Chinese Academy of Arts in 2007 in an old middle school site. A related variety model, its ambition is to become a leading creative design and service centre for Zhejiang brands in fashion, architecture and interior design, film and TV production services, home furnishing, environmental art and modelling agencies.

One of the curious features of Hangzhou's aspirations to be cultural centre of China is what might be called the 'rent-a-celebrity' campaign. There are currently a number of celebrity-endorsed 'creative projects' under construction including the Xixi Wetlands Cultural Creative Industries Park. Xixi National Wetland Park is located on the western edge of Hangzhou at the southern tip of Hangzhou-Beijing Canal covering an area of 13 square kilometres. It includes thousands of ponds, networks of streams and rivers, extensive reed beds and ecological areas. The

Plate 3.1 LOFT 49 Hangzhou design studio (photo by Wen Wen)

Wetlands is a major tourist attraction and a place where many locals come to be married. In 2009 I took a boat tour with Du Yubo of LOFT 49 who pointed out the frenetic construction of celebrity houses. Sites have been set aside for former TV personality and CEO of Sun TV Cybernetworks, Yang Lan, for the popular Taiwanese cartoon artist Zhu Deyong, and according to Du, there is even a site reserved for John Howkins, the so-called 'father of the creative industries'.

The transformation of Xixi Wetlands from a quiet nature reserve to a creative industries production and consumption zone is not without controversy. Television and film companies have been allocated space for studios. An international architectural firm Bagot Woods has landed the contact for the overall design of the Xixi Wetlands International Tourism Region. Another project with ambitions to capture celebrities is called Phoenix Creative International. Jointly developed by the West Lake District and China Academy of Art, the project's slogan is '3 in 1 Structure', namely creation + production + living. The park offers studio space to the Taiwanese animator Tsai Chih-Chung and the Japanese designer Kijyo Rokkaku.

Perhaps the most ambitious project is the White Horse Lake Creative Eco-City. The White Horse Lake (WHL) area is located in the southern rural Hangzhou High-tech Industry Development Zone (Binjiang), a National High-tech Zone accredited by State Council. The publicity for the High-tech Zone (Binjiang) resembles many innovation park projects in China. The zone promotes impressive development in industries such as micro-electronic information, biomedicine, optical-mechanical-electrical integration and various computer applications. In November 2007, the

High-tech Zone signed a project authorisation document and design contract with China Academy of Arts (CAA) to develop the White Horse Lake area into a cultural and creative industries park. The White Horse Lake Creative Eco-City (Creative-Eco City for short) has a designated area of 20.5 square kilometres, making it the largest cultural and creative industry area in terms of scale and industrial infrastructure in Hangzhou. It involves 18 villages and a total population of 52 000. The construction is scheduled for completion in 2014.

The promotional material provides an expedient mix of business and political realities. The overall strategic goal is described as providing the 'four comforts' (*siyi*), namely, 'a right city for residence, for business, for travel and for culture'. With a view to the larger picture rather than just a state-level cultural and creative industries district, the project identifies the construction of travel and leisure resorts as well as business centres with elaborate architectural design. In a sense the White Horse Lake has selectively borrowed ideas and slogans. The chief design consultant of the White Horse Lake Eco-creative City is the China Academy of Arts (CAA). Its 'experimental' SOHO Creative Park (SOHO Park) in Shanyi Village offers reconverted farmhouses, an opportunity to work in a natural environment while maintaining a fashionable work style. The second attraction is that the farmhouse SOHOs are offered to eligible creative teams for free for three years. The admission criteria are: (1) the participants must be involved in one of the eight subsectors of cultural and creative industries recognised by municipal government; (2) they must attain an annual production value of RMB 5 million (excluding start-up businesses).

With the endorsement of the CAA, 30 teams, including at least one from each cultural and creative sector, soon signed contracts with the CAA Creative Industries Development Co. (CAACID). Close examination of the teams reveals preferential treatment – about half of the work studios are owned by deans, accomplished painters and designers of CAA. A few institutions, such as the CAACID and an Atelier Pierre Bleue founded by the dean of School of Arts and Design of CAA, are even nominated as the 'CAA practice base', offering internship to students or graduates from CAA.

The appeal of the model fits the expectations of the community, one long accustomed to planning, and long dependent on government. The cultural and creative industries precincts are viewed as a development method that fits the Chinese way of doing things; people generally believe in the 'clustering' approach; after all, it is a form of collectivism; it has references to the past when city people were sent down to the countryside to engage with nature.

The appearance of better-educated creative professionals is intended to have an 'uplifting' impact on the villagers, for instance, to make many work and lifestyle possibilities, rather than just farming, more accessible.

In turn, it is assumed that the rural lifestyle may have some influence on the creative workers. Some reports of the Eco-creative City project use the gimmick 'celebrities are moving to the countryside to be farmers'.[1] Being trapped in the crowded, noisy and air-polluted city, people are hoping for a sea change effect by going back to the countryside, being closer to nature and communing with good-natured 'down to earth' farmers.

While following the national development script of clustering Hangzhou has diversified its cultural strategy, incorporating tourism and leisure. The renowned film-maker Zhang Yimou has also been active in Hangzhou with his production of *Impressions West Lake*, a spectacular performance on the West Lake that incorporates elements of Chinese traditional culture, pop music, pyrotechnics and dance. Zhang's fantasy, the Xixi Wetlands Project, tea house culture and the current 'top ten' cultural and creative clusters, are the key elements of Hangzhou's culture that are packaged, recombined and offered to visitors and tourists as a taste of 'creative China'.

Clusters and predictability

As I have shown in this chapter, the development of cluster projects in China has followed a predictable course. The central government initially endorsed the cluster plan as a new collectivist model to transcend the limitations of an immature cultural market. In most cases, however, developments have been expedient, based on real estate speculation, gentrification and the generation of tax revenue for local governments. As an economic development model there is great value in promoting cultural quarters and attempting to construct viable creative industrial parks. However, a cluster, if it is to reflect the adjective 'creative', should be principally about the development of ideas, technologies, innovations, businesses and markets. The Foshan model is certainly set up to exploit these opportunities. However, its future will depend on maintaining a delicate balance between the cultural quarter (the Nanfang Ancient Kiln) and the industrial cluster.

Strategic considerations also pertain to the design of creative work space, which is often not well considered. Clustering often involves replication of business models; for instance the practice of following the lead of other districts and other clusters even when their success is not demonstrated. The process of transforming science parks into creative parks, or cultural quarters into creative clusters requires more rethinking about both the creative process and different types of knowledge involved. There is substantial scope for creative clusters to fail due to failure to adopt appropriate business models associated with adaptive and learning organisations.

As the examples in this chapter have shown, the same points apply for local and regional governments. The extent and distribution of benefits differ between cultural quarters and industrial clusters. Both create opportunity for rents through various mechanisms (licences, taxes, etc.), and there will be instances when a cultural cluster will yield higher immediate returns than an industrial cluster, as well as more direct and obvious public goods as cultural goods. The missing model is in fact the creative cluster. Few of these are operational. Yet creative clusters have the most to contribute to ongoing public revenue and economic growth and development through their role in the creation and development of new ideas and their contribution to innovation (Potts and Cunningham 2008; Bakhshi *et al.* 2008). This does, however, require clear recognition that creative clusters work only when they function as dynamic spaces for learning, experimentation and innovation within and between businesses. This is difficult to achieve in China where the emphasis is squarely on short-term benefits and where district governments are driving the proliferation of clusters without a clear vision, aside from real estate speculation.

4 Beijing: creative capital or state-managed openness?

I first visited Beijing in 1989, entering the city from the north. It's how I imagined the Mongol emperor Genghis Khan would have come to his ancient capital, Dadu, in the thirteenth century. In 1989, the modern capital was entering into a frenzy of construction. As the Trans-Siberian rail wound its way slowly through a landscape of old buildings, factories, alleyways and apartments to Beijing Central Station, a fellow traveller, who had been to Beijing before, reminded me: 'this is *the* authentic Chinese city, the cultural and spiritual capital of China'.

In this chapter I want to look at how Beijing has repositioned itself as a creative city, rather than a historical, cultural or political city. Politics permeates daily life in Beijing more so than in any other Chinese city. Innovations in management of media and cultural activities, including clusters, are therefore more likely to happen elsewhere. Accordingly, I will examine contradictions that come with the popularisation of 'creative industries' within local growth coalitions.

Growth coalitions in Beijing have benefited from the dissemination of the concept of creative industries. With the Ministry of Culture in Beijing prescribing the use of the term 'cultural industries', it is therefore pertinent to compare Beijing's experiences with those of Shanghai, where the municipal government has openly endorsed the 'creative industries'. While I will discuss Shanghai's experience in Chapter 6, my purpose here is to explain why some cultural and creative sectors are concentrated in the national capital, and what living in Beijing means for the fulfilment of creative aspirations. I briefly discuss the cultural heritage of Beijing including its popular culture and iconic landmarks. This entails an examination of significant changes in urban planning over the past several decades. This then leads to a case study of Fangjia 46, an inner-city cluster located in a traditional *hutong* (alleyway) in Dongcheng District. In describing the evolution of the Fangjai 46 project I draw some comparisons with a nearby high-profile cultural district called Nanluoguxiang hutong (South Gong and Drum Laneway).

My interest in Beijing's emerging clusters brings together three lines of enquiry: the first, as I have just mentioned, the comparison with Shanghai and other large cities, or to put it more succinctly, where exactly is Beijing's creative edge? (Liu Kai 2008). As the capital city, Beijing is representative of the nation. Yet the capacity of Beijing people to generate criticism of government is constrained, particularly within media sectors. The paradox is that Beijing is home to the nation's largest media cluster and its most diverse avant-garde arts and music scene.

My second concern is the role played by epistemic communities in informing cluster developments and urban policy. Epistemic communities can be defined as groups or networks of people who perform exploratory learning. Such groups engage in activities at the interstices of various disciplines (Nooteboom 2008: 125). The role of epistemic communities comes into operation when they are useful to bureaucratic entrepreneurs and growth coalitions. The example that best illustrates this relationship is the International Creative Industries Alliance (ICIA), a growth coalition that emerged from an epistemic community called the Creative China Industrial Alliance (CCIA). I will show how this group participated in the proposal for the Fangjia 46 cluster project.

My third line of enquiry brings us to the often fraught relationship between culture and creativity. In short, Beijing's officials have prioritised culture over creativity. Evidently there are political considerations at play. The latter term has an international cachet. In times of change, the discourse of creativity is championed by city government officials and entrepreneurs; it has been heralded as a miraculous 'ingredient' which stimulates the production and dissemination of ideas, a symbol of the new economy, post-Fordism, flexible labour, creative classes, portfolio careers, increasing returns, sustainable development (for instance see Rifkin 2000; Caves 2000; Florida 2002; Howkins 2001; Bilton 2007).

In China the concept has been used by reformers to critique hierarchical management in some industry sectors. Chinese cultural officials have decried the lack of creativity in mainland China's media content industries, which are forced to compete with imported Korean, Taiwanese and Hong Kong programmes (Keane 2007). In contrast to the people-oriented, time-honoured and collective notion of 'culture', which reaches deep into the spiritual wealth of China's history, creativity is a recent Western construct. It is about the process of discovering more so than preserving, challenging norms rather than observing them. Advocates of the creative *zeitgeist* in Beijing as well as other Chinese cities regard the cultural industries as elitist, predictable and state managed, as opposed to the internationalising potential of creative industries.

Finding the creative edge

A provocation to begin:

> Shanghai is a cosmopolitan entrepreneurial metropolis. It has historically embraced international ideas. Beijing is the national capital of China. It has historically resisted foreign ideas. Shanghai is the city that looks outward: Beijing is a political capital which looks inward. Beijing is a great city of culture; Shanghai is a modernising creative city.

In the course of my fieldwork in Beijing and Shanghai, these kinds of comments surfaced regularly. On the surface such perceptions, if true, would account for many differences between Beijing and Shanghai. Depending on where the informant was located, the perceptions varied. Some informants from Beijing argued with justification that Beijing is China's most cosmopolitan city and conversely that Shanghai is insular and dominated by government. Indeed, in collating evidence from a range of cultural activities, the stereotypes of Beijing as excessively bureaucratic and Shanghai as open and entrepreneurial run into exceptions.

With the possible exception of Shenzhen in south China, Beijing is China's most multi-cultural city. People are drawn to Beijing for a variety of reasons. In modern times, the city has absorbed migrant populations; up to one-third of Beijing's population are now classified as migrants or 'floating population' (Dutton 1998). This is no better illustrated than in Zhejiang Village, a community situated at Dazhongmen in Fengtai District 5 kilometres south of the centre of Beijing. During the 1990s, the area had become a locus for small-scale clothing businesses from Wenzhou, a city in Zhejiang Province. Despite eviction due to local government pressure in 1995, the migrants returned the following year to set up close relations with the local people, eventually establishing a cluster of clothing production factories. The cluster is now recognised by the Beijing municipal government. The cases of the art villages Caochangdi and Songzhuang, discussed in the next chapter, also illuminate the hybrid and often transitory nature of Beijing's population.

Beijing's proximity to Mongolia and the former Manchuria (the region now collectively termed Dongbei) has contributed to its ethos. Li contends that 'the border location of the city not only served strategic purposes but also fostered cultural creativity' (Li et al. 2007: 27). The absorption of diverse elements adds to the Beijing's complexity. Compared with the popular perceptions of Beijing as a regimented political city due to it being the centre of government, Chen Guanzhong, co-author of *Bohemian China*, suggests that Beijing illustrates complex hybridity and tolerance to social diversity: 'whether you have long hair or a shaved head, whether you wear well-fitting clothes or clothes whose style and colour don't match, in public Beijing people are indifferent'. He also adds, 'Beijing is "cool", like New York: you can praise or deride Beijingers. They just don't care' (Chen 2004: 54).

In many respects Beijing has shaken off much of its typecasting as a cautious city dominated by conservative Communist Party officials. While much policy innovation occurs outside Beijing, bureaucrats in the nation's capital actively engage with entrepreneurs in the interest of growth politics; entrepreneurs in turn employ consumer lifestyles factors to influence development decisions. In 2008, I was surprised to be given an extensive explanation of 'long tail theory' as it applied to the cultural industries by a Chaoyang district propaganda official.[1]

Cultural consumption, and the association of art with social capital, is a factor in real estate speculation. Wang Yingyao (2006) writes how real estate advertisements in Beijing work to upgrade China's 'new rich' to the status of culturally and historically rooted aristocrats by endorsing their aspirations for success. She says that the conspicuous display of real estate advertisements allows affluent classes to obviate anxiety brought by urbanisation and modernisation. One could also argue that many real estate projects offer an unreal promise, spaces free from the stresses of migrant populations, places where creative aspirations can be fulfilled; for instance, within or near art zones.

Avant-garde art and rock music has contributed much diversity to the Beijing ethos. As I discuss in the following chapter, Beijing describes itself as the capital of contemporary art: hundreds of art communities feed into the two most prominent clusters, 798 Art Zone and Songzhuang Capital Arts District. The city maintains a strong gay culture despite the government's spiritual civilisation edicts against bohemianism and homosexuality. Beijing is well known for its progressive rock scene, a reputation dating back to Cui Jian, a folk rock musician whose lyrics drew on generational ennui, culminating in idiosyncratic performances during the Tiananmen Square protests of 1989 (Huot 2000). Bar areas like Sanlitun (Chaoyang District) and Houhai (Dongcheng District) attract a mix of artists, musicians, tourists and entrepreneurs. Beijing's media production capacity is supplemented by its literary scene, particularly with many of China's television serial dramas emanating from Beijing production houses. Perhaps the most well known Beijing director is Feng Xiaogang, whose collaboration with the 'hooligan' writer Wang Shuo produced the classic TV comedy drama *Scenes from an Editorial Office* (*bianjibu de gushi*) (Keane 2002). Feng Xiaogang also directed the TV serial *Beijingers in New York* (*Beijing ren zai Niuyue*), 'a stranger in a strange land' narrative that was itself a reflection of Beijing's own economic transformation (Keane 2001).

Beijing has more top-ranked universities than any other Chinese city. Its art academies are supported by an infrastructure of world-class performing arts and convention venues, ranging from the spacey National

Theatre for the Performing Arts in Xicheng District known as the Bird's Egg to the very solid concrete Workers Stadium in Chaoyang District. In addition to its cultural assets, Beijing is the central node in the Chinese communications industries. As one informant remarked, 'We are engaged in a telecommunications business and we need relationships with the Internet, broadband and mobile companies.'[2] Telecommunications companies based in Beijing include China Telecom, China Mobile, China Netcom and China Unicom.

Drawing on information provided from a leading Chinese data and directories provider called YIBAI, Kai Liu (2008) argues that Beijing overall has more large creative industries businesses than Shanghai, although Shanghai has the edge in designer fashion segments. The businesses surveyed are those who are listed in the top 500 by aggregate annual turnover. This 'index' was compiled by the researcher to fit the 13 DCMS categories developed by the DCMS in Britain. With a large number of state-owned enterprises, regulatory agencies and large media businesses, Beijing would be expected to be the leader in gross output and value added. A recent study conducted by the Renmin University on China's Cultural Industry Development Index (Renmin 2011) confirms Beijing's premier position in four categories: comprehensive development, cultural industries productivity, cultural industries influence and cultural industries driving force. The results of both studies need to be evaluated with care: the first study mentioned doesn't capture the small and medium enterprises that account for so much value and contribute the most innovation to their respective sectors, whereas the Renmin study is obviously inclined to a cultural industries approach, thus building into its date the significant impacts of tourism. As mentioned above, when it comes to tourism, Beijing leads.

Beijing: exotic utopian urban dreams

Many people I interviewed in Beijing during the course of my research reflected on cultural memory, the architectural traces of the city's past and their untimely disappearance. In 2003, the journalist Wang Jun published *Beijing Record*, an account of the transformation of Beijing over the last 50 years. Wang raised the question of why so much historical architecture has vanished: including city ramparts, gateways, old temples as well as the urban fabric of Beijing's famous *hutong* (alleyways) and *siheyuan* (courtyards surrounded by four buildings). Wang is direct in his condemnation of the problem: 'real estate capital has completely administered the deathblow to the ancient city' (Wang Jun 2006: 77). Change is driven by developers as much as Beijing's elite who yearn for a version of modernity that assembles past, present and future in a hybrid East Asian dreamscape.

Zhou Rong, a professor at the School of Architecture at Tsinghua University in Beijing, provides another perspective on change. He describes 'three vernacular and exotic urban dreams' (Zhou 2006). His first utopia is a nostalgic vision for the ancient city – the city as symbol of ritual, representing the hierarchy and ordered relationship of an ideal society. This is also Wang Jun's disappearing 'old Beijing', reflecting the city's geo-spatial planning in the Ming Dynasty of the fifteenth century. As well as serving as a fortified northern boundary against barbarians, the Ming Dynasty planners reopened the Grand Canal leading south and connecting the city with Hangzhou. Beijing became a capital with a new topography, a geo-architecture that included the Great Wall, the Grand Canal, and a number of prominent symbolic manifestations of imperial power, the altars of the Earth, Sun and Moon in the north, east and west (see Zhu 2003).

Despite claims that the spatial topography of modern Beijing resembles a sprawling pancake (Mars and Hornsby 2008), the city is based on a symmetrical design: a 7,500-metre axis runs north to south as well as east to west. The imperial Ming capital comprised four distinct enclosures: the Forbidden City at the very centre, the Imperial City, the Capital (Inner) city and the outer city (Zhu 2003). The Forbidden City was the apex of power. The centre reflected its moral status in height rather than area of its structures, walls and palaces. Next to the Forbidden City was the Imperial City, an extension of the imperial household, a series of lakes, gardens, palaces and temples. The next layer, the capital city, formed the commercial centre while the outer city collected and distributed the lower classes. The population of the outer city comprised merchants, visiting students, sojourners and officials. It was a zone of restaurants, brothels, street markets, tea houses and theatres (Zhu 2003). As we shall see in the next chapter, the outer zones are now sites for bohemian art communities.

The second utopia is the 'grand socialist' city, a development model imported from the Soviet Union in the 1950s, with visual manifestations of baroque cities such as long axes, symmetrical forms, and monumental landmarks (Zhou 2006). This sacrifice to the 'political gods' is evidenced by the grandiosity of Tiananmen Square and the baroque splendour of the Great Hall of the People. When Communist Party revolutionaries reclaimed Beijing as the capital in 1949, they initially considered moving the central business district to the west, if only to save the historic centre from the fate of modern development. According to a planning proposal advanced by the founder of the School of Architecture at Tsinghua University and a passionate advocate of preservation, Liang Sicheng, 'The Proposal allocated an area of 14 square kilometres between the Altar of the Moon and the Tomb of the Princess, in the western suburb for the Administration Centre, providing sufficient land for construction and reserve, the basic prerequisite for favourable conditions for a "Political centre of modern efficiency".' To the north and west of the Administration

Centre, residential areas for the staff of these government institutions and reserved land were planned' (cited in Liu 1997: 252).

While much of the political power and money gravitated to the northwest of Beijing, the Central Business District remained intact. Beginning in 1953, a series of Master Plans was implemented. Mao and Jin (1997) note that the vision was to serve ordinary working people as well as facilitating the growth of industries. In effect, this served the needs of the central government. Beijing was set to become a national economic centre with a strong industrial base, as well as being a national political and cultural centre. Old buildings and civil engineering structures – those that were seen to impede these objectives were demolished, a precursor of things to come in the post-Mao era. Development in suburban areas progressed largely through the establishment of manufacturing industries, with the exception of the city's northwestern sector where an independent university and research zone were established. Urban infrastructure, such as roads and public transportation, was categorised under government provision. The priority project of assuring urban water supply received considerable attention in the first Master Plan owing to water shortages in the area.

The early years of the new republic witnessed a considerable influx of people into the big cities, the urbanised proportion of the total population doubling between 1949 and 1960 (Friedmann 2005: 11). The first Five Year Development Plan (1954) had led to the expansion of several industrial districts, a socialist strategy to transform cities into productive centres (Visser 2004; Friedmann 2005). This collectivist vision gained traction in the ensuing People's Commune Movement which began in 1958. The Chinese Communist Party's utopian plan to catch up with the developed capitalist countries during the Great Leap Forward (1958–1961) led to the elimination of difference between workers and peasants, between urban and rural, and between intellectual and workers.

A draft of Beijing's Urban Plan released in 1959 underscored the template for the producer city (shengchan chengshi). An excerpt from the plan provides insights into Mao Zedong's vision of 'a forest of smokestacks' (Mangurian and Ray 2009: 427):

1 Guideline: to serve the need of the future republican era, city construction should serve the goal of establishing an industrialized capital city, an industrialized commune and an industrialized agriculture.
2 City layout: by adopting 'the dispersal group type', especially for the industrial layout, balance should be achieved between having both reasonable unity within the group, and having both industries and agriculture inside each. Land between the 'groups' should be filled with vegetable gardens, farmlands and forest, forming towns and residential areas of different sizes around the urban areas.

Already the city was experiencing the strains of population pressure. City migration was held in check by a household permit system introduced in 1958. Devised to restrict mass urbanisation, the *hukou* or registration system effectively divided the population into two – 'the haves' (urban households) and 'the have nots' (rural households). A *hukou* permit provided residents with greater social freedom; for instance, the right to purchase a vehicle, to receive education and health welfare. Migrant populations without a *hukou* lacked many rights.

A new phase of urban transformation followed during the 1980s. During this decade, Beijing set its sights on asserting its authority as China's cultural and political centre. The centre of Beijing expanded into the suburbs and a major subway system was built. Private capital stimulated the architectural transformation of the Central Business District, concentric ring roads were added, and highways constructed to link Beijing with southeastern Tianjin and northern Shijiazhuang. The factories that twenty years previously had symbolised socialist productivity were shifted further to the margins. Relaxations on migration saw many more pouring into the capital looking for economic gain. By 1995, over a quarter of the population was made up of migrants from the countryside (Visser 2004: 284).

The third vernacular is the so-called 'Modern Utopia'. In the early 1990s the Beijing municipal government issued a document called the Overall Plan for Beijing City 1991–2010. The plan envisaged Beijing becoming 'an international and modern metropolis' within 20 years. Concurrently, a document was released promoting the preservation of Beijing as a historic city, nominating 25 designated protected areas. Despite the intent of preservationists, however, Beijing's yearning to be an inventive city provided permission for international architects and designers to construct elaborate iconic structures. These include Rem Koolhaas' CCTV towers, ironically referred to by many locals as *da kucha*, 'the big trousers', the Paul Andre designed National Theatre for the Performing Arts affectionately called 'the 'Egg', and the National Olympic Stadium, known as the Bird's Nest.

The current phase of urban development recognises the dual impact of modernisation and urban congestion. Beijing's 2004–2020 City Development Plan articulates a sustainable vision for the city. The Beijing Plan document emphasises economic use of resources and ecological sustainability (Beijing City Plan 2004–2020). It argues that the capacity of land, water and ultimately productivity is contingent on natural resources and the reduction of pollution. These diminishing natural resources contrast with the 'increasing returns' of knowledge-based industries, service industries and cultural industries. By 2006, the proportion of Beijing's economy occupied by services was 70.9 per cent. Tourism accounted for almost 22.9 per cent of Beijing's GDP (Beijing Statistics Yearbook 2007). Figures such as these should be noted with a degree of critical distance. The idea of service industries incorporates everything from housekeeping to foot massage. Unquestionably, however, Beijing and Shanghai are the centres of producer services such as management and public relations, consulting, advertising and education. Increasingly, however, the city trades on tourism: its resources include The Great Wall at Badaling, the Forbidden Palace, the Summer Palace, Tiananmen Square, the Temples of Heaven and Earth and the Ming Tombs. In the past few years a new destination has been added to the tourist must-see list – the 798 Art Zone at Dashanzi.

In 2003, the Chinese Academy of Social Sciences calculated the value-added contribution of culture to Beijing's economy at just 4.89 per cent, less than Shanghai at 5.84 per cent. By 2005, a new data calculation system had recalibrated Beijing's cultural value added as 10.2 per cent (Keane 2007).[3] In 2010 the value-added contribution of these industries to Beijing's GDP was 12.3 per cent, a total of USD 26 billion. During the Eleventh Five Year Plan period, one which saw the success of Beijing Olympics and a major spike in tourism, the average yearly increase was 20 per cent while income of cultural and creative enterprises in Beijing in 2010 was USD 85.5 billion. The city's cultural ministry spokesperson has revealed Beijing's intention to focus on building three major national centres in the upcoming Twelfth Five Year Plan: a performing arts centre, a centre for R&D, technology promotion and product exchange in animation, and an art trading centre. In addition the city's press and publication industries will undergo substantial systemic reform in management, content, and technology (Beijing International 2011).

Cultural and creative industries policies

The recognition of the potential value of Beijing's cultural economy led to series of policies. In 2006 the creative industries momentum was quickening in Shanghai. In response, the Beijing Municipal Commission of Development and Reform released its first policy statement,[4] in which 35 measures were advanced to improve the environment for business. The measures included relaxed market entry access; support for R&D and innovation; protection of intellectual property; increased financial support channels; promotion of domestic and international trade; strategies for developing talent and research; and improving co-ordination mechanisms among different sectors. Specifically an annual Special Fund of RMB 500 million was made available. The designated areas for support were art performance, publishing, TV and film, animation and online games, advertising, exhibitions, antiques, design and cultural tourism. The 'special funds' would focus on projects that had 'guiding significance, independent innovation and proprietary intellectual property rights'. The Beijing Cultural and Creative Industry Promotion Centre subsequently signed an agreement with the Bank of Beijing and the Bank of Communications Beijing Branch in October 2007 with the Bank of Beijing agreeing to provide an annual credit limit of RMB 5 billion for creative industries enterprises in Beijing. In 2010 the Beijing government contributed a total RMB 600 million towards fixed asset investment on twenty-two projects in ten of Beijing's cultural clusters (Beijing International 2011).

Concurrently, a policy on foreign investment was released[5] which allowed approved private and international businesses to invest in animation, video games and publishing sectors, as well as in a range of 60 sub-sectors. However, openings were provisional according to four categories: encouraged, permitted, restricted and forbidden. The market openings did not include audio-visual content production and Internet content provision.

The next phase in the evolution of Beijing's cultural and creative industries policy came with the Beijing Eleventh Five Year Plan document released by the Beijing Municipal Commission of Development and Reform in September 2007.[6] The 'plan' articulated a grand vision for Beijing as a creative city during the eleventh five-year period. Beijing would 'seize the opportunity of the Olympic Games' and would become the 'national centre' of art and performance, publishing and copyright trade, radio, TV, film production and trading, antique and artworks trading, design, cultural tourism and cultural sports and recreation.

While many of the documents are phrased in terms of great expectations and national leadership, a further policy document on investment from the Beijing Cultural and Creative Industry Leading Group Office is relevant to the ensuing discussion. Released in April 2008, the 'measures' allocated authority to the newly formed Beijing Cultural and Creative Industries Promotion Centre to administer discounted interest.[7] The BCCIPC (see below) would then delegate authority in each district to a 'District Cultural and Creative Industries Leading Group'. Effectively companies or projects which received project loans from commercial banks in Beijing would be able to obtain discounts on interest, from 50 per cent to 100 per cent of the total loan interest over the duration of the loan.

The International Creative Industries Alliance

The institutional infrastructure of these policy decisions had the earmarks of a bureaucratic nightmare. According to Chen (2004), 'inner and outer factors' (*neibu waibu yinsu*) play a key role in cultural and urban policy in Beijing. The tension between inner (political conformity) and outer (the interests of people) is more evident in Beijing than elsewhere in China. Mindful of the authoritarian legacy of the past six decades, policymakers working in the cultural and media industries in Beijing are beholden to national agendas, while at the same time cognisant of the expectations of local government officials.

In November 2006, at the same time as the first wave of Beijing's cultural clusters was unveiled in a ceremony at the Hilton Hotel, the Beijing Cultural and Creative Industries Promotion Centre was established. The first annual budget of 500 million RMB (US$ 71.5 million) was made available. Shortly after, the Beijing Gehua Cultural Development Group was tasked with the role of guiding and co-ordinating Beijing's projects. The Gehua Cultural Development Group was set up in 1997 as part of an initiative to restructure many of the city's cultural assets (Chang 2008). The sibling organisation of this group is the Beijing All Media and Cultural Group (BAMC), which regulates cable TV networks in Beijing. The BAMC is a separate institutional entity from the national and local TV broadcasters, CCTV and BTV respectively. While it has considerable financial assets, the Gehua Cultural Development Group cannot directly engage in profit-driven business activities due to its status as *shiye* (public institution). The administrative centre of the Beijing Cultural Development Group is located at the Gehua Tower in Dongcheng District near the Lama Temple.

Charged with administering the Beijing Cultural and Creative Industries Promotion Centre, Gehua moved to set up an independent platform in 2007, a non-profit organisation that would draw international expertise and lead the development of the city's cultural and creative industries (Chang 2008). This organisation was called the International Creative Industries Alliance (ICIA). The concept had been promoted by Su Tong, a local entrepreneur who headed up the Creative China Industrial Alliance (CCIA), a 'think-tank' and epistemic community which provides design concepts for cluster projects under the name of CRE.CO as well as operating a branding enterprise called Baroque. In 2004, the group initiated the slogan from Made in China to Created in China, which in time would be adopted by a number of government and commercial entities. As I discuss in Chapter 8, the slogan was originally embedded in 'the creative China plan', an initiative that failed to capture the attention of conservatives in the Ministry of Culture.

The ICIA was a bold initiative with a big vision. It was launched in November 2007 in a lavish ceremony attended by local media in the Gehua Towers. The ICIA had eight founding members of which five were international organisations: the Hong Kong Design Centre, Made in China (UK) Ltd, the Corporate Design Foundation (US), the Da-Tong Foundation China Desk (Netherlands) and the Queensland University of Technology's ARC Centre of Excellence for Creative Industries and Innovation (Australia). The ICIA's stated aim was to act as a think-tank and consultant to government. However, the organisation soon discovered that its parent, the state-owned Gehua Cultural Development Group, was unable to respond to its demands for autonomy. The first issue was that the ICIA was unable to be registered as a non-profit organisation due to legal issues. And because it was not officially registered it subsequently could not have access to a legal stamp to receive member fees (Chang 2008). With this income stream denied, ICIA was beholden to Gehua to provide funds. These were not forthcoming, partly because the global financial crisis impacted on Gehua's bottom line, and partly because Gehua was unable to shake off its bureaucratic identity. Under these operational difficulties the energy for the ICIA eventually dissipated. In effect, it was Gehua's status as a state-owned enterprise that derailed the good intention of the ICIA.

Fangjia 46

The ICIA nevertheless had impact. Members continued to use the name to promote projects. One of the projects in which ICIA members were involved is Fangjia 46, a renovated factory cluster in a *hutong* (laneway) in Dongcheng District close to the residence of the famous Chinese writer Lao She, the Imperial College (*guozijijian*) and the Confucius Temple. Fangjia laneway dates almost 750 years to the Yuan Dynasty and is classified as one of 25 conservation areas earmarked by the Beijing municipal government in 2002 (Beijing Municipal Planning Commission 2002). The development project known as Fangjia 46 accommodates more than 40 businesses, a blend of local and international. These include the Beijing Modern Dance Company, a training and consultancy company from Hong Kong, a media consulting company run by Taiwanese and Japanese-American partners, a New York-registered architectural services company, several design and fashion companies, advertising companies, a film-maker, a photography studio, a restaurant and a lighting company. Fangjia 46 comes under the administrative jurisdiction of the Zhongguancun Yonghe Technology Park, one of Beijing's authorised cultural and creative industries clusters.

Before discussing Fangjia 46, it is worth recounting the evolution of a successful nearby laneway, also in Dongcheng District. *Nanluoguxiang hutong* (South Gong and Drum Laneway) received special commendation as a model creative industries cluster from the Beijing municipal government in 2008. Approximately 800 metres long, it is located between East Gulou St. (*guloudong dajie*) and Ping'an Avenue (*pingan dadao*) in the vicinity of the Drum Tower (*gulou*) and the popular Houhai bar and tourist area. The lane is intersected by sixteen branch parallel alleys, illustrating a 'classic fishbone pattern' (Wu 1999).

The Nanluoguxiang preservation area occupies a total of 39.54 hectares and contains more than 1,200 courtyard houses known as *siheyuan*, many of which have been appropriated by real estate developers in recent years (Shin 2010). Courtyard dwellings in Nanluoguxiang have been either demolished or given a makeover as part of the local district's gentrification of the area. Residents of Nanluoguxiang are mostly long-term occupants of the area; some have taken the opportunities on offer through 'upgrading' to either become landlords or start small businesses. Some of the refurbished dwellings fetch up to RMB 20,000–30,000 per month.

Nanluoguxiang's commercial activities span the length of the *hutong*, generating a 'milieu' effect due to the number and variety of participants. More than 120 shops are registered in the area: these include fashion boutiques and handcraft stores, bars, coffee shops and restaurants. The success of the project has come with costs: Nanluoguxiang is often noisy and crowded; it attracts a steady flow of tourists who more than likely purchase some items. As well as steep increases in residential rents, the rental costs for shop owners have soared: one shop owner complained that his rent has increased tenfold; from RMB 1,000 per month in 2005 to RMB 10,000 in 2009 (Zhao 2009).

As a creative cluster, however, the area has succeeded beyond expectations. A study conducted by a team from Peking University claims that Nanluoguxiang is a seedbed for independent creative activities, particularly film-making; in particular, underground and part-time spin-offs from local arts institutions (Wang *et al.* 2010). Proximity to the Central Academy of Drama means abundant human resources are on hand to participate in creative projects. The popularity of the locale with international artists and designers generates face-to-face interaction, the kind of 'buzz' that is celebrated in studies of innovation clusters (Storper and Venables 2004; Gertler 2008). In addition to its sociable atmosphere, the abundance of bars, coffee shops and craft shops, the lane draws on atmospheric traces of old Beijing, ready-made scenery for film production. The authors say:

> the cafes and bars became a window to history and to former artists... The cafes and bars also brought the elegant art down from the altar and made it accessible to the public. Everyone could be an artist, and in this sense creative production process was not something mystic. The customers in the cafes and bars usually engaged in the process of creation unconsciously, and with a sense of fun.
>
> (Wang *et al.* 2010: 18)

The day-to-day governance of Nanlouguxiang's commercial activity is handled by the municipal government's Jiaodaokou Street office. In 2009, the vice-director of the office, Yu Yongjun, endorsed the municipal government's intention to 'upgrade' the Nanluoguxiang Culture and Leisure Street, saying: 'To play up to the cultural aspect of the area, we would prefer to co-operate with entertainment companies and performance theatres with a strong cultural background' (Zhao 2009). The official promised that RMB 13 million would be used to 'develop the quality and the diversity of culture represented by the street in 2011'.

In contrast to the exuberance of Nanluoguxiang, the Fangjia 46 cluster illustrates a quieter ethos, described by its initiators as a 'creative neighbourhood'. One of the instigators of the project is Zhang Changcheng, known as 'Great Wall'. Zhang is manager of the Beijing Modern Dance Company. Zhang's role was to act as a cultural intermediary because of his close association with officials at Gehua and the team of designers who contributed to the revival of the hutong. Zhang continues to act as an intermediary and an event organiser.

The cheap rent at Fangjia 46 is a bottom-line factor for many of the occupants. Residents of Fangjia 46 view the success of nearby Nanluoguxiang precinct as indicative of commercialisation; most are ambivalent about this tourism development model. Moreover, the intentions of the owners of Fangjia are to avoid complications with excessive development. The investor is the Beijing Fengbaoheng Creative Investment Corporation, a company purportedly specialising in the transformation of old buildings. According to Su Tong, a member of the International Creative Industry Alliance under Gehua and the director of CRE.CO, Fengbaoheng received advice in February 2008 that the local government was intending to redevelop the Fangjia hutong area. They then invited CRE.CO to participate. Su told me:

> At that time, we pooled a lot of resources for the project. In the planning process, we were the creative force, the company was the investor, and the administrative committee of Yonghe Park of Zhongguancun Science and Technology Park was the representative of the government. Fangjia could enjoy preferential policies as it is in the Yonghe area. But we had to use the idea of creative industries to negotiate with the government.
>
> (Interview, 11 March 2011)

Su believed that the good relationship with government and investor was instrumental in the project receiving the green light. CRE.CO proposed the concept of 'creative community' (*chuangyi jiefang*) in order to accommodate the strategy of the Beijing municipal government. Another key element of the proposal was the cultural context. Su believes that the missing dimension in creative clusters in China is community. Rather than proposing to 'attract investment' (*zhao shang*), the proposal aimed to 'attract creativity' (*zhao chuang*). Su says: 'The slogan was "Come to the creative community, cluster with creative neighbours".'

The growth coalition in this instance was constituted by Beijing Cultural Creative Industry Leading Group, the International Creative Industries Alliance, the Beijing Cultural and Creative Industry Promotion Centre and the administrative committee of the Zhongguancun Yonghe Technology Park. The administrative committee of the Yonghe Park provided assistance regarding registration of companies in the cluster and implementation of policies.

Su says:

> This explains why we need to talk to the government at first. In other words, the growth coalition must involve the government. You can't just do your work by yourself quietly. The government, the expert team and the investors make a composite structure like Chinese checkers. 'Attracting creativity' (*zhao chuang*) involves six parts, the marketing director, design director, investment, construction, purchase, and project management.

Su concedes the project has been relatively successful in bring together a 'creative community' although his optimism towards the investment company's motives has diminished over time. In spite of using the lever of creative industries to get approval, the investor has so far failed to follow through, acting as a landlord rather than a facilitator. As well as office space made available from the old factory, the site has a rundown hotel, which doesn't appear to fit the new creative neighbourhood ethos. Like many other cluster projects in China, it seems that having enough paying clients is the game plan for the owners. From one perspective, the land use is now effectively real estate, although many of the resident businesses are happy with a hand's-off approach. The owners of a design studio called Lee Space Design appreciate the ambience of the space and the sense of history but felt that the 'seedy' hotel was in need of upgrading. Gao Yin and Da Li met in Birmingham in the UK when they doing Masters degrees in design and IT respectively. They said they were enticed back to Beijing by the idea of creative industries, which they came across in the UK. The prospect of starting a small design business in a new location was exciting to them. They 'discovered' Fangjia 46 through a friend who introduced them to the Dongcheng local government representative. They now employ ten young staff members; most come from design schools or have arts majors.

Fangjia 46 includes a number of non-Chinese businesses. InFocusAsia (IFA) was set up in Hong Kong in 1995 and has offices in Singapore and Bangkok. The business in Beijing is managed by Shaun Chang and Arito Go. On its website, IFA China is described as 'an independent television production company that provides quality programming, crew solutions and production facilities across China'. The company also works on longer-format factual entertainment for the international market, and produces corporate films and video news releases for NGO clients in Asia. Most of IFA's work is for overseas clients and networks including BBC, Discovery Channel, Animal Planet, Channel 4 and CNN. The company writes stories and develop treatments of subjects which they pitch to these networks.

Plate 4.1 Fangjia 46 cluster certificate (author photo)

As I discuss in Chapter 7, the description 'independent TV production company' is a relative one in China. For a foreign-owned and operated company to be classified as independent in China requires reading 'between the lines'. In actual fact, InFocusAsia is classified as a business consulting company with a sub-category of 'business operations in video promotions and related categories'. The main reason IFA came to Fangjia 46 was to register as a wholly owned foreign enterprise (WOFE). Registration required office space which was much cheaper in Dongcheng than Chaoyang. The actual registration process is also less problematic than in Chaoyang. IFA is therefore able to produce content due to its flexible classification and at the time of our interview was negotiating with China Central Television on a documentary project. Shaun says that 'getting the word video into the classification opens up a range of activities'.

The low-profile relationship with the investment company, the local officials, and Gehua seems to suit the company's mode of operation. Despite a lack of promotion on the part of the cluster management, Shaun Chang says that brand recognition of Fangjia 46 seems to have moved ahead of its own accord. The relationship with fellow resident businesses is about synergy rather than collaboration; there are not enough companies

94 *China's New Creative Clusters*

Plate 4.2 Fangjia 46, Beijing (author photo)

in the same industry at Fangjia 46. As such, the spillovers occur incrementally through friendships with people that have similar creative interests and outlooks and an emotional investment in the precinct: photographers, designers, film-makers.

According to Arito the companies in Fangjia 46 are low key, the stakes are not high and while they do interesting things there is no real temptation for corruption or *guanxi*. Part of IFA's work schedule, as defined by their registration, is consultancy: that is, they act as an intermediary or co-production entity for international companies seeking stories in China. IFA liaises with the international partner, suggests topics and schedules, arranges interviews with experts or local celebrities, and even accompanies the overseas production team to the interviews and shoots. There may be follow-up work in relation to translating. Leading up to the Beijing Olympics in 2008 the company had a busy schedule.

Another non-mainland incorporated business now registered in Dongcheng is Acewood (Beijing) Consultancy. Roger Lee came to Beijing from Hong Kong in 2007 after spending several years as a celebrity fashion photographer. At Fangjia 46 he works with his sister Linda. Acewood's business logo is 'we train and entertain'. Linda does the training and Roger concentrates on children's photography, a strong market segment in China due to the one-child policy. Roger likes the pace of the city and the quiet environment at Fangjia 46. Coming from Hong Kong he is perhaps more aware of government; he believes that when government is close, people tend to behave. Moreover, he is ambivalent about the landlord's lack of interest but agrees that Fangjia 46 needs more gala events: 'No-one knows that you are here.' The bottleneck in China, he says, is the promotional channel. 'The government aims at the bottleneck in order to get control; they don't want you to get on twitter, on Google.' In relation to Beijing, he believes that people are more cultural than in Shanghai: he believes they know a lot of the history about China and how to integrate into their personal life, to make it a philosophy.

Wei Na and Christopher Mahoney are principals of Elevation Workshop, an architecture and urban design company founded in New York; they have been working at Fangjia 46 since 2009. Born in Beijing, Na graduated with a Bachelor of architecture from Tsinghua University before attending graduate school at Yale University. From there she worked in New York for several years before becoming involved with a company in Rotterdam that had a design project in Shenzhen. Following this experience, she decided to return home to set up a business. Christopher joined her in Beijing and they looked for premises similar to their home office in New York, which was also a renovated factory in a quiet neighbourhood. The atmosphere of the hutong had appeal to both of them. Na likes the 'fabric of old city area'. She says that it is good to be able to see and interact with local people:

> You see a mixture of people; you see young people, old people, and foreign people. When we had our previous location not far from here I used to go to Houhai where I would see elderly people mixing together singing Beijing opera, young people carrying guitars going to a rock and roll concert.

Both recognise the attractiveness of Nanluoguxiang; they believe that it promotes Beijing culture to people who are not local but at the same time they are wary of the model being replicated at Fangjia and at other hutong. In relation to creative industries projects, they believe the role of government is to intervene only at appropriate times. Christopher adds:

> The real inception of a creative community happens completely separate from government intervention: it provides artists relatively inexpensive places to live where they might find a community of other people and potential to grow...and then the government might get involved, easing up on the zoning etc.

They are satisfied with the relative invisibility of officials at Fangjia 46, but believe more can be done with the spaces, for example having more events. This is a view shared by several others although the relative tranquillity of the area is something that all residents like. During one of my visits to Fangjia 46, I met the representative of the local district government who clarified that the residents' interests were never far from the minds of local officials, who like her had the common goal of promoting the cluster and finding solutions to problems such as car parking and scheduling of events. In order to 'serve' better they had set up a website with instant messaging affordances such as QQ and MSN. Residents and businesses could visit to see just how the local government was attending to their interests. The design of the site is fairly basic with a distinctly political message: the home page has a poster-style image of a People's Liberation Army soldier reading a story about China's revolutionary heroes to a group of smiling young children.

Concluding remarks: A city in motion

For Chinese people anywhere, Beijing is the spiritual centre of China. It is a metropolis where tradition and modernity are in a state of constant conflict and negotiation. The vernacular and exotic dreams of Beijing residents are blended into a diverse cultural landscape, one populated by more officials and artists per square kilometre than any other Chinese city. The high proportion of officials and bureaucrats delivers a twofold effect: development projects can be caught up in Beijing red tape: on the other hand the presence of more officials means more opportunities exist for epistemic communities to propose solutions to Beijing's and China's development dilemmas.

Cultural quarters, parks, bases and zones appear and compete for recognition in Beijing. Unlike Shanghai there is a limit of 30 accredited clusters and these generally larger and far more dispersed, taking in satellite districts like western Shijingshan and northern Huairou. Beijing's clusters include high technology parks and 'incubators' – the Zhongguancun Software Park and the Tsinghua Science Park (in northwestern Haidian District). Aside from the Chaoyang International Media cluster (see Chapter 7) film, TV, animation and new media bases are located in southeast Daxing District (National New Media Industrial base), western Shijingshan (the Cyber-Recreation District), northern Huairou District (China Audio-visual Base), and northwest Dongxiaokou (Shangpo Animation and Gaming Industry Park). Design clusters are found in the central west district of Dongcheng (the Beijing DRC Industrial Design Creative Industries Base) and in southern Fengtai (the Dahongmen Clothing Apparel Creative Industries Cluster). A number of designated art clusters exist, although as I will show in the following chapter there are also many unofficial communities. The primary designated art zones are in the east: Songzhuang Capital Arts District in Tongzhou District and the 798 Art Zone in Chaoyang. The quota of 30 clusters is filled out by an assortment of music clusters (the China

Entertainment Cultural Creative Cluster in northeast Pingu District); writing (the Wayao Writers' Village in northwestern Changping District); publishing (the Beijing Publishing and Distribution Centre in eastern Tongzhou District); and arts and crafts (Panjiayuan flea market in Chaoyang District).

Cultural tourism constitutes a large component of Beijing's clustering map: from Great Wall culture in Badaling and Gubeikou to the Fangshan Historical Tourism Cluster in the southwest and the Ming Tombs and a European Castle Theme Park in northwestern Changping District. The inclusion of tourism as a key driver of Beijing's cultural economy has the effect of diluting the emphasis on creativity, in comparison to what we see in Shanghai. The overrepresentation of artists in Beijing, as we will see in the following chapter, provides a dynamic tension around the fringes of the city. Elsewhere creativity is added like a façade to show loyalty to the Eleventh Five Year Plan, and to the upcoming Twelfth Five Year Plan.

On a district government level 'cultural creative industries' is an expedient term to justify real estate speculation. The scale of urban development during the past two decades has been extraordinary. Construction workers have razed old buildings and alleyways to construct high-rise apartments; historic factories have been demolished or turned into centres for creative industries. The view flying into Beijing resembles a pancake-like development sprawl dotted with five-star tourist hotels, modernist business centres, hyper-modern television towers, eye-catching sports complexes, overpasses, underpasses, ring roads, technology parks, theme parks and convention centres. Meanwhile the city's streets are congested by cars, residents suffer increasing instances of respiratory illness and traditional ways of living vanish amid the dust of bulldozers. This is progress Chinese style, reflecting the idea of modernity as 'a coming into being', as process, rupture and even disruption. It is also an unprecedented phase in China's history as the nation harbours aspirations of becoming a world power, a harmonious civilisation and an advanced society.

5 Art districts: the pin-up child of the Chinese creative economy

Art districts zones are a visible expression of China's culture-led economic renaissance. Considering the many troubled relationships between the state and artists in recent Chinese history, these projects appear to vindicate the government's commitment to ongoing social reform. In this chapter I look at the historical development of art districts since the late 1990s, focusing on 798, Songzhuang and Caochangdi in Beijing and Dafen Art Village (Dafen cun) near the southern city Shenzhen. 798 is frequently referred to as an Art Zone; more specifically, it is a group of galleries, bars, design studios and cafes which developed in the late 1990s; by 2007 it had become a commercial venture with the full support of the local government.

The second case, Songzhuang Capital Arts District, is a state-administered contemporary art commune further to the east of Beijing. Its origins date to 1993. It is also referred to as the Songzhuang Original Art Industrial Base. Caochangdi is an art village not far from 798 on Beijing's northeastern fringe; its status remains unclear despite attracting an international reputation as a creative milieu.

Dafen's success tells a much different story: how the industrial organisation of art can regenerate a rural community. The Dafen model is supported by cultural entrepreneurs from Hong Kong, who have set up production studios there, assembling teams of workers to 'reproduce' well-known art works. Many artists in Songzhuang and Caochangdi have distanced themselves philosophically from the overt commercialisation of 798 and the 'copy culture' of Dafen.

In this chapter I investigate two issues: first, the industrialisation of 'art worlds'; second; how creativity is viewed as 'resource' in urban fringes. In the case of Songzhuang I am concerned with the relationships between local residents and the new creative classes, many of whom have no direct affinity with the locale. The challenge of rural regeneration is an important one, particularly as a great deal of rural land is rezoned. In 2009, Li

Wuwei, a vice-chairman of the Chinese People's Consultative Reform Committee and a vice-director of the Revolutionary Kuomintang Party, published *Creativity is Changing China* (*chuangyi gaibian Zhongguo*) (Li Wuwei 2009, 2011). The book presents a case for a new China, a China that is open, and on the brink of becoming an innovative nation (*chuangxin xing guojia*). As might be expected from a senior official, the account is optimistic. One of the positive aspects noted is the role of rural projects, which are adjudged to illustrate 'creative agriculture':

> The development model of creative agriculture is characterized by the ability to construct a multi-level, panoramic industrial chain. It will combine cultural and arts activities, agricultural technology, agricultural products, farming activities and market demand to form an interactive industrial value chain. This will open up new opportunities for the development of agriculture and the development of the countryside. This will also maximize industrial values.
>
> (Li 2011: 74–75)

Art worlds

In his seminal study of 'art worlds', first published in 1982, Howard Becker draws attention to multiple environmental factors that allow creative ideas to be conceived, executed and distributed (Becker 2008). In regarding art production as collective activity, Becker identifies 'art worlds': these are populated by various agents whose activities are necessary to the production of works that are deemed to be 'art', whether such judgements are made by connoisseurs, critics, peers or consumers. Aside from these obvious members of the field, an expanded list of persons associated with visual art worlds would include workers who make canvasses and supply paints and frames; impresarios who mount exhibitions; curators, auctioneers and even caterers; landlords who rent studios and work spaces; cultural bureaucrats who administer public funds; and policymakers who define boundaries of expression.

Becker's sociological approach is at variance with many accounts of art which privilege the originality of the creator; for instance, the celebration of stylistic breakthroughs. Richard Sennett, among many others, has voiced suspicion of the concept of originality. While he says that 'art seems to draw our attention to something that is unique or at least distinctive', he believes that originality is a 'social label'; it conjures up an image of sudden appearance, arousing wonder. And yet all art, even avant-garde expressionism, is based on existing foundations and tradition. The work of great artists and major thinkers sets the 'terms of reference' (Sennett 2008: 79). In the first instance one might have an idea; however, this must fit standards or conventions in order to be evaluated.

Becker notes how conventions place strong constraints on artists.

Conventions emanate from the field itself, from critics and connoisseurs. Conventions are maintained by gatekeepers. From a market entry standpoint we can contrast 'art worlds' with the 'world of entertainment'. Whereas the world of entertainment, for instance popular music, is directly responsive to consumers, entry into arts worlds is determined by actions of curators, cultural lobbyists, politicians and bureaucrats (Andersson and Andersson, 2006). Understanding how these gatekeepers function often requires deep knowledge of the field. Indeed, many entrants come from educational institutions specialising in fine or performing arts.

Conventions are often set by the state. State intervention in 'art worlds' takes many forms; these include open support, censorship and suppression. In fact conventions, subventions and interventions are linked. Subventions represent the many ways that government provide funding for artists according to designated criteria; for instance, whether or not the work reflects government social campaigns. In contemporary China the state has maintained a close interest in the subject matter of artists; in turn artists have been willing to produce the kind of work expected by the state. In the 1950s the popularity of oil painting was a direct consequence of the state's need for political posters; the Russian social realist style became a benchmark. By the end of the 1950s as the Chinese state headed in its own nationalistic direction, oil painting came to be seen as a 'foreign' capitalist art form (Clunas 2009: 215). Those artists whose work failed to meet the party's requirements came under suspicion.

In justifying intervention, states will legitimate their actions as in the public interest, to protect public morality and well-being. However, as Becker points out, 'the state acts because it has interests of its own' (Becker 2008: 180). The important point to note here is that government support is conditional; it can change suddenly in response to public sentiment or in response to elite pressure. However, implementation of censorship in China is rarely clear cut. In *The Party and the Arty* Richard Kraus notes three reasons for diminishing state intervention in the arts in China; first, there is a degree of indecision within China's political elite about what to allow; second, the rapid commercialisation of cultural products and the sensationalisation of contemporary popular culture, such as reality TV shows, has rendered censorship more difficult; and third, censorship is poorly institutionalised. The lack of consistent norms provides artists with a degree of latitude during times of social change (Kraus 2004: 108).

The challenges of maintaining ideological control were summarised in the introduction to the *Blue Book of China's Creative Industries* (Zhang 2009). In noting 30 years of cultural reform, the authors point out that ideological conflicts that were important in the past do not exist today. They also note that commodification of cultural expression generally entails products that do not have an ideological sense. Moreover, digital technology has resulted in a greater diversity of media products, which makes the task of government intervention into the marketplace more problematic. Finally, because people have the means of technical reproduction – that is the ability to rapidly copy and disseminate – maintaining control is difficult.

Artists' and farmers' lives

The image of the artist as 'outsider', a strong theme in many Western liberal accounts of creativity, from Van Gogh to the Beatles, entails celebration of autonomy; namely, the belief that good work emerges when artists are left alone by the state, and in many cases by the demands of commercial agents. Works that might subsequently have claims to originality often emerge from the edges of conventional practice: such 'marginal works' are in turn legitimated by the mainstream.

Contemporary Chinese art worlds have been readjusted due to a sudden interest in the artist as an economic entity. While artists have experienced a fraught relationship with policymakers in the past six decades, artists were not lacking social and political distinction in traditional Chinese society.

The definition of 'artist' in China requires some investigation before we proceed. Throughout Chinese history many artists, writers and poets lived adrift from mainstream society, often finding inspiration in nature, music and wine. However, many others were absorbed directly into positions of power, beneficiaries of patronage from the imperial courts and rulers who sought out learned counsel; they were acknowledged as *shi*, a term to describe 'gentlemen'. Many of these gentlemen came from the ranks of the gentry; their lives were devoted to learning and understanding of the Confucian classics. Such *shi* were positioned atop a social hierarchy that included farmer, artisan and merchant. According to tradition there were injunctions against these four groups mixing. One account dated 306 BC describes the expected living arrangement of the four groups: *shi* resided in 'pure' surroundings, farmers in the countryside, artisans in official buildings and merchants in market centres (Lloyd and Sivin 2002: 19).

In investigating the peri-urban fringe community of the Capital Arts District in this chapter I am therefore cognizant of long-held tensions between city and country people. I use the term 'mentalities' to describe this tension and I contrast it to the modern political concept of governmentality (Foucault 1988) (i.e. literally govern/mentality). 'Mentalities' was used by Lévy-Bruhl (1923) to explain perceived differences between pre-logical (primitive) populations and those of civilised countries (i.e. France), or at least the implication that people have different mindsets and worldviews. It has transferred into psychological and educational debates, as well as into cross-cultural debates (Nisbett

2003). At stake is whether apparent differences in belief systems reflect differences in the content of thoughts or whether they correspond to different ways of thinking. Stereotypes of urban–rural differences remain even in a modern age when city and country populations are deeply interconnected. Are people more inclined to be honest and trustworthy in the countryside, where co-operative forms of social capital have a longer history? Are city people smarter but less trustworthy? We might ask: what determines differences in our mindsets: is it social persona, upbringing, values, the societies we belong to, the languages we speak, or some combination of all these factors (Lloyd 2007)?

Invariably, history has shown how the domain of culture has been subject to a process of 'splitting' – into high and low culture, elite and mass culture, civilised and primitive culture, intolerant and tolerant culture (Bennett 1997). Chairman Mao Zedong, voted by a survey of students from mainland Chinese and Hong Kong universities to be the most creative person in recent Chinese history (see Yue and Radowicz 2002) was known for generating 'dialectical' oppositions and then administering political programmes to resolve these. Mao's views on the urban classes of the revolutionary period (1930s–1976) provide an example of splitting and resolving oppositions. Mao asserted that the urban literati who aspired to take an active part in the revolution were as much in need of reform as the bourgeois culture they espoused. Mao viewed such 'petit-bourgeois intellectuals' with distaste: '(they) stand aloof from the masses' and 'lead empty lives' (Mao 1940, cited in Denton 1996).

Mao's idea of a 'revolutionary peasant culture' collapsed the opposition between the literate high tradition and the unsophisticated common tradition, to forge a 'national, scientific and mass culture' (Denton 1996). Using the theory of dialectical materialism, contradictions between intellectuals and peasants would be dissolved: the masses would become the object (*duixiang*) of cultural government. The normalising role of culture established models; in doing so it allowed cultural programmes to perform the task of raising the level (*suzhi*) of those sections of the population deemed to be backward, dysfunctional or recalcitrant.

Now the object of reform in China has changed. Modernisation, urbanisation and economic reform have shifted the balance between urban intellectuals and peasants back in favour of the former. Artists have become useful and productive members of Chinese society while the social status of peasants has suffered. The association of peasants with floating populations, migrant labour and even petty criminality has targeted them as an increasingly marginal social formation (see Li 2001). Meanwhile, artists have moved closer to the mainstream, thanks to their association with post-industrial transformation.

This image of the artist as *shi* underwent refashioning as a result of Mao's cultural reforms. Enlisted as a 'cog in the wheel' of socialist development, artists became responsible role models. The reward for this elevation was not material wealth but a sense that they were part of history. Artists enjoyed a new kind of intimacy with government patrons, with propaganda cadres. By the 1980s, revolutionary socialism had faded into economic reform. The Chinese state lost its direct interest in the production of art and the management of artists. In this interregnum a commercial world of art began to emerge. Kraus writes: 'artists (and other intellectuals) have established a new and more autonomous relationship with the state. The price of this growing independence is financial insecurity, commercial vulgarisation, and the spectre of unemployment (Kraus 2004: 28).

In turn, Chinese artists have resorted to organising themselves in new networks. Many operate autonomously, displaying their wares in areas frequented by tourists, churning out replicas of works by well known artists. Others have formed into collectives. China's art communities have taken various forms – from decidedly imitative, best illustrated by Dafencun Artists Village in southern China – to presumably original, typified by the Beijing's Industrial Centre for Original Art located at Songzhuang. While I will discuss elements of the Dafencun 'model' in the second part of this paper, my focus is Beijing as a centre for contemporary art.

Beijing's art communities began to emerge in the mid-1980s, spurred on by a group of 'would-be poets, painters, sculptors and writers' calling themselves the Stars. Karen Smith (2008) writes about how they took up residence at Fuyuanmen Village, close to the ruins of the Yuanmingyuan, the Ming Emperor's Summer Palace in Beijing's northwest Haidian District. The group included artists like Fang Lijun, Qi Zhilong, Ding Fang and Yang Maoyuan. Initially, a certain rapport, or at least tolerance, existed between the artists and the more 'down to earth' locals. These were exhilarating times. They were punctuated by the emergence of 'culture fever', an intellectual scepticism brewing in some of Beijing's elite universities and new forms of popular culture, best illustrated by the hooligan writer Wang Shuo. Artists saw themselves in this vanguard. In describing lifestyles of the artists in this area, the renowned art critic Li Xianting has said:

> In the crowded living quarters parties were never-ending. Wine, lovemaking and raucous exchange stimulated art...it seemed that wine and women heated the passions all day long. However, to describe this lifestyle as romantic would be too elegant, glorifying what was a debauched lifestyle.
>
> (Li, introduction vii in Ma 2008)

Eventually the initial goodwill that existed between artists and peasants began to evaporate. The intoxicating lifestyle afforded artists led to social division. Rubbish, including beer bottles, began to line the streets; villagers complained that their stockpiles of winter cabbage were disappearing (Smith 2008). Parties were noisy affairs and went long into the night. The painter Xu Ruotao reminisced: 'We were poor but we were relaxed. You didn't have to be a great painter as long as you were doing your own thing. It was a lifestyle that was entirely new in China' (cited in Smith 2008: 112). This bohemian lifestyle eventually merged with the tides of migrant workers that were congregating in the city fringes in the wake of economic reforms.

Even though the artists were not from peasant stock, their itinerant lifestyle meant that could be dealt with in similar ways. Without a local residency permit, they could be moved on. Local authorities, concerned about the impact of artists on the development blueprint of Zhongguancun, the emerging IT hub, saw reason to relocate these risky communities to other parts of Beijing. The move saw art activities return to the east of Beijing, traditionally the focal point of artists. Some prominent artists had set up a 'collective' in East Village (*Beijing dongcun*) at a location just past the third ring road in Chaoyang District. This settlement was short lived, no doubt due to the propensity of many of the leading performance artists there to push the limits of public acceptance. In particular, a performance art piece by Zhang Huan attracted notoriety, even though few were there to witness. The artist sat naked covered in fish entrails on a village latrine for an hour attracting a huge volume of flies. In other 'memorable' performances at the East Village artists appeared naked, attracting the attention of Public Security officials and charges of 'pornographic acts' (Smith 2008: 115).

While the lifestyles of artists in Beijing had become a problem for officials, the government saw something of interest unfolding behind the problem. Chinese art had unexpectedly captured the attention of international buyers. Until the 1990s the only Chinese artist to achieve international success was Chen Yifei, who was known for his depictions of 'nubile women lounging in Asian bordellos and corny depictions of Tibetan villagers' (Pollack 2010: 28). By the time the East Village community had made its presence felt, Chinese artists, particularly art movements labelled Cynical Realists and Political Pop, were being discovered by international connoisseurs. Prices for Chinese contemporary art began to spike.

The management of the Chinese contemporary art scene since the early 1990s shows how the state moved quickly to monitor valuable economic resources. The value of the Chinese art market rapidly increased in the 1990s, initially stimulated by the reputation of expatriate Chinese artists in New York and Paris. Artists such as Xu Bing, Zhang Huan and Cai Guoqiang captured the imagination of Western art critics and connoisseurs. In 2006, China's share of the global art market was 6 per cent; by 2011, this had increased to 23 per cent (McAndrew 2011). The artist, once marginalised, has become a valuable industrial commodity, one that requires enough freedom to be 'productive' and enough management to restrain the 'disruptive' artistic passions that led to the demise of the Yuanmingyuan artists' village and the East Village. This has entailed a new strategy of governance. Ulfstjerne (2009) describes how the former intimate relationship between artist and the party-state under revolutionary socialism changed as private investors and corporate collectors emerged. While the survival of Chinese visual art still relies on the hand of government, there is greater arm's-length supervision. Barbara Pollack, a US-based art critic who first visited China in 2004 writes:

> Once government censors saw their job as protecting the people from the destabilizing influence of contemporary art. Now they have been won over by the screaming success of their nation's artists in the international art world and embrace this home-grown talent.
> (Pollack 2010: 12)

The 798 Arts District

The name 798 is well known internationally. A former electronics factory designed by East German engineers in the 1950s, 798 is a tourist attraction for many international visitors to Beijing. For both artists and visitors alike the district has become a symbol of Beijing's openness. The evolution of 798, from spontaneous artists' collective to the commercial hub of Chinese contemporary art, is a familiar one: a disused industrial space is occupied by artists seeking low rent, the artists' presence attracts visitors, the value of the land rises, local government officials become interested; some groups prosper, others become disillusioned. For some 798's success is symptomatic of its failure.

798 is situated within a larger industrial cluster initially called Joint Factory 718 between ring roads 4 and 5 on Beijing's central northeast, occupying a total land area of 290,000 square metres, 225,000 square metres of which are occupied by buildings. The area originally contained multiple factories designed in the Bauhaus style by East German architects in 1952, occupying 93,000 square metres of the whole factory complex. In 1964, the 718 Joint Factory was disbanded and six sub-factories (700, 706, 707, 718, 797 and 798) took on their own lives.

The area was initially used for public art projects by the Beijing Central Academy of Fine Arts when it moved during its transitional period to the Beijing Municipal Semi-conductor Parts Factory in 2000, before its eventual relocation to Huajiadi. The idle 798 factory in Dashanzi meanwhile drew a number of well-known contemporary artists and media practitioners, led by Sui Jianguo and the magazine publisher Hong Huang. In 2001, the writer and musician Liu Suola, the art publisher, Robert Bernell and artists Huang Rui, Bai Yiluo and Chen Lingyang came to 798. Xu Yong, who had initiated 'Houhai culture' in the adjacent district of Dongcheng, rented a large factory. This would become known as the 798 Art Space. In 2001, the factories joined together under the name Seven Stars Science and Technology Co., Ltd (*qixing huadian jituan*).

Within two years the area had transformed into an exhibition space featuring many of China's avant-garde artists. The design of 798 was further enhanced by Chinese artists who had experienced loft-style living overseas (He 2004). Bérenice Angremy, director of Thinking Hands Co. Ltd., an international art consultant, worked for five years in 798. She notes: 'In the first phase, 2002–2005, we moved into a largely empty factory and organically turned it into an art district. The first galleries entering here had a mission, to fill a space in Beijing's creative society.' During this phase 798 was open to all, the occupants believing that it would soon be demolished. After three years, participation in the project was subject to a renewing yearly contract. Angremy continues, 'In the second phase, after 2005, the Seven Stars Group stopped renting to foreigners and artists' (cited in de Muynck, 2007). This was the beginning of big expansion plans for 798.

On 28 March 2006, the complex came under the joint management of the Chaoyang government and the Seven Stars Group. The local government officially designated the area as The 798 Art Zone. A management group called the Beijing 798 Arts District Construction Management Company was formed. From 28 September to 14 October of that year, the site hosted the '2006 Beijing 798 Cultural Creative Festival'. In December 2006, the site was officially celebrated as one of Beijing's first wave of designated cultural creative clusters. The following year represented 798's initiation as a global centre for contemporary art. While there were some 400 registered organisations filling out the art district, the basic infrastructure was still a work-in-progress. This was to change within a year as preparations took place for the Beijing Olympics.

In 2007, the Ullens Centre for Contemporary Art (UCCA) opened in 798. The centre is funded from the art speculation of Baron Guy Ullens, a person who made his fortune in foodstuffs. The centre attracted a deal of criticism from some Chinese critics for its lack of attention to Chinese mainstream art. Can Xin, one of a group who came to 798 from the East Village, offers the following commentary: 'art is a commodity that has no relationship to mass taste, it has all the hallmarks of the upper classes and so you get this sort of problem. In Europe the Ullens are part of the elite and the things they do are in line with the expected way of doing things but in a Chinese environment the same things will stand out, be more jarring and make people uncomfortable' (Can 2008: 151). In April 2011, Baron Ullens began to divest himself of his Chinese art assets, as well as relinquishing his role in the management of the UCCA amid speculation that the 798 centre had run into managerial and political difficulties. Ullens refuted these suggestions, maintaining that: 'The Chinese have been nice, we've had very nice relationships; we've never had censorship. The problem is they have structures and you need to have Chinese partners to navigate the structures. So it's true, to some extent it's true' (cited in Ruiz 2011).

In response to the question of whether 798 is a creative cluster or an art district, there have been a number of responses, some ambivalent, others contradictory. Predictably, non-Chinese participants in the designated parks are sceptical. Alexander Ochs, founder of White Space Beijing at 798 says: 'I don't understand the term "creative industries park" because art and culture are not things you can produce on an industrial scale' (Ochs 2008: 186). Monica Piccioni, a Director of offiCina, an Italian art organisation, expresses the concern, shared by many, that something has been lost in the haste to turn 798 into a commercial attraction:

> The quality of infrastructure like lighting and the roads has improved, but the overall fresh charm has disappeared because too much space has been rented out to that kind of people; they have no taste or experience and they are even more clueless in the way they renovate art galleries.
> (Piccioni 2008: 162)

Yet when asked if government support for 798 as a creative industries park was contradictory to the ethos of art worlds, Piccioni expresses the view that 'turning 798 into a "creative industries park" did not go against the original function of the district. Inherent in this kind of response is the sense that the elite of the international art world – high-minded, richly experienced specialists and vigorous business people – have much to offer Beijing. Robert Bernell, the founder of Timezone Books, one of the earliest non-Chinese participants in 798, sees no problem with the idea of a 'creative industries park'; for Bernell it is a commercial endeavour but one that leaves room for some experimentation. The time to worry, according to Bernell, is if it turns into 'a curio market where they sell Mao badges and Little Red Books' (Bernell 2008: 146).

Similarly, Li Yilin, the Director of the Asia Art Centre, believes that art districts do not have a strong commercial atmosphere, whereas a creative industries park, such as 798, does; in turn this allows greater diversity of production, and according to Li this is a good thing (Li 2008). However, a different view is expressed by the artist and critic Shu Yang, who believes that creative industries should reflect individual creativity, not industrial organisation. He says that the line between culture and commerce is not drawn by the artist in 798 but by the management and by the local government, which has the power to determine the branding of 798.

The Capital Art District (CAD)

In 1993, a handful of artists set up makeshift studios and workspaces in Songzhuang village, a rural locality some 30 kilometres east of Beijing's

CBD in the district of Tongzhou. The scale of the Capital Arts District (CAD), sometimes referred to the Industry Base of Original Contemporary Art, is difficult to imagine in developed countries. In the Jin and Yuan Dynasties (twelfth and thirteenth centuries CE), the Tongzhou region formed the northern axis of the Great Canal leading south to Hangzhou. Up until a decade ago Tongzhou's economic success had come from high-tech industries, manufacturing, and food processing and garment production. The district is about 20 kilometres from 798 Art Zone, with which it maintains an ambivalent relationship. Many Songzhuang-based artists take the opportunity to exhibit in 798 but many are equally critical of what they see as artists taking short cuts; that is, producing derivative commercial art. According to the Songzhuang artist Wu Zhenhuan (2007: 2):

> Many contemporary artists use 'contemporary' and 'avant-garde' as their excuse for self-appropriation, deceiving themselves and others as well. Someone has once said that 80 percent of contemporary art is trash. Personally I would say 99 percent of them are.

In 2004, the activity of artists at Songzhuang attracted the attention of local government officials who conducted an analysis of the economic potential of the art industry to the district and subsequently implemented a long-term development plan culminating in 2020. According to the deputy party-secretary of Songzhuang the plan outlined five urgent projects. The first, beginning in 2004, saw the establishment of the Songzhuang Arts Promotion Committee, a co-ordinating group responsible for providing infrastructure facilities such as road construction, water projects, as well as internet and telecommunications infrastructure. The newly constituted committee allocated subsistence allowances to struggling artists.

A second project in 2005 saw the establishment of an annual Songzhuang Cultural Arts Festival which provides exhibition and trade opportunities; after the first art festival, 100 galleries and 14 arts museums were established. The largest arts museum is 20,000 square meters. These facilities were designed to promote exhibitions and tourism, and to develop supporting service industries. A third project was a dedicated Cultural Industries Fund to assist industry development; the fourth project was the official Songzhuang website, which has provided an online exhibition and trade platform. The final project, according to the official, was the Cultural and Creative Industries Investment Company, which functions as a financing platform.[1]

In 2004 there were 316 artists at Songzhuang and neighbouring villages. According to the official there are now over 4,000 artists, most of whom are professional art workers.[2] In the same year efforts were made to brand the region. In 2004, the brand China Songzhuang was registered and now

Art districts: the pin-up child of the Chinese creative economy 109

Plate 5.1 798 Art Zone, Beijing (photo by Yeshi Tsering)

provides IPR protection for more than 40 brands in the region. The official was quick to empathise with concerns of local artists: 'Instead of following the commercialization path of SoHo and 798, Songzhuang intends to retain original art work creation as its defining characteristic'.³

The question that arises is: what kinds of spillovers are evident in this cluster? Are there mutual benefits from the confluence of artist and peasant communities? Firstly, it is evident that the open and natural environment of the district has attracted many younger artists. The infusion of artists from all over China, as well as from outside China, has generated an aesthetic apparent in the design of shop fronts. In comparison with the disorder that led to the removal of artists from Yuanmingyuan, the externalities are positive. Artists have provided a makeover for this former agricultural and industrial area. Some artists see advantages accruing to the villagers. An artist from Ningxia, a northwestern province deep in the 'socialist countryside', was unaware of any noticeable transformation in artists' mentalities as result of exposure to local life. In response to a question: Do villager's thoughts influence the artists' work? He replied:

> I would say normally not. Artists are trained in thinking and skills; they won't change because of farmers' mentalities. There might be some artists who pay attention to social problems but usually they care about higher level things.⁴

In this account, 'higher things' implies non-material values associated with aesthetics. When pressed about the reverse effect he was more forthcoming:

> Do the artworks influence farmers' lives? It is not necessary a good thing: there might be a gap between backward and advanced thinking. For instance, farmers can see some artists who are very rich and who have a very different life; they may not notice the 'down-to-earth' attitude of the artists. These things appear suddenly and affect their lives; it takes away their simplicity and honesty. An example is that houses are built roughly for renting – they used to build good houses.

One might expect a different perspective from the management of the community, whose goal it is to promote harmonious relationships. The social and economic benefit of artists to the welfare of the locals was expressed by the local party official as follows:

> Combining rent and consumption, we have calculated that each artist spends 60,000 yuan in the region. Furthermore, local people not only work for the artists, but also have collaborated with artists to open the 'Farmer's Gallery'. With over 500 exhibitions already held in this area, some local farmers have set up the 'Farmer's Supply Company'. Some run stores selling painting materials. This has changed local people's life and work.[5]

On the issue of occupational externalities the pitch is even more upbeat: 'The cultural and creative industries bring jobs. If one artist can bring 6–7 jobs then 4,000 artists will bring over 10,000 jobs.'

As to the question of how the mentalities of locals are transformed, the response is predictable:

> Working and living with artists has a great influence on local peoples' lifestyle; for example, they decorate their houses more nicely. The artists have great influence on youth. The Arts Promotion Committee introduces the Jilin Art School into Luzhou High School in Tongzhou; in recent three years, 100 per cent of the students specialised in art have passed the Entrance Examination (*gao kao*). This is the social effect.

The effectiveness of the social transformation from farming life to 'art world' is evident in Songzhuang's neighbouring village of Xiaobao. In 1993, a total of 703 persons, 100 per cent of the workforce, were engaged in agricultural production. In 2007, the total workforce of 682 persons was employed in service-related industries such as restaurants, cleaning and gallery maintenance (Kong 2008). The per capita income in Xiaobao increased from RMB 7,992.9 in 2002 to RMB 13,607.1 in 2006. In 2002, there were no street lights; now there are street lights and a bus service. Villagers own motor vehicles. Before there was no village square; now there is an art square and an 'art street'. Where once the village livelihood was farming, its integration into the artworld has created new possibilities and new income streams; farmers have become entrepreneurial, renting out their houses and building additional structures.

However, like many cluster projects in China, the bottom line is real estate speculation. According to a number of interviewees Songzhuang has profited by developing the real estate business more than art. In the main commissions and tax from sales of art don't remain in local hands. Before the 'art industry' gained a foothold in Songzhuang, artists merely lived in villagers' homes and used these for workspaces. One view is that the government pushed the development of the art business because Tongzhou is a newly developed district which needed the fame of art to drive land prices higher. In turn the real estate profits are turned back into building galleries and museums.

Hybrid spaces between city and country

The Songzhuang Capital Arts District in Tongzhou District illustrates the expansion of the cultural and creative industries beyond urban enclaves. Organic beginnings were followed by official intervention: the rationale of intervention is to help manage the affairs of the artists. Songzhuang made its reputation on the back of the unprecedented boom in Chinese contemporary art from the late 1980s (Pollack 2010; Smith 2008). Sensing an opportunity to adjust the 'art world' of Songzhuang to the aspirations of the local community, a correction that accords with the Chinese Communist Party's theme of 'harmonious society' (*hexie shehui*), and the 'new socialist countryside', officials conducted research carefully. They became knowledgeable connoisseurs of art; they exercised restraint in managing the lifestyles of artists; in short, they have worked hard to provide the impression that this is a project that brings together locals and artists with mutual benefit. For the artists, however, the association with both officials and villagers is more a necessity than a duty; officials and villagers are essential to production, they are part of the artworld of Songzhuang; the locals provide many of the support services including the production of canvas, frames and art materials, the provision and maintenance of artist spaces, galleries, as well as modelling for artists and manning restaurants to service the new community. The officials set the rules; they provide pastoral care of their congregations.

However, to see Songzhuang and 798 as illustrative of Beijing's contemporary art scene would be to disregard the messy nature of urban development in which artists and villagers are often victims rather than heroes. The example of Caochangdi (literally 'grasslands') on Beijing's northeastern fringe provides a salutary example of the sprawling nature of Beijing's artist villages and their temporality.

Reminiscent of the Yuanmingyuan commune in many ways, village life in Caochangdi is a hybrid of floating urban populations, villagers and farmers, taxi drivers, gallery owners, rich and poor artists and assorted industry occupations. Village life takes place surrounded by rapid development – ring roads, expressways, suburban villas for the wealthy, high-end international galleries as well as factories and agriculture. The heterotopia is well illustrated in Mangurian and Ray's account of Caochangdi:

> A mule cart rolls by a parked Bentley and then through an impromptu market. There is a mix of original village structures, ad hoc shacks, brand new multistory buildings built by entrepreneurial farmers, and the 'high architecture' studios and galleries designed by Ai Weiwei and FAKE.
>
> (Mangurian and Ray 2009: 429)

Caochangdi evolved in the 1980s when Deng Xiaoping ordained the socialist commodity economy. Like many fringe areas around China's cities, Caochangdi attracted private entrepreneurs who set up factories which in turn eroded the farmland. According to Robert Mangurian and Mary-Ann Ray: 'this has produced a unique kind of space under the influence of a hybrid experiment that is part capitalist, part communist, and part socialist' (Mangurian and Ray 2009: 425).

The internal complexity of Caochangdi seems to add to its dissonance, its fragile nature adds to the creative ethos. Unlike 798 and Songzhuang, Caochangdi it is not an 'official' cultural cluster: the studios and exhibition spaces that exist there are classified as illegal. Streets are not named; addresses are simply numbers. At the centre of Caochangdi, at least for many international observers, is Ai Weiwei's FAKE studio. According to reports plans have been made to name the streets of Caochangdi beginning with Ai Weiwei Way (Mangurian and Ray 2009: 430). Ai is China's most celebrated artist, a person who has found himself on both sides of political boundaries. Celebrated as an artistic consultant for the iconic Bird's Nest Olympic Stadium in Beijing's Chaoyang District, Ai Weiwei quickly fell out of favour following a series of open criticisms of China's human rights, urban planning policies and state corruption in the wake of the Sichuan earthquake in 2008. As Ai Weiwei's political notoriety increased, the future of Caochangdi has become a problem for Beijing's planners. Another nearby artist village, Suojiacun, suffered threats of bulldozing in 2005, following a dispute over land use regulations; according to officials the land was designated as 'agricultural land', and had not been accordingly rezoned. Following undisclosed discussions between officials and developers the village was allowed to reopen in 2007 (Mars and Hornsby 2008). Anticipating the temporality of Caochangdi as an art community, Ai Weiwei wrote in 2009:

> There is an S village in B city. Many artists lived there until one day their residences were forcibly demolished because they were illegally constructed. B City is the capital of C county. It means nothing to tear down a few old buildings.
>
> (Ai 2009: 420)

Art and imitation

The modernisation of Chinese cities, together with increases in international tourism brought about by the 2008 Beijing Olympics and the 2010 Shanghai World Expo, now provides numerous opportunities for Chinese artists to reach prospective buyers. Entering into many small street galleries, one is struck by the similarity of the art on display; not only are styles similar to Cynical Realism and Political Pop but a great many contemporary art works are passed off as original when they are clearly imitations of successful artists like Zhang Xiaogang and Wang Guangyi. Chances are many of these artworks are reproduced in Dafen cun (Dafen Village), a model 'cultural industries base' on the fringes of the southern city of Shenzhen. Dafen is sometimes called the 'copy capital' of China, a term that is often unkindly accorded Shenzhen itself. Whereas Songzhuang positions itself as the Original Art Industrial Cluster of China, Dafen is unapologetically imitative. As I found out, raising the topic of Dafen in Songzhuang arouses expressions of contempt among the 'professors' there. Part of the reaction has to do with the extraordinary success of Dafen and the fact that the majority of painters at Dafen are former farm labourers and factory workers.

One of the highlights of Shenzhen is the Overseas Chinese Town (OCT), which covers 9 square kilometres and includes two theme parks and three scenic towns. One of these is called Interlaken, a Chinese replica of the Swiss holiday resort, complete with villas, golf courses and inns. Replicas are not confined to architecture. Over the past decade Dafen has become the world's largest production cluster for oil painting with up to 6,000 practitioners, more than the 4,000 artists currently resident at Songzhuang. The success of Dafen generates a degree of ambiguity in relationship to Shenzhen's aspiration to be a global creative city.

Every year the city of Shenzhen hosts an International Cultural Industries Fair (ICIF). Shenzhen claims to be China's city of design (*sheji zhi du*) and has received recognition from UNESCO as a member of its 'creative city network'. One of the reasons for Shenzhen's prominence in design has been its proximity to Guangzhou and Hong Kong. In 1986, the first graphic design consultancy in China was established in Shenzhen by

Wang Xu and Wang Yuefei, who worked in the state-owned Guangdong Provincial Packaging Company. Zhang Hongxing (2008) notes that by the end of the 1990s Shenzhen's graphic designers had come to exert an influence in other cities throughout China. Zhang uses the term 'paradigm' to describe Shenzhen's breakthrough design culture. With all this emphasis on creativity and design, one needs to ask: how does Dafen fit in; what paradigm is being shifted here?

To understand why Dafen is touted as a success story, it is necessary to provide some background of Shenzhen. Arguably China's most culturally diverse city in terms of population, the story of Shenzhen began in 1979, following its inception as the first of China's Special Economic Zones (SEZ). The SEZs, which were created to bring foreign investment into China, initially included Zhuhai, Xiamen and Shantou. Hainan Island became an SEZ in 1988. By 1984 there were also 14 'open coastal cities', which like the SEZs had considerable autonomy in fiscal and managerial matters (McGee et al. 2007). The rural areas around these cities ultimately witnessed complex forces of migration. Industrial zones (*kaifaqu*) were set up to attract foreign investment; these ultimately attracted workers from many parts of China. Hong Kong provides a good co-ordination point for many Shenzhen exports. In 1978, the population of Shenzhen was 30,000. By 1994, following Deng Xiaoping's 'southern tour' of SEZs, it had jumped to 3.3 million (Liang 1999: 116). Shenzhen developed a reputation as a frontier city, a place where experiments could happen, where money could be made. It attracted young Chinese from other provinces as well as many speculators.

Opportunities quickly arose for entrepreneurs in Shenzhen due to its openness and its proximity to Hong Kong. A 40-minute bus trip can bring tourists from Hong Kong or take local business entrepreneurs to Kowloon or Hong Kong Island. Shenzhen quickly became a mainland stopover for tourists to Hong Kong, a chance to pick up bargains, often counterfeit goods. In recent years Shenzhen has developed a reputation as the home of *shanzhai* culture. Shanzhai, literally 'stronghold of mountain bandits', refers to goods that are cheap copies of well-known electronic brands. One anecdotal account of the origin of the term *shanzhai* is in fact Shenzhen products; when spoken in Cantonese this sounds very similar to the mandarin 'shanzhai'. While shanzhai is associated with 'passing off' and counterfeit, it also bears a connotation with cleverness. The fact that *shanzhai* products are cheaper and often better than mainstream brands conjures up a link with *Outlaws of the Marsh* (*shuihu zhuan*), China's classic tale of brigands and bandits.

Dafen's exports are oil paintings. In the 1980s Hong Kong dealers saw an opportunity to exploit the low cost of labour in Shenzhen, setting up reproduction factories. By the 1990s the locus of activity had moved to Dafen village where the rent was cheaper than the city. The production of art, or more specifically the reproduction of art works, is broken down into work groups that paint different components of the work, for instant skies, trees, houses. By 1999, local authorities had recognised the value of the art village to the local economy and subsequently set in place plans to regulate the environment by distributing licenses and making available preferential business, tax and custom policies. The rehabilitation of Dafen from a poor fishing and agriculture village to an international hub in the global art market has been legitimised through a website whereby anyone in the world can buy a Dafen copy painting, pay by credit card, and have it delivered to their front door. Prospective buyers can browse by artist (van Gogh, Monet, Picasso), by style (Realistic, Impressionism, Morden Art [sic], by subject (Mediterranean scenes, landscape, pop art) and size (extra large, large, medium). While this conjures up an obvious association with take-away pizza, the value of the art market is significant. According to the Director of China's Cultural Trade Centre, Li Huailiang, many Dafen art works make their way out of China:

> Clusters like Dafen Village have already improved our cultural exports. It is estimated that Chinese products captured 70 per cent of the oil-painting product market in the US but by the US official estimations, it was only 1 per cent. The fact is that it does not show the original production location in the art works. Many Chinese oil-painting products are bought by British or Cantonese in Hong Kong and then sold into US market.
> (Interview with author Beijing, 18 March 2011)

If the commercialisation of 798 evinces scorn from the professors of art at Songzuang, the mention of Dafen evokes the homophone *dafen*, literally 'big shit'. However, as Michael Ulfstjerne (2009) writes, the art scene of Songzhuang is itself not immune from imitative and exploitative practices. With so much at stake in breaking through, artists will often find themselves lured into business contracts. One way this occurs is when brokers artificially inflate the bidding price of a painting at auction. This 'false buy' is an arrangement with auction houses or galleries, art brokers and investors (*touzi men*) and artists. While artists who engage in these activities get the benefit of an increased profile, this comes with obligations. The existing artworks of the artist involved are usually handed over to the investor to dispose of, and the artist might be advised to produce more works of the same, even a series of works in the same style, in effect imitating one's own works. Another form of commercialisation is 'taking short cuts' (*zou jiejing*), usually by catering to market tastes, precisely the same practice that Songzhuang art critics have levelled at 798 artists. As well as artists imitating each other, they are not averse to producing parodies of Chairman Mao or 'agonistic comments' on earlier political events. These have a kind of market appeal for tourists and many such works find their way into 798 galleries.

In Caochangdi the culture of the copy is encapsulated in Ai Weiwei's FAKE studio and its repertoire of architectural designs. An ironic comment on the artistic predisposition for isomorphism and taking 'short cuts', FAKE architecture has been mimicked by villagers.

Concluding remarks: artworlds in collision

The entrepreneurialism of arts villages in China illustrates the contradictions between world factory and world studio. In the Chinese creative ecology the factory is the baseline, a physical production space for fabricating, processing, copying and a range of OEM activities. The catalyst for the expansion of such spaces was the introduction of land use tax in 1989. All work units or individuals were then obliged to pay for land use (Liu Chang 2008). This levy substantially changed the productivity of land outside cities or at least perceptions of how such land might be converted to better use. Within a few years an amendment was introduced that allowed profits from land use transactions, effectively encouraging the reuse of farming land and in turn allowing local governments to make money.

The rezoning of farmland and its conversion into high-profile projects is accompanied by great fanfare; local peasants are encouraged to believe that these new projects will raise their standard of living and provide new forms of housing. Local governments play a part by planting trees and building new roads. However, for many of the peasants the loss of land means that they have no clear means of subsistence; they have to learn new skills, provide services to the new creative classes, or leave the area. Many of the refurbished properties are sold or rented out to wealthy business people who aspire to have a rural address and to live among 'professors', an accolade dispensed to many of the educated classes; for instance more than a half of the registered artists at Songzhuang are deemed to be 'professors'.[6] With the introduction of educated and titled residents, the land values rise, rents increase and tax benefits to the local district bureau (*dishuiju*) increase. If the businesses are successful, more tax is passed to the local coffers. If businesses are unsuccessful, they are encouraged to pay for professional services which are provided by cluster development companies (*kaifa gongsi*). Because local tax revenue derives from the registration of businesses, the cluster managements seek out small local companies rather than businesses registered in other jurisdictions. Effectively, this model, with its focus on real estate speculation, constrains innovation.

The problematic aspect of clustering, both from a civil society perspective as well as from a business perspective, is that they remain regulated, although for many incumbents the regulation appears to be 'at a distance'. People's mentalities, and their conduct, are effectively governed by appeals to economic creativity. For some this is a social contract they are willing to endure; the promise of tourism adds to the incentive model. For others the issue is one of loss; they feel displaced by the incursion of art and its international connections. Ai Weiwei writes:

> There are many things that B City does not understand. For example, that art districts are not circuses and that the protection of ancient structures is neither for the sake of sightseeing nor a city's competitiveness, but the people's need of memory. When dealing with old cities or ancient structures, there is only discussion regarding its commodifiable cultural value rather than dealing with true cultural issues.
>
> (Ai 2009: 420)

6 Shanghai's cluster-led creative renaissance

> Perfection, creative experience centre,
> Tobacco unique fragrance fills the air.
> Glasses and brandy interlock.
> Blues broadcast from the record player.
> Time seems to go back to 1933, Shanghai.
> While the leading actors are city nobles of the 21st century.
> *1933 Old Millfun Launch promotional brochure*

In this chapter I look at Shanghai's prominent role in establishing and renovating creative clusters. Creative parks are a feature of Shanghai's post-industrial urban landscape. Some bear colourful descriptive titles like Creative Warehouse, Creative Garden, Creative Shanghai Riverside and Media and Culture Park; others like Bridge 8, New Ten Steel and M50 retain a visible link with the industrial heritage of the past.

I begin with a brief cultural history of Shanghai in order to frame the city's contemporary foray into contemporary fashion and design industries. The discussion then moves to several varieties of creative parks in Shanghai; these are the Knowledge Innovation Community (KIC), Tianzifang, 1933 Old Millfun District, and M50. KIC is a large aspirational project in Yangupu District initiated by the Hong Kong-based developer Shuion Land; Tianzifang is a consumer-focused milieu in the French Concession District on Taikang Road; the 1933 project is a high-profile architectural conversion of a old abattoir built by British engineers in 1933 in Hongkou District; M50 is located in the Suzhou Creek vicinity in the Putuo District and it is owned and operated by Shanghai Textile Group, a Chinese Fortune 500 listed enterprise with a stake in Shanghai's fashionable 'makeover'. In the final section of the chapter I look at a much different model of creative clustering called Xindanwei, literally the New Work Unit. Xindanwei is a co-working space located in the French Concession area. Xindanwei is not an accredited creative cluster. However, its operating model is arguably more likely to engender innovation than most of the designated government parks.

The broader question I want to canvass in this chapter is: to what extent does Shanghai exemplify China's engagement with the international discourse of the creative economy? Shanghai's cultural officials were the first to recognise the importance of this idea and were quick to engage the resources of the city's Economic Committee and establish a co-ordinating mechanism for clusters, the Shanghai Creative Industries Centre. By 2010, there were over 80 creative clusters. The active involvement of local state actors in the designation, accreditation, regulation and promotion of creative clusters points to the concept of the 'entrepreneurial state', where local government officials wear 'two hats': 'one of the official and one of business – embarking on profit-seeking and risk-taking endeavours by investing in real estate, bars and restaurants' (Zheng 2010: 144). However, as Zheng (2010: 163) points out, 'the local state does not act as the unitary force in local government: there is a high degree of competition among district governments as well as occasional conflicts with "street offices" (*jiedao banshi chu*). This then leads to the question: with so many clusters sanctioned by government compared with other Chinese cities, can Shanghai really be considered as a city where independent creativity flourishes?

Shanghai's cultural legacy

Shanghai is a metropolis with a population that is believed to exceed 23 million. Taking into account the inflow of rural workers from neighbouring provinces, this figure is probably conservative. It is one of four Chinese municipalities, the others being Beijing, Tianjin and Chongqing. Shanghai is the core of an extended metropolitan region that includes the Yangzi River delta. While Shanghai people have acquired a reputation for business acumen, the popular culture of the city reflects its reputation as China's most international and entrepreneurial city. Shanghai transformed from a trading city in the nineteenth century to a Treaty Port in 1895 following the Treaty of Shimoneseki, which allowed foreigners to set up factories. The growing city attracted industrialists and fortune hunters who took advantage of its status as an open city. By the 1930s, the population stood at almost 3.5 million, at that time the fourth largest city in the world. In 1933, there were 70,000 foreigners living in Shanghai, resulting in a mixing of cultural genres, a 'fusion' of styles, a creolisation of language and a transfer of technologies.

The interplay between foreign and Chinese populations gave rise to a prosperous publishing industry, including a genre of fiction called Mandarin Duck and Butterfly, which provided avid readers with tales of dangerous liaisons and *ménages-a-trois*. The first Chinese feature film, *The Difficult Couple* (*nanfu nanqi*), was produced in Shanghai in 1913. Isabel Wong's study of Shanghai's early music scene, 'The incantation of

Shanghai', details the influence of foreign styles and fashions (Wong 2002). By the 1930s theatres were exhibiting the latest Hollywood movies. European classical music, Broadway musicals and Hollywood songs were mixed into the lexicon of social life. Shanghai's music scene incorporated influences from jazz and palm court orchestras while areas such as the French Concession were frequented by courtesans and prostitutes. Women imitated Western fashions (Wong 2002). While cabarets were variously classified as 'high class, low class and no class' the description of Shanghai as the 'Paris of the East' seemed entirely appropriate. The area around the Bund and Nanjing Road was known as the 'ten square mile foreign zone' (*shi li yang chang*).

Such escapist pursuits distracted attention away from the reality of foreign occupation. But Shanghai had already made its mark in Chinese political history. The Chinese Communist Party was formed in Shanghai in 1922. Nevertheless the social scene continued to thrive. In 1946, following the defeat of the Japanese the previous year, the foreign concessions were closed down. Much of Shanghai's 'bourgeois culture' was purged during the heady years of revolutionary socialism. A large number of film-makers, writers and artists migrated to Hong Kong, a metropolis with a similarly eclectic fusion of east and west.

Shanghai's re-emergence as a cultural city was put on hold until the 1990s, a decade which saw the development of the new Pudong area, the construction of the Oriental Television tower, and the re-fashioning of Nanjing Road as a consumer mall. In 2004, the Shanghai municipal government made a bold move by endorsing the international concept of the creative industries. As discussed in Chapter 1, the ideological battles between cultural and creative are played out differently in China by way of comparison with most international cultural policy jurisdictions. In China the distinction between culture and creativity embodies a distinctly political edge. Shanghai's strategy was clear. The 'creative industries' was an international discourse, well suited to Shanghai's aspirations and entrepreneurial identity.

One of the iconic figures in Shanghai's creative rebirth was the artist and entrepreneur Chen Yifei. Chen's career symbolises the shifting cultural tides of contemporary Shanghai. Born in Ningbo in Zhejiang and passing away in Shanghai in 2005, Chen graduated from the government art academy in Shanghai in 1965 and was admitted to the Shanghai Institute of Painters at the age of 19. Honoured with the title of Revolutionary Socialist Artist, he spent the following ten years churning out large portraits of Chairman Mao and scenes from revolutionary history – epic canvases with titles like *The Seizing of the Presidential Palace* (1971), which hung in great halls around China (Darwent 2005). During nearly 20 years working in the US from 1980 he developed a style he called Romantic Realism. While this hybrid aesthetic failed to captivate the purists back home in China, his paintings fetched extraordinary prices in international art auctions, enabling Chen to return to Shanghai in the late 1990s whereupon he launched a fashion boutique called Layefe, a home furnishings line, and a fashion magazine, *Vision*, which was later sponsored by the Shanghai Communist Youth League. By 2003, Chen's empire was valued at US$ 25 million (Darwent 2005). At the time of his premature death at 59 Chen was producing films about Shanghai's cultural legacy.

The creative industries moment

The Shanghai Creative Industry Centre (SCIC) was established on 6 November 2004 and began its operation on 8 January 2005. Within a short space of time the SCIC became the principal administrative and promotional body of the local state under the developmental umbrella of the creative industries. In August 2005, a delegation from Shanghai visited London to gather knowledge under the sponsorship of the British Council. The British recognised an opportunity and offered expert advice. In November 2005, another delegation from Shanghai visited Hong Kong where a large consultancy project, *The Hong Kong Creative Industries Baseline Report*, had just been published based on the UK parent model. Following this, Shanghai published its strategic plan. The Shanghai Creative Industries Association, a planning think-tank connected to the Shanghai's Academy of Social Sciences under the leadership of Li Wuwei, identified five key sectors: industrial design and design industry research and development, architectural design, culture and media industries, consumer fashion and business consultation and planning services. These sectors are ostensibly characterised by creative inputs into production rather than the exploitation of existing cultural resources as evidenced in Beijing. The omission of tourism from Shanghai's list contrasts with other regional policy jurisdictions that collapse cultural and creative as 'cultural creative industries' (see Appendix 1). While missing cultural tourism and the significant value that this contributes to regional branding, the inclusion of R&D in Shanghai's list of creative sectors provides an alternative example of category elasticity. R&D includes a buffet of pursuits including artwork and craft design, computer software and internet technology, R&D laboratory activities, architectural design and advertising (Zheng 2010: 158).

In February 2005, the Shanghai Economic Committee announced the launch of the Shanghai Creative Industry Clustering Parks. The 14 clusters in this 'first wave' were mostly disused industrial spaces in high-value commercial districts. Many were already operational and the term 'creative industries' seemed appropriate to describe their activity. Zheng (2010) describes three kinds of users that constituted early tenants. As in most international cultural quarters, the first and arguably most representative group were artists seeking cheap and quiet locations with large work spaces. The unused factory spaces owned by state-owned enterprises (SOEs) provided such opportunities. The second user group were start-ups, usually small enterprises, often formed by persons returning from Europe and North America with new ideas, stimulated by the sudden surge of interest in the creative industries. A third demand for space came from fine arts departments of universities. The term 'incubator' is applied loosely to describe the relocation of applied innovative pursuits, often in the field of design.

By the end of 2005, Shanghai had earmarked 36 creative industry parks. Old plant buildings, warehouses and disused buildings made up two-thirds of these. By 12 December 2006 the Shanghai Municipal Economic Commission had authorised 75 creative industries parks (Keane 2007). Within two years the number had risen to 83.

Shanghai's creative clusters

While most of Shanghai's clusters are reconverted factories and relatively small scale, some are ambitious projects. The KIC project in Yangpu District aspires to brands itself as an 'innovative milieu, a hybrid of digital incubator and talent park'. Occupying 84 hectares, the Knowledge Innovation Community was conceived by the Hong Kong-based developer Shuion Land which had previously developed the fashionable Xintiandi precinct in downtown Shanghai. Noted for its traditional *shikumen* (stone-gated) houses in Shanghai's historic French Concession district, Xintiandi was targeted in a major urban regeneration project which saw the displacement of 2,300 resident families. The Hong Kong developer brought in an American architectural firm to oversee the restoration. When construction finished in 2000, Xintiandi had transformed into an elegant and intricate version of repurposed historical retail developments. Commercially Xintiandi appears to be successful, despite having preserved only two-storey buildings in an area dominated by high-rise towers. Xintiandi is generally regarded as a commercial success; that is, if success is measured by increases in real estate values.

Shui On Lands' KIC is a major urban renewal project. It promotes itself as a place where people live, work, and play.

> At KIC, individuals can come together in groups to collaborate and foster creativity through formally scheduled programs; for example meetings can be held in conference centres, exhibition halls, clubs or restaurants. Or informal chance interactions can occur in public and civic spaces such as sidewalks, elevators and transit stations.[1]

The KIC incorporates a 3,300 square metre Talent Plaza. These kinds of developments symbolise the high-value end of the spectrum. Foreign investment and human capital are the key ingredients. Drawing directly on Richard Florida's creative class, the KIC promises a place where you will find technology, talent and tolerance. International technology companies such as Oracle and Smith Street Solutions have already located in the park. In 2010 the KIC management, trading as the Shanghai Yangpu Centre Development Company Limited, entered into a MoU with Kong Kong's Cyberport Management Company Ltd. The Cyberport is a major digital technology project wholly owned by the SAR Hong Kong government but which has largely failed to capture the imagination of Hong Kong residents. According to Tommy Chung, General Manager of KIC Commercial, the MoU

> will also serve as a platform to share our talent and expertise, and to exchange ideas across borders – ideas that will generate new insights into the facilitation of innovation and creativity.
>
> (Digital 21 2010)

The KIC is an aspirational cluster for Shanghai's internationalised creative class. The promotional video taps into the *zeitgeist* of creativity, linking the once impoverished site with Paris's Left Bank and Silicon Valley. When I visited the KIC in 2009, I was informed by Shui On Land's public relations officer that the project was linked to the creative industries strategy of the Shanghai municipal government. The main problem, he told me, was that they didn't know how to identify and recruit creative people.

Creative clustering parks range from the resolutely industrial to fashionably conspicuous consumption enclaves. An example of the latter is Tianzifang in the Taikang Road precinct of downtown Luwan District. To a large extent the emergence of Tianzifang from six old factories to a fashionable tourist enclave extending into residential areas, occurred with minimal government planning or intervention. The catalyst for the makeover of Tianzifang occurred in 1998 when Chen Yifei opened a studio space in an old factory site. Chen was reportedly enticed to Tianzifang by Wu Meisen, a local artisan, in order to stimulate the reputation of the emerging arts community (Shinohara 2009). In time the area attracted more established artists, names such as Huang Yongyu, Wang Jieyin and Er Dongqiang (Zheng 2010). Cafes, bars, restaurants, small galleries and fashionable boutiques, many leased by international tenants, were quickly added as Tianzifang extended its development into several linked alleyways and lanes. This gentrification was not without problems. The old stonegated *shikumen* tenement buildings housed many elderly residents whose lives were affected, for better or worse by the influx of businesses. The area was officially designated as a 'creative industries' cluster in April 2005. By 2005, the Taikang Road Art Street accommodated 105 enterprises, contributing RMB 1.38 million worth of taxes to the state and generating 550 jobs (Zheng 2010; Cao 2005: 10). As of July 2009, 350 out of 641

124 China's New Creative Clusters

residences had been leased to enterprises engaged in some form of artistic activity or associated services (Shinohara 2009).

The governance of Tianzifang currently functions on three levels. (Shinohara 2009) On the first level is the Administrative Committee of Taikang Lu Art Street (*jiedao bansi chu*), which is responsible for the

Plate 6.1 Tianzifang, Shanghai (photo by Elaine Zhao)

management of the factories, their leasing arrangements and for monitoring market activities. The governance is generally conducted at arm's distance and does not directly impact on business operations, except when there is cause to intervene. The Shikumen Owners Management Committee is the second level of governance, assuming responsibility for management and leasing of the old gated tenements. Because of the heritage attributes of the Shikumen buildings, the Committee works with tenants to ensure that renovation work does not transform the urban character of the area. The Shikumen Owners Management Committee together with the Administrative Committee mediates on issues of noise, a problem that has encroached on the daily lives on many older residents. Indeed, this is a delicate matter as the nightlife economy provides much-needed tax revenue to the district government. The third level of governance according to Shinohara is the self-organising capacity of residents who identify with the character of Tianzifang. Like many urban gentrification developments elsewhere in China and globally, there are apparent strains: rents rise, developers make constant pitches to upgrade the built environment, and tenants engage in activities that are deemed 'out of character' to the ethos of the community.

Arguably the most iconic of all Shanghai's clusters is 1933 Old Millfun. Situated in Shajing Road in Hongkou District, the building was originally a slaughterhouse designed by British architects. The spaces are now occupied by members of China's creative class: graphic designers, fashion boutiques and marketing companies. The curiously titled Old Millfun is managed by the Old Millfun Creative Industry Management Co. Ltd., a group linked to the Shanghai Automotive Asset Management Company. The project's investors were the Shanghai Creative Industries Investment Co. Ltd., and Jinjiang International Enterprise Co. Ltd. The Shanghai Creative Industries Investment Company is an investment and cluster management company established in May 2005. It has three partners: Shanghai Automobile Assets Management Co. Ltd., Shanghai Creative Industries Centre and John Howkins, the British consultant, although Howkins' involvement to date has been primarily an international expert role. According to reports RMB 70 million was invested in the project (Zheng 2010) to create a flagship landmark. The large sunk costs, combined with the prestigious location, have however led to rents exceeding those of adjacent office space.

The 1933 Old Millfun project has drawn much attention for its 'tasteful' restoration of a heritage site. According to one account, 'with its most advanced architectural techniques, as reinforced concrete structure and beamless roof, it became the largest modern butchery – Municipal Committee Butchery – in the Far East' (Tang 2007). The construction comprises two parts: an inner circular tower and an outer rectangular ring. The floor space of 1933 is 31,000 square metres while the labyrinth design resembles a basilica with 24 sides. In the original slaughterhouse cattle would move upward through the outer ring via ramps. At the top, they would cross bridges to the inner core before proceeding downward to meet their fate. The irony, however, is that creativity was a dangerous preoccupation under Chairman Mao Zedong's version of social progress. In the 1950s, many bourgeois counter-revolutionaries actors were rounded up like cattle and executed.

The reconstruction evokes Shanghai's western past, its golden years. Echoing nostalgia for the age of palm court orchestras and courtesans, the promotional material announces:

> Consciousness is unlimited, thought territory has no boundary
> To capture the sparks of thought
> To realize life's highest value
> Condense the faith of innovation
> To free the straight jacket of soul
> Beautify the world with the new angle of view
> Make the life more beautiful with new experience
> In the Holy Land of creativity
> Pursue ideality, forever.

In November 2007, the Old Millfun project was ceremoniously revealed at the launch of the Shanghai International Creative Industries Week. The event featured a Hollywood-style red carpet and an audience made up of business entrepreneurs, local officials and academics. A-list celebrities and special guests were introduced to muted applause, each receiving a sculptured glass plaque as souvenir. A fashion award performance followed which was hosted by media personalities from Channel Young, a local TV channel that focuses on fashion and urban lifestyles. Despite the Hollywood-style launch and the central location, the venue has not lived up to the promotional material; many of the spaces remain empty due to the cost of space. The lack of patronage is not only a problem for 1933 but for a number of other high-profile projects. Bridge 8, the former Shanghai Automobile Brake Factory on Middle Jianguo Road, has been criticised by former tenants for its escalating rent. The lack of public interest in facilities such as 1933 and Bridge 8, and the amounts of money invested nationally in similar lavish 'image projects', has drawn the attention of senior leaders. Chinese National Academy of Arts researcher Wu Zuolai has captured the sentiments of many observers of such projects: 'It's necessary to build cultural institutions and facilities. But they should be neighbourhood and community-based rather than luxurious and inaccessible to ordinary people' (He 2011).

Whereas Old Millfun aims for a distinctively upmarket segment of the market, the Shanghai Chunming Metropolitan Industrial Park presents a more unvarnished industrial façade. Rebranded as M50 Creative Garden, it is now regarded as a creative cluster success story. M50 is situated on

Moganshan Road (*moganshan lu*) in the vicinity of Suzhou Creek in the inner northern Putuo District of Shanghai. M50 is noteworthy because its existence as an art zone predated the interest in rezoning industrial and rural land for creative parks. Sometimes referred to as Shanghai's 798, M50 occupies almost 24,000 square metres. It is well known internationally and in recent years has established a growing reputation in Shanghai's cultural circles, although the presence of a number of aspiring art clusters means that M50 has had to work hard to maintain its identity in an increasingly crowded cluster market. According to the management of M50, the brand is an extremely valuable commodity for its owners (interview with author October 2010).

The old factory site is owned by the Shanghai Textile Group, a China Fortune 500 ranked company, whose board members include leading business and political figures. The company is also involved in designing and manufacturing car interiors, particularly carpets. It supplies Shanghai Volkswagen as well as Shanghai GM, Honda, and Toyota. Known as Shangtex, the group operates four creative clusters and has developed a network of affiliated fashion industry production, retail and training sites, bearing names such as Huifeng Creative Park, Huizhi Creative Park, and Xinlin Creative Park. Many of these are located in former industrial premises; other premises have been acquired by the company due to its active involvement in the creative industries. Among the cluster parks M50 has the highest profile. Others are the West Bank Creative Industry Park in Xujiahui; EP700, which houses a range of enterprises in multimedia, business consultancy, advertising, project design and software development near downtown Xintiandi; and the High Street Loft (Shangjie LOFT). The High Street Loft is an attempt to project high-end local design but according to the management it has met with resistance from consumers who prefer to spend their earnings on international brands (interview with author October 2010).

Factory production ceased operation at the Moganshan Road site in 1999 and the premises remained dormant until a local artist took up residency in 2001. Attempts were even made to entice Chen Yifei to M50. At that time there was no talk of the space being anything other than a cheap workspace for a few artists. The old buildings with their industrial past and high ceilings provided ambience; a gallery was subsequently introduced, which led to more people gradually finding out about the space. In 2002, the local government began to notice the activity and provided recognition of M50 as an artists' zone; however, this required changing the nature of land from industrial use (*gongye yong*) to commercial use (*shangye yong*). A plaque was erected by the Shanghai municipal government in 2004 to officially register M50 as one of a Shanghai's certified creative clusters. Inevitably real estate developers saw opportunities; refurbishments to the site proceeded and restaurants and coffee shops were added.

Despite the encroachment of developers the management has tried to keep rents relatively low. According to the management, this is possible because Shangtex is the landlord and can amortise rising costs. The precinct belongs to a division of the Shanghai Textile Group called the Creative Fashion Group. While Shangtex says there is no direct relationship between artists and the parent company, there is considerable interest in using M50 to highlight Shangtex's corporate contribution to culture. The group's interest in the creative industries and its association with Shanghai's blueprint as a 'fashion city' entails the provision of visible support for fashion and associated sectors.

Of the residents of M50, 70 per cent are galleries and artists while 22 per cent are affiliated creative businesses such as advertising, architectural design and cafes. Brand development is a key strategy for the company. At the moment the image of M50 is contemporary art. The company is seeking to reposition the brand image as 'modern art, creation and life'. This entails the integration of the M50 brand with its online platform, the cluster, performance spaces and a flea market. While there are two websites for M50 there is no interactive platform that might be used as a discussion forum. The management considers such as communication mechanism as problematic due to 'security regulations'. The company maintains a close relationship with both the local and Shanghai municipal government, and the respective 'supervisory bureaus'. The Shangtex representative assured me that the Chinese government is 'changing their way of doing things'. The Ministry of Culture sees M50 as tangible evidence of its national cultural industries planning; meanwhile the Shanghai municipal government embraces M50 as a local creative industries success story; finally, the district government sees it as a local economic resource and a means of generating tax.

In terms of the governance, it is clear that Shangtex plays the role of landlord and patron; the management of M50, which comprises 20 people, is drawn primarily from the Creative Fashion Group; there are no representatives from businesses. However, the M50 landlord takes advice from the residents and claim to have their interests at heart. The company generally adopts an arm's distance approach to the business practices although it does assist in policy areas when asked, such as providing advice on human resource policy. In many instances enterprises need to apply for a Shanghai residency permit (*hukou*) for out-of-town employees.

There are plans for further renovation to provide a better working environment. There is now an internal group called the M50 Alliance which will compete for projects in the market. The businesses in M50 have begun to work together more; however, the main form of interaction is between galleries; sometimes they work together on a project. Identification with the future of M50 has led to some co-operation; one of the architecture studios has played a key role in the design of the renovations. In addition, M50 has worked to build its relationships with the local community by providing a physical space for charity auctions. As management put it to me: 'This is all part of making M50 a total brand.'

Xindanwei co-working centre

Unlike creative clusters that are accredited by the Shanghai Creative Industries Centre and sponsored by district governments, Xindanwei, or New Work Unit, is an autonomous co-working enterprise. The bricks and mortar that form Xindanwei are located at 50 Yongjia Rd in the Xuhui District of Shanghai. From the outside it looks like just another multi-level tenement building. Moving closer to the glass window facing the street, one can see people huddled over work stations; again this is nothing unusual in urban China, except that many of the co-workers are not Chinese.

Xindanwei is a place where individuals come together and share ideas. The philosophy behind it draws on 'sharism', a term used by Isaac Mao, a Chinese venture capitalist, blogger and director of the Social Brain Foundation. Mao describes sharism 'as a mental practice that anyone can try, a social-psychological attitude to transform a wide and isolated world into a super-smart Social Brain' (Mao nd). Essentially sharism develops its philosophical foundations from copyleft movements like the Free Software Foundation and Creative Commons. The affinity with user-generated content and digital technology makes sharism a radical concept while at the same time it has a traditional appeal, people helping each other with projects and sharing resources. In a collectivist society like China, sharism would appear to make sense. For instance, the cultural legacy of Confucianism suggests that people are inclined to co-operate if they feel they are part of a community and especially if there are reciprocal obligations; on the other hand, the rapid escalation of the market economy in China has led to a tendency not to share ideas for fear that they will be commercialised by others. Reciprocity is replaced by fear of piracy and collaboration becomes problematic. In this scenario, creativity is diminished or kept within enclosures.

Another person who espouses collaborative values is Charles Leadbeater, the British thinker who coined the term 'we-think' (Leadbeater 2008). Echoing the theme of social connectivity, Leadbeater says that contemporary sharing practices draw on traditions long established in villages and communities. The difference with these past 'commons' however, is that information today is pervasive and often freely circulated; the kinds of conversations that occurred in small face-to-face communities now manifest in online forums. It is not just an increase in online communities but the connection between online and offline activities, in other words, there is a shift from *collective sociality* to *collaborative spatiality* (Shang *et al.* 2009). Hubs or nodes of innovation appear that are linked into multiple networks globally, allowing almost instantaneous feedback.

Leadbeater argues that collaborative models of working allow ideas to be tested 'from a larger, more diverse set of vantage points more quickly and with ideas continually passing between the tightly knit core who develop them and the crowd who test them out' (Leadbeater 2008: 74). In a recent publication he maintains that 'a combination of mass self-expression, ubiquitous participation and constant connection is creating *cloud culture*'. The metaphor of cloud culture refers to 'cloud computing', the technological capacity to download information from massive servers in cyberspace just like turning on a tap. The ubiquity of networks and devices has ramifications for the kinds of traditions referred to above. Leadbeater says: 'If culture provides much of our sense of identity, then creativity helps to give us our sense of agency: who we want to be, what mark we want to leave. Culture gives us roots, creativity a sense of growth. Creativity gives us a way to add to and remake our cultural stock: it allows us to escape being entirely defined by our traditions' (Leadbeater 2010: 36).

The founders of Xindanwei are Liu Yan, Chen Xu and aaajiao. Yan grew up in Amsterdam, a city that has a long history of sending and receiving ideas. In 2006, she returned to China. While working in the Netherlands Yan witnessed the emergence of a number of interdisciplinary projects such as the V2_ Institute for Unstable Media in Rotterdam and Picnic in Amsterdam. Members of the V2_ Institute are interested in relationships and interactions between different media and in the relationship between art and scientific disciplines. V2_ is supported in part by the Dutch Ministry of Culture, the City of Rotterdam and corporate partners. Picnic began in 2006 in Amsterdam; it is now an annual three-day festival that blurs the lines between creativity, science, technology and business. Yan says she was stimulated by the Dutch way of organising events across domains and helped organise Chinese participation in Picnic 2007. Could such things happen in China?

In the initial stages Yan looked for opportunities in Beijing while acting as an intermediary for Dutch cultural entrepreneurs who had become interested in projects in China. 2007 was a time when there was a great deal of interest in initiating clusters. Projects on the drawing board at the time included the no. 3 Beijing textile factory in Chaoyang District and the Fangjia development in Dongcheng. It was about this time that she began to think of doing something that was not necessarily aimed at making profit. A little bit disillusioned with the bureaucratic way of doing things in Beijing, or perhaps 'not-doing things' (projects getting stalled), Yan moved to Shanghai in 2008. She believes that Shanghai is a city that looks towards the future, an international hub, a place that encourages the flow of ideas. She says 'In Shanghai relationships are businesslike and it is

Plate 6.2 Xindanwei, Shanghai (photo by Joy Zhang)

easy to get around geographically whereas Beijing is very spread out and grid-like.'

Xu Chen is a native of Shanghai who spent a deal of time in the UK. She has worked closely with John Howkins and in the past accompanied him whenever he went to China, which was often several times a year. With an MA from King's College, London, she has collaborated with BOP Consulting, an agency that was instrumental in introducing the creative industries concept into Shanghai. Xu has been part of several cultural and creative industries research projects in China working with international teams. She decided to return to Shanghai in 2009. Xu Wenkai, known as aaajiao, is one of China's foremost digital artists, bloggers and free culture developers. He comes from Xi'an, one of the ancient capitals of China, a city rich in tradition. In 2006 he founded the Chinese take on the blog we-make-money-not-art: We Need Money Not Art.

The first incarnation of Xindanwei took the form of salons in which artists, designers and even academics would speak. However, the founders of Xindanwei realised they needed a physical space; they researched co-working models in the US and Europe. In most instances, co-working models are about communities of people hanging together, essentially non-profit organisations. The exception is an organisation called The Hub, which began in London and then began to franchise its operations; there are now more than 35 co-working Hubs around the world. The slogan of the Hub is 'an inspiring place for people with ideas for a better world to work, meet, lean and connect'. Yan visited the Hub co-working space in Amsterdam Westerstraat and learnt that the operators were interested in forming a Hub franchise in Shanghai. The Hub franchise model promised investors and knowledge but the fee was too much to pay. In the case of the Xindanwei founders, it was more a case of taking one step at a time.

According to its founders Xindanwei operates in a kind of parallel universe to the official creative industries of Shanghai. Essentially grassroots, it began as a few people wanting to have some 'creative fun' and then realising that this fun needs to be turned into a viable business. The project seemed to have a natural affinity with government but in the end this turned out to be an illusion.

In China creative endeavour is dispersed over three levels. On the top government aspires to turn cultural resources into value by adding creativity. Similar to many other governments around the world, bureaucrats need ideas which are provided by think-tanks, coalitions of artists, academics and entrepreneurs, often with connections to a government official. On the market level there are a multitude of businesses scrambling to make money but encountering difficulties because market players either lack autonomy or are engaged in low-value activities. On the grassroots levels thousands of artists, would-be entrepreneurs and amateur producers form a large 'creative community'. This is where there is greatest potential. Bringing it to market and getting it recognised by government is the problem.

When I first interviewed the team in 2009 Xindanwei had set up on the third floor of a building in an old factory site in Changing District. The cluster, IINShanghai, is one of the many emergent clusters that the municipal government talks about. IINShanghai has about 40 businesses and despite the out-of-the-way location and the industrial facade there was promise of developing a community. Like a lot of the clusters in Shanghai, the site has a mix of occupants, both Chinese and international. There was a mess of rubbish left by the previous occupant. The makeover took place quickly and the Xindanwei business model began to take shape, both physically and virtually. The Xindanwei promise was 'a workspace within a community' with opportunities 'to share knowledge face-to-face and to get inspired through collaboration with other members'. Xindanwei membership was to be evaluated and adjusted based on the value of each member's contributions and interactions in the community.

Expectations were high at the time about working co-operatively with the local government. A local celebrity photographer turned entrepreneur, Song Bo, had been discussing the Xindanwei model with the district officials. There was talk of taking the Xindanwei co-working model and using it to identify creative talent, not only in the cluster but in a number of other locations. Song Bo had spent time in England in 2002–3 where he had come into contact with the idea of co-working spaces. When I spoke with Song in September 2009 he was optimistic about the link to government. Xindanwei seemed like a good 'model', a good 'platform'; it was something that he believed might work as Shanghai's primary spokesperson for the creative industries, Li Wuwei, was advocating the benefits of diverse and tolerant creative communities. Li Wuwei described his idea of creative communities as 'cells in the organisational system of creative industries', which were represented by networks, platforms, theme activities and exchange mechanisms, and which were dynamic, often loose and even virtual (Li Wuwei 2009).

In comparison with many official cluster projects that function as real estate developments, Xindanwei is innovative, in theory at least. In order for a niche idea like this to impress officials, however, it had to be linked into a pragmatic plan. The proximity to Donghua University was an advantage, Song argued, showing me a video he had made of his extended creative cluster: this included shopping malls and fashion lofts and of course the obligatory creative incubator. He says 'Government is interested if they can see some tangible outcomes.' Eventually the Xindanwei co-founders realised they were closer to market than government. However, this closeness did not translate into returns on investment. The market in China is less convinced by intangibles. China's wealth has come from manufacturing 'things'. Moreover, the co-working model is in competition with other office rental businesses and many of these have a property developer background. The rent paid by some of these companies is cheaper but they charge similar prices as Xindanwei. Yan says:

> On the market level people tend to bring a lot of creative new models in markets but it's very different to find people willing to pay for it; people perceive traditional services like real estate; for instance this is an office, but if you talk about networks, how to connect people's minds, it's hard to get them to pay for it; so it's very hard to come up with something new and innovative and get support from the market.

According to Yan and Xu the value of networks, and the concept of 'sharism', need to be quantified. The people are customers on the one hand but they are co-building the soft values, the soft infrastructure. The issue of sharing inevitably raises questions about ownership – and reciprocity. Yan and Xu agreed that intellectual property remains a challenge: if you charge money to use the network and expect users to share their valuable ideas it may become tricky. In relation to privacy, there is no compulsion to publish. They believe there is a need to develop a new currency for sharing in China. Ideally people will identify with the community ethos and work collectively to build an intelligence system that contains everyone's ideas. By contributing to the Xindanwei network, they will build a 'commons'; for instance, members are networked in a similar manner as Facebook; if they need resources they can ask for help. When members log in, they are visible to all members and presumably to any members with government affiliations. For this reason it is necessary to get to know the people who use the co-working spaces. A careless remark or a reference to Free Tibet, for instance, could bring the local security bureau knocking on the door. Yan describes how she and Xu have been invited to drink tea (*he cha*) with local officials, a euphemism for quiet discussions about Xindanwei's activities. They believe the place is constantly monitored and because of its difference from other legitimate clusters it could be shut down suddenly without a reason given.

Initially the proportion of foreigners at Xindanwei to locals was 80/20. Yan believes the reason for this was that many local people were just not used to just sitting next to one another; for locals there was no real need to connect with other local people. Those that came generally spoke English and saw the venue as a means to connect with 'foreign' expertise. One local member of the community had set up a Chinese language-teaching course and was paying to use space as a classroom and using members to bounce ideas off.

While the rent was cheap at Changning, the flow of co-workers was slow. Moreover, organising events proved to be a little difficult in this location. The opportunity to move to Xuhui district came up and even though the rent was considerably higher the location on Yongjia Road was good. It meant shifting from a horizontal space in a factory environment into a vertical space, a six-level 1930s building on a busy road in the fashionable French Concession District.

The move paid off. The layout of the new space allows more services to be added such as food and drinks. In addition, the ratio of locals to foreigners has increased. Locals turn up at Xindanwei events; most are entrepreneurs with start up aspirations and are aged between 25 and 35; word of mouth is complementing the Xindanwei virtual community. One of the goals has been to maintain a quantity of co-workers who are willing to pay for an hourly space or even a monthly space. In addition, Xindanwei holds regular salons, hosting international and Chinese designers, artists and free thinkers. Sometimes these salons draw unexpected crowds; according to Xu sometimes very clever people find themselves talking to a small group. Guests are charged RMB 30 yuan for admission, a radical move considering that many similar events in Shanghai are free. When speakers from IDEO gave a presentation about *shanzhai* as an open platform for design in January 2011, people were still paying for admission after the talk was finished. Likewise when a speaker from IKEA was advertised on the virtual notice board, the room was packed.

How creative is Shanghai?

Finally, I want to run an alternative perspective on Shanghai. Does Shanghai's engagement with the creative industries, one characterised by more than 80 accredited clusters, reflect the city's progressiveness or does it merely signal that the city has managed to utilise the international discourse of creative industries more effectively? Shanghai's advantages are fairly obvious: a municipal government that has ridden the wave of this international policy discourse and district governments that have been quick to exploit post-industrial real estate, sometimes termed 'creative estate' (Zheng 2010).

Shanghai presents itself as China's most entrepreneurial city. On the surface the creative industries discourse fits like a glove. Growth coalitions – real estate developers, district governments, powerful state-owned enterprises and academic think-tanks – provide the momentum. Artists and creative start-ups are purely bit players. Yet is this so different from anywhere else in China? Justin O'Connor and Xin Gu question assumptions that the proliferation of cultural districts and clusters in China will generate innovate milieu: they say 'the creative class may turn out to be as socially and politically conformist as the "bourgeois bohemians" in the West' (O'Connor and Gu 2006: 277). Reflecting on the launch of the first Shanghai Creative Industries Week in 2005, they noted: 'This programme is almost entirely real estate driven and spaces are only available to those with money and *guanxi*' (281).

Indeed, the promotional material published by the Shanghai Creative Industries Centre for 2007 Creative Industries Week launch at 1933 Old Millfun provides insights into the power structures underpinning the serious business of creativity in Shanghai. One of the participants named was the aptly titled Shanghai Creation Investment Management Ltd., which pitches its operations as commercial real estate, specialising in the 'Creation' series of creative industries parks. Another participant 'evaluated and certified by the Shanghai Economic Committee was the Chenkai Arts Innovation Studio, an enterprise sponsored and supported by the Committee, by the Yangpu District government and by the Shanghai Textile Holding (Group)' (Creativity Brand Lifestyle 2007).

The question: 'how creative is Shanghai?' cannot be resolved simply by a cursory examination of the city's creative clusters. However, the survey of clusters in this chapter does reveal the ubiquitous hand of government, albeit at a greater distance than in the past. Writing about what he sees as a misplaced international image of Shanghai, Yasheng Huang notes: 'Despite a rich history of business creation and risk-taking, entrepreneurship is almost completely missing in Shanghai' (Huang 2008: 177). Huang targets heavy-handed intervention by the state in micro-affairs of the economy. Compared with the neighbouring province of Zhejiang where industrial clusters developed and have been largely private enterprises,

Shanghai's capitalists are government agencies. Moreover, in the creative industries a similar story is unfolding. In spite of the proliferation of creative clusters and a higher number of international creative businesses in Shanghai than Beijing (Liu Kai 2008), the city may be just too regimented – or paradoxically as O'Connor and Gu (2006) suggest 'too commercial' for the creative industries.

7 Media districts, parks and bases

The usual way to approach the media industry is via *media sectors*: broadly speaking, print-based products (books, newspapers and magazines) and electronic products (film, TV, radio, music, internet and mobile content). Media industries first and foremost provide content, and so we often hear the term 'content industries' rather than the creative industries. This content may be news, entertainment, sports or data. In most models, and in most countries, content is provided for a price to audiences or readers: sometimes it is free, and sometimes it is premium, charged according to perceived market value. The most important idea about the media industries, as distinct from the automobile or the textile industries, is that media content is a public good; in other words, it is not used up in consumption and it can be reused without incurring additional production costs.

Media are a risky business, compared with manufacturing components or widgets. Most media rely on advertising. Demand is uncertain, chance often plays a role in success, and differentiation is important when similar media products are offered at the same price. Because of high sunk costs many media products are based on formats and genres. Consequently, under-capitalised media industries tend towards conservatism – following the leader, copying, making sequels, prequels, spin-offs and reversions. When media are public funded, as in the case of public broadcasting, this is often justified as a mandate to take risks and be innovative in the context of systemic market failure. For all these reasons the media are atypical industries. But, for a number of reasons more to do with ideology and national stability, the fundamental ideas of competition and risk do not carry as much importance in China. Until recently, China has valued content for its use value rather than its exchange value (to use a standard Marxist line).

In this chapter I examine the proliferation of media clusters in China. Media clusters are a common model of industrial organisation in many countries. Film and television clusters can be found in Canada, Australia,

Germany, Great Britain, New Zealand, Romania, South Africa and many developing countries. Obviously the most well-known media cluster is in Los Angeles. Allan Scott (2004) has shown how Hollywood's pioneering model of film production generated an expanding system of agglomeration economies. Scott says that agglomeration economies and localised increasing-returns effects are the glue that holds Hollywood together as a spatial unit and endow producers with potent competitive advantages.

Numerous media production centres, bases and zones, both large and small, have sprung up in Chinese cities and around the fringes of cities. Do these generate increasing returns for China's media content industry or do they serve to diminish returns and homogenise? The Hengdian World Studios inland from coastal Zhejiang Province brands itself as 'Chinawood', a not so original but still highly effective way of claiming pre-eminence in a competitive regional production environment. Despite the Hollywood allusion, Hengdian's business model is based on low-cost production; in other words, competition on price. Its many sets and backlots provide opportunities for East Asian production companies to produce TV serial dramas, many of which inevitably compete against domestic dramas for the hearts and minds of viewers. As I have discussed elsewhere (Keane 2007), Hengdian's investors hope the cluster can be more than a low-cost location by developing a comprehensive media production, post-production and investment system. The problem, however, is that because media production bases have become such a dominant feature of the clustering landscape the core business model is to attract a quantity of paying business. For most, outsourcing is their bread and butter, and for this reason there is strong cost-cutting pressure rather than open sharing of ideas and joint ventures.

Aside from the obvious benefits that might flow to local economies, the national rationale for constructing media clusters, or bases (*jidi*), is to find and attract 'talent'. A second reason for bases is to 'upgrade' China's production capacity to supply national media channels with 'good content'. A third justification is that the alignment of productive and creative forces might just change international perceptions of Chinese media content as dull, propagandistic and unprofessional. If this were to occur, then China might become a net exporter of culture rather than an importer. The variable here, however, is the definition of 'good content': should content be good for Chinese audiences or good for export audiences? Can China become a regional player in media and in doing so reverse its media trade deficit?

Media industries in China illustrate a particularly salient point about governance, namely acts of government by the state. Media industries globally are subject to a range of regulatory policies designed to both limit concentration of ownership, to regulate public taste and to provide opportunities for independents. In order to contextualise the clustering effect that has been visited on Chinese media, I begin with some background to China's media reforms over the past decade. Following this I revisit the innovation ecology concept that I set out in the beginning of this study (see Chapter 1) and its relationship to the clustering of cultural production. I believe that the ecology model fills in many gaps in Chinese media research. Furthermore it explains why clustering has emerged as a preferred solution to the challenge of 'upgrading' the nation's media export capabilities.

The remainder of the chapter focuses on two media clusters. The first study is the Beijing CBD International Media Industry Cluster, sometimes called Central Media District, other times referred to as the Capital Media District, a mega-cluster of production, post-production and ancillary services in commercial Chaoyang District. In order to understand Beijing's ambition to lead in media I draw on Michael Curtin's idea of media capital. Curtin (2007) argues that creative talent is central to success of Hollywood, Mumbai and Hong Kong. Curtin goes a step further and argues that success is more than just the attraction of talent. He says that successful media capitals have come into being through 'logics of agglomeration' and 'forces of socio-cultural variation'. Whereas logics of agglomeration are standard cluster effects – for instance, concentrations of capital and regulatory bureaus – socio-cultural variation implies a capacity to produce a diversity of forms that can serve both domestic and international audiences. Beijing has talent and a high degree of media industry concentration. Its weakness is its ability to generate cultural diversity in media content. I argue that the principal reason for Beijing's inability to command 'forces of socio-cultural variation' is its status as an administrative centre of media.

The second example is the Suzhou National Animation Base located in the Suzhou Industrial Park, 100 kilometres west of Shanghai. Animation is a highly protected creative industries species in China. Central and regional governments have invested a great deal of money in attempting to lift China's cartoon and animation industries to compete with Japan, Korea and the US. The State Administration of Radio, Film and Television (SARFT) has accredited 19 'national animation bases' in various provinces of China since 2004. In addition, more national animation bases and training bases are ratified by the Ministry of Culture and the General Administration of Press and Publications (GAPP), the latter entity taking responsibility for combined online games and animation projects. As I will show, with few exceptions animation companies struggle for survival in a poorly functioning market. In a conversation with a leading media official in Beijing I was told of a popular joke that was circulating. The gag is that an appropriate punishment for young criminals is subjection to constant screenings of Chinese animation. It seems that while clustering may be a means of increasing the production output of animation, it is not the solution to making it competitive.

Media businesses essentially deal in human attention. As Philip Napoli (2003: 5) points out, 'human attention represents a much more abstract, elusive and intangible product than, say, steel, insurance, or legal services'. Producing content that consumers want in the face of stiff competition from Taiwan, Korea, Hong Kong SAR – and even the US media – is a key to a competitive Chinese media environment. If innovation is the mantra of competitiveness in the age of media volatility, how does China innovate in its media? Where do we find creativity in China's media industries?

While China's media industries are fragmented across three levels – national, provincial and metropolitan – their combined value is significant. In 2009, the most authoritative *Blue Book* report estimated the overall output as US 72 billion (RMB 490.8 billion), double the figure of 2005 (Cui 2010). Media production is no longer dominated by party propaganda although tensions persist in relation to balancing commercialisation with public interest, and independent production with state-owned national champions.

Table 7.1 Key moments in the China's media reform (compiled by the author)

Date	Key moments in Chinese media reform
1978	*The People's Daily* announces the policy of 'institutional units, enterprise management' (*shiye danwei qiye guanli*), the first step in changing the model of media management in China
1979	The first television commercial is broadcast in China
1983	Article 37: The four-tier administrative policy for broadcasting (*siji ban*) establishes a decentralised system of financing and management (central, provincial, municipal and county)
1992	Deng Xiaoping's 'southern tour' leads to media reforms: broadcasting is recognised as a service industry (*guanyu jiakuai disan chanye fazhan de guiding*)
1996	First newspaper group formed (*Guangzhou ribao baoye jituan*)
1999	First broadcasting group formed (Wuxi Radio and TV group)
1999	First provincial group formed in Hunan Province (*Hunan guangbo yingshi jituan*)
2002	State Administration of Radio Film and TV releases *The Tenth Five Year Plan for Film and Television Animation Industry*
2003	Doc 105 (12/31) *Promote reform of the cultural system, uphold enterprise development and enterprise transformation* establishes momentum to transform public institutions into 'industries' (*chanye*) and enterprises (*qiye*)
2004	First cross-regional print merger; China Youth News Media Development Co. established; 60 per cent China Youth News and 40 per cent Beida Qingdao Pty Ltd.
2004	SARFT approves establishment of first batch of nine national animation bases
2005	Notice on preferential tax policies for cultural institutions converting to enterprises during the course of cultural system reform *(guanyu wenhua tizhi gaige zhong jingyingxing wenhua shiye danwei zhuanzhihou qiye de ruogan shuishou zhengce wenti de tongzhi)* (Ministry of Finance, the General Administration of Customs, and the State Administration of Tax)

China's commercial media effectively began in 1979 when the first television commercial was aired. Since that time international media conglomerates have attempted to move into the Chinese market. Perhaps the best illustration of such attempts has been News Corporation's aborted ambitions to become a player in Chinese media. Over a period of two decades Rupert Murdoch has attempted to win the support of Beijing's media power brokers, people like former Propaganda Head Ding Guan'gen. Murdoch's limited success has come from his operations in Guangdong province (Dover 2008). However, Murdoch is one of many 'foreign wolves'. Foreign incursions into Chinese cultural space became a major concern for propaganda officials and Party conservatives leading up to China's accession to the World Trade Organisation in 2001. The theme of 'cultural security' (*wenhua anquan*) arose among conservatives who argued that China needed to strengthen quotas on overseas media content while developing more traditional cultural themes that would appeal to domestic audiences. The enemy in waiting appeared to be Hollywood. However, the escalation of South Korean content from the turn of the century alerted China that its competitors were Asian. It was Asian culture, not Western culture, that was the new Trojan Horse. The nation's regional soft power needed a shot in the arm (Keane 2010). Ultimately, the cultural and creative industries advocates with their theme of 'soft power' and Asian markets won the day over those who called for increased cultural protectionism.

According to Li Huailiang, the Director of the National Cultural Trade Research Centre in Beijing:

> The Chinese government has always regarded the export destination as the western mainstream market so markets in developing countries have not had enough attention. I think markets in developing countries will increasingly be export destinations for Chinese cultural products. Because there is more similarity in the development between China and other developing countries, it is easier to exchange cultural products.
>
> (Interview with author, Beijing March 2011)

The innovation ecology revisited

Reasons for the neglect of Asian markets until recently have much to do with the ideological divide between socialist China and the free West. It was imperative for the media to compete on the propaganda front and this meant sending messages to the 'West'. Because of the importance attached to the media as the mouthpiece of the Chinese Communist Party and government, there was reluctance on the part of writers and producers to experiment with new genres. Media workers were not employed to show initiative but to follow formulas. In the initial stage of commercial media production which lasted until the mid-1990s, many participants waited for officials to determine the form and prescribe the content. Paradoxically, this willingness to follow instructions became a competitive advantage. China was able to supply low-cost labour for international media, cultural and design companies, sometimes in sweatshop environments. From the mid-1980s China's animation studios operated as processing factories; they engaged in painstaking inking and cleanup work for Disney as well as for Japanese animation companies. Many animation 'factories' set up in Shenzhen. While the technicians in these work units received higher salaries than other factory workers in Shenzhen, the problem was that the 'talent pool' was absorbed into menial repetitive tasks rather than in original concept development.

The second stage of the ecology saw producers imitating; a 'follow the leader' pattern ensued. Little risk-taking occurred during the 1990s and there was little recognition of intellectual property. The weaknesses of China's institutions with respect to intellectual property rights and rule of law mean it is far easier to copy than to innovate. Broadcasting networks copied foreign television formats in the hope that they would be able to minimise development costs and maximise commercial returns; domestic networks copied each other's programmes. The problem was there was no incentive to move to a robust rights system because of the fragmentation of channels and the meagre returns for original content. According to standard theories of intellectual property, profit-driven firms are unlikely to invest in innovation unless a strong intellectual property system ensures they are rewarded for their investment in the form of content or format licensing fees. China's weak system is often blamed for the absence of innovation and commercial risk-taking (Montgomery 2010; Montgomery and Keane 2006).

The third and fourth stages saw Chinese producers entering into co-production and knowledge-sharing arrangements with foreign players. This occurred more rapidly in non-sensitive media such as advertising and video games as China entered the World Trade Organisation (WTO) in 2001. The rapid rise of the Korean wave soon alerted Chinese media players and policymakers that their most valuable markets were in Asia, not the West. As China became more closely integrated into a global economy, the possibility of economic gain resulting from the export of creative content and the inward flow of expertise and investment associated with East Asian media entrepreneurs strengthened. While efforts to pressure the Chinese government into stricter enforcement of intellectual property rights have had little impact on attitudes towards violation, the knowledge transfer associated with East Asian media entrepreneurs is producing change in the role of copyright in China (Montgomery 2010). There is now widespread awareness of how the international media work. The difficulty is translating these practices into the Chinese system.

If the fourth stage was recognition of Asian markets and copyrights, the next move was the formation of numerous media bases and clusters, co-opting investors and personnel from East Asia. These media bases range from medium to large-scale agglomerations of businesses. Policymakers believe that this clustering strategy is a way to upgrade creativity (the term 'upgrade' is frequently found in policy reform blueprints). In changing the culture of production in Chinese media the key elements are found the stages three, four and five of the ecology, which may be expressed as:

$$Cooperate \leftrightarrow Trade \leftrightarrow Differentiate$$

Uncertain independents and soft power

Framing China's media ecology in this way draws attention to the juxtaposition of the terms 'creative' and 'industry'. Industry began to find its way into policy and academic discourse in the 1990s; creativity came later in 2005. As Chinese media began to 'industrialise' in the late 1990s, media groups (*jituan*) formed; this momentum was followed by bases. Along with the creativity discourse, the popularity of the concept of soft power modified the media production focus from domestic to international (Sun 2010; Keane 2010). Soft power is not a new idea. Coined by Joseph Nye in the early 1990s, it has been applied broadly in the field of international diplomacy (Nye 1990). One of the key elements of soft power is cultural exports, and in this respect China is now attempting to follow a path paved by its Asian neighbours. As discussed in Chapter 1, Japan has expressed its influence through popular culture (its so-called 'Gross National Cool') and South Korea has exploited the Korean wave, its emergence coinciding with another global sporting event, the 2002 World Cup.

In May 2005, Ministry of Culture officials reported China's poor cultural export performance to the media. Aside from the success of Chinese cinema, buoyed by blockbusters such as *Hero* and *House of Flying Daggers*, the story was not good reading for cultural nationalists. The 'cultural exports deficit' (*wenhua maoyi chizi*) became a call to action, in many sectors precipitating a 'base mentality': that is, a belief that industrial clustering would solve the problems. A year later China's television exports were RMB 16.9 million while imports totalled RMB 33.7 million (Zhang Xiaoming 2008). This imbalance provided an opportunity for cultural reformers to link China's economic internationalisation strategy – the 'going out strategy' (*zou chuqu*) – with the development of soft power (Ding 2008; Keane 2010; Sun 2010) and creative industries (Li Wuwei 2009; Keane 2007). It is important therefore to see the ideas of soft power, content reform and innovation/creativity as strategic 'industrial development' initiatives.

Much has changed in China's producer communities over the past decade. Up until the early 2000s, Chinese broadcast production was almost completely dominated by large broadcasters, notably China Central TV (CCTV). According to reports there are now approximately 4,000 production companies in China (SARFT 2010: 1). Many of these companies offer specialist production, post-production and ancillary services to broadcasters (Tang and Li 2005). This has coincided with the clustering of media production in Chinese cities (Keane 2009a). The State Administration of Radio Film and Television (SARFT), China's principal broadcasting regulator, reveals that demand for broadcasting content in 2009 was 10 million hours per year. Domestic TV stations could only supply 2.6 million hours (SARFT 2010: 33–4). Because of the shortfall, TV stations have increasingly sourced content 'outside the system'.

The most significant change in the Chinese media industry over the past decade is the rise of independent companies. Independent television production companies have existed in mainland China since 1994 (Lu 2005). Independent cinema had an even earlier incarnation. In 1984, the state withdrew substantial funding from the film sector forcing elite directors to purchase studio logos as a way of making films. In the early 1990s many young directors, unable to get production licences to make films, began to make 'underground' productions and target these towards international film festivals. From an international perspective, therefore, mainland Chinese media production is not independent, certainly not in a political sense. However, the term 'independent media' is relative. Globally many independent companies are part-owned by broadcasters; in many instances they are heavily subsidised by states (Taub-Pervizpour 2004).

As noted earlier, China's media have progressed through a series of structural reforms intended to separate 'public institutions' (*shiye*) from 'commercial industries' (*chanye*). From an international perspective this is similar to the distinction between public broadcasting and private media networks, the key difference being that in China the infrastructure of broadcasting is still owned by the state. Despite this, however, there are many new private companies providing production services while competing with large players like China Central TV and Shanghai Media Group.

Independent production in mainland China is embryonic, and it is hindered by strict censorship and uncompetitive models of market organisation. According to administrative regulations, the production of Chinese TV, animation and documentary is categorised as in-house production and outsourced (Lu 2005). In-house is where all aspects of production (including pre-production and post-production) are planned, monitored and executed within a state broadcasting entity (e.g. China Central TV, Shanghai TV). Outsourced includes: (1) directly state-owned or with partial government ownership (such as ownership by the People's Liberation Army); and (2) completely privately owned (*minying dianshi*).

Many companies from Taiwan, Hong Kong and Korea have set up in Beijing, Shanghai, Hengdian and Guangzhou, or have entered into various models of co-operation with Chinese companies (Davis 2010). One of the key reasons for this East Asian 'migration' is economic decline in Hong Kong and Taiwan, together with a substantial shift of media production to the lower-cost mainland. Preferential business policies on offer plus an availability of human capital (especially technical resources) make the mainland an attractive destination. Because market entry costs are lower than in Hong Kong, Taiwan and Korea, many cultural workers and managers are moving to the mainland. Entrepreneurs from East Asia can be found in private media companies in China, and particularly in Beijing. Their roles are creative, managerial, consulting and technical, providing professional expertise, alternative approaches to human capital management, and new ways of solving problems. These persons act as intermediaries, bringing ideas, investment and know-how into the sector.

In addition, many Chinese natives are returning home with overseas experience and determination to form their own companies. Policymakers are allowing these media entrepreneurs to generate ideas, to offer solutions to revitalise stagnant Chinese productions. The hope is that an increase in domestic quality, brought about by the new independents, may counter the cultural exports deficit; that is, by providing 'good content' to fill the schedules. Alternatively, the definition of 'good content' as determined by the Chinese government may in the end – as it has in the past – impact on confidence of producers.

From an outsider perspective China's media organisations are protected species within a walled garden. Direct competition from within China – and particularly from international media – is limited. One view among observers in China is that if full market competition were unleashed the resulting 'gales of creative destruction' would result in thousands of bankrupt media institutions. While there are many advocates of greater competition within China's media industries, few want an open playing field. This is unlikely to occur. Rigid organisational forms will continue to coexist with flexible and unorthodox business practices.

Understanding Beijing's media agglomeration aspirations requires us to take into account the idea of structured uncertainty (Breznitz and Murphree 2011). Together with Michael Curtin's three trajectories of 'media capital', this concept demonstrates the complexity of Beijing's media. Bresnitz and Murphree define structured uncertainty as 'an agreement to disagree about the goals and methods of policy'. They argue that structured uncertainty is ever present in China because of extensive cross-alliances, tangled matrices of authority, numerous organisations lacking institutionalisation, and strong reliance on personal authority and network consensus. Uncertainty plays a decisive role in restricting experimentation in Chinese media production.

Uncertainty occurs in all policy regimes internationally but in China it operates in four main ways: first, businesses are asked to be innovative but the limits are defined so vaguely that different regions and actors take greater or lesser risks; second, there is complexity in regulation because different ministries and bureaus cross over; third, powerful players like party secretaries have veto powers which together with *guanxi* effects (*quid pro quos*) lead to constraints on risk-taking; and fourth, the ambiguity of policy is exacerbated as reform goals (the goalposts) keep changing. Structured uncertainty leads to short-term behaviours and promotes imitation (which is safer) over innovation (which is inherently riskier). Although Bresnitz and Murphree's study concerned the IT industry, the framework is applicable to media content and creative industries, and particularly to understanding the complexities of Beijing's emerging media cluster.

Animation provides a classic example of structured uncertainty in the media content industries. The Ministry of Culture rather than the State Administration of Radio, Film and Television (SAFRT) is the leading national body responsible for the animation industry in China. It has the power to ratify industry bases. The general Administration of Press and Publication is responsible for managing – and censoring – the publication of animation software and online formats. Meanwhile SAFRT takes charge of animated films and TV programmes as well as online animation videos. The problem with so many bureaus having control is that businesses have to apply for multiple licenses and permits. In turn, this creates uncertainty. As one Beijing animation company proprietor put it:

> Right now, the Ministry of Culture, the Ministry of Finance and the National Tax Administration are carrying out joint certification work on animation enterprises and providing favourable policies and subsidies. However, *guanxi* affects this practice. This phenomenon is very fierce but inevitable in China. In China all business is based on *guanxi* and friendship. They won't necessarily approve us just because we are qualified when we are applying for something from the government. We have to ask a friend inside to submit the application.
> (Interview with author 15 October 2009)

Beijing: the aspirant media capital

The company in question had moved to Chaoyang District two years earlier. The Beijing CBD International Media Industry Cluster is a large area of approximately 4 square kilometres surrounding the China Central Television (CCTV) twin tower building in the eastern and northeastern district of Chaoyang. From 2006, media companies began to drift their operations eastward. By March 2008, 824 media enterprises, including 45 journalism and publishing organisations, 27 radio, TV and film organisations had relocated or established there (China Publishing Net 2011).[1]

The Beijing CBD International Media Industry Cluster now houses numerous media support services including advertising agencies, animation, post-production and special-effects companies as well as talent agencies and studio equipment suppliers. The reasons for the geographical clustering of media in the past have had much to do with the location of China's major broadcasters, CCTV, Beijing TV and Phoenix TV. Until 2008, broadcasting was concentrated in the western districts of Xicheng and northwestern Haidian. Xicheng District, a centre of political power long before the Communist Revolution, includes Finance Street (*jinrongjie*) and the Xidan Commercial District, as well as Liulichang, a traditional culture and antiques district. China's national media regulators including the State Administration of Radio Film and TV (SARFT), the Ministry of Information Industry (MII) and the General Administration of Press and Publications (GAPP) are located in Xicheng. Adjacent to Xicheng is northwestern Haidian District, a powerful cluster for new media and IT start-ups. By way of contrast, the Ministry of Culture is located in Chaoyang.

In 2004, China Central Television announced its move into Chaoyang District. The construction of the new headquarters was approved in 2003, a time when the Municipal Committee of the Chinese Communist Party of Beijing recognised the importance of reasserting Beijing's pre-eminence as the national centre of media production as well as administration. The CCTV redevelopment project included the new CCTV towers, a Television Cultural Centre (TVCC) and a media park. The project was designed by Ole Scheeren (OMA) and Rem Koolhaus and engineered by Ove Arup in partnership with the East China Architectural Design Institute (ECADI). The CCTV 'twin tower' structure comprises two 230-metre edifices that rise from a common base connected at the top by an 80-metre construction extending outwards. The intended effect is to create a three-dimensional arch. Unfortunately the effect has not resulted in admiration from Beijing residents, who like to refer to the edifice as the 'big trousers'. The Television Cultural Centre holds a 1,500-seat theatre along with convention centres, a luxury hotel and a visitor's centre while the Media Park covers 25,600 square metres and is intended to provide open-air green spaces for the purposes of entertainment. The foreign design consultants have attempted to integrate traditional Chinese elements and a modernist paradigm, somehow befitting the way that the government imagines CCTV interpelating its audiences in the new era of Chinese soft power. Unfortunately, a fire that broke out in the tower in 2009, reportedly started by Chinese New Year's Eve revellers, had the effect of diminishing the authority of the project in the minds of locals.

Notwithstanding ambivalence towards the CCTV tower and the power that it symbolically represents, a number of businesses I spoke with in the area are optimistic about the future of the media cluster, while unsure if Beijing will ever be a media capital. Happy Go (*kuai le gou*) is a TV online shopping enterprise owned by the Hunan Broadcasting Media Group, a powerful provincial network in south China. According to The CEO of the Beijing operations, Ms Peng Yang, there were three main reasons for relocating in Beijing. The first is human capital. Peng believes Beijing is where most internet 'talent' clusters; secondly, Beijing has key resources such as telecom operators, the company's business partners; and thirdly, as the political centre of China, Beijing is where media policy is made. For internationals as well locals, centrality is crucial to understanding the winds of policy change. Beijing provides best access to officials, a point also noted in Breznitz and Murphree's study of the IT industry. The authors note a multinational company lab director who believes more policy flexibility exists outside but proximity to policy decision-makers means 'sometimes you can do bigger and better things' (cited in Breznitz and Murphree 2011: 105).

Another perspective comes from Beijing Lanyuegu, a start-up company specialising in animation but pitching their product to teenagers through cinema networks rather than TV like most animation companies in China. The company began in the 798 Art Zone at Dashanzi in 2007 but moved to Chaoyang a year later. According to Lanyuegu's CEO, Luo Xuan, he and his partner Wu Qiongli considered moving their office to Songzhuang Art District (see Chapter 5) where there was a lot of talk circulating among officials about merging the cartoon and art industries. Luo believes commercial animators and visual artists are not necessarily good bedfellows, the artistic community generally holding 'cartoon artists' in low regard. Luo says that location in the CBD allows his small company to come into regular informal contact with other industry players, particularly mobile phone and advertising companies. Despite the higher rents, the result of such untraded interdependencies can broaden horizons and learning opportunities. He says, 'most companies in this area are top companies'. Luo says there are two types of cities in China: those with centralised power, which have a concentration of resources, and coastal cities that have gained good business opportunities thanks to their export channels, such as Shanghai and Guangzhou. Beijing is the former with over 2,000 agencies or offices of regional governments.

Tom Wang runs an animation and film company called iMotion. His business is located in nearby Dongcheng District where he and his brother Jerry work closely with the Ministry of Culture. Jerry's focus is on providing approved video content for internet cafes. Both brothers say that many cultural companies are located in the east of Beijing because of proximity to internationals, resulting in a more cosmopolitan environment than in the west or north of the city. Tom says 'you can have the biggest power of speech in China in Beijing'. The reason people are here and working in the media cluster, he says, is that you can influence more people. Originally educated in Shanghai, Tom and Jerry believe that Shanghai has missed the opportunity to be a media capital:

You have to be in a city where your voice can be heard in order to achieve your goal. In Beijing it is very likely you will run into a journalist from CCTV, some famous film director. If the government can be more open, allow different voices to be heard and set up a rating system as soon as possible, Beijing is very likely to be a media capital.

(Interview with author, Beijing October 2010)

Animation: struggling to compete

Animation provides a window on media industry development in China and China's relationship to its East Asian neighbours. Animation has come of age during the past decade, evolving from children's cartoons to adult anime, and from 2D to 3D. Moreover, the number of animated films released internationally has increased steadily since the 1990s. China's animation industry is regarded as strategically important by the Ministry of Culture. The principal reason for animation's rise in status is a sense of indignation caused by the success of large overseas media companies who have used Chinese traditional culture as a creative resource for their work, in the process adapting the traditional values of the stories to suit international audience tastes. The success of Disney's *Mulan* and Dreamworks' *Kungfu Panda,* as well as Japanese and Korean renditions of *The Journey to the West*, together with derivative online gaming products, led to a series of urgent strategic measures to revive the former glory of Chinese animation. By this, China's cultural officials are referring to trailblazing animators such as the Wan brothers, who produced the first full-length animated movie in 1926, *Princess Iron Fan* (*tieshan gongzhu*) (Lent 2001). Ironically, the success of *Princess Iron Fan* was influential in shaping the style of Tezuka Osamu, who became Japan's leading animator, later producing *Astro Boy*, which caused a sensation when it was broadcast on Chinese television screens in December 1980. By the end of the 1980s foreign animation was decimating China's fledgling industry, which was tied to propagandist themes determined by the Ministry of Culture. Animation was deemed to be suitable programming for young children and accordingly the content needed to be appropriately national and pedagogical.

While the principal outlet for animation work in China is television, most income is generated by skilled technicians who provide low-cost services for international companies, including animation, rendering and compositing. According to the director of an aspiring Wuxi-based business, the industry is differentiated by the *animation production business* and the *animation business* (interview Shi, 7 May 2008). In the first of these categories original content is created for domestic outlets or fabricated for outside contractors. Content producers can offer their work to TV stations in exchange for rights. The most important buyers of content are CCTV Children's Channel, Hunan TV Golden Eagle Channel (Jingying), Shanghai Xuandong Cartoon Channel and Beijing TV Cartoon Channel. Because Chinese stations are unwilling to pay reasonable prices for animation, the companies invariably look to other ways to make returns. The second category, the animation industry, uses content to manufacture branded product lines, everything from foodstuffs to apparel. I will discuss this model later with reference to two of China's leading animation companies.

Animation production is challenging for a number of reasons. It is difficult to create a popular animation, one that colonises the imagination of children. According to government pronouncements the prescribed 'market' for animation in China is children, not teenagers or adults (see Donald 2002, 2005). This policy view was mentioned by survey respondents as a limit to business model development. In other words, to attain government subvention, producers aim at the juvenile school market. It is not only officials that view animation this way. Many people with whom I spoke remarked that parents regard animation as just 'cartoons', for kids. This reflects the way the animation industry is currently organised in China.

However, not all industry participants accept the view that animation has limited audience appeal. Outside the policy-defined industry there are alternative consumption patterns. Many youth and older consumers, particularly university students, are aficionados of *anime* developed with adult audiences in mind. Many produce such *anime*, mostly of a non-commercial or experimental nature, and this suggests there may one day be a viable Chinese animation industry over and above 'kids' cartoons. At the moment, however, the question is how to commercialise this nascent fan 'market'.

While most companies focus on producing what many in the industry regard as just 'fodder' for the domestic market, following the symphony of 'autonomous innovation' led by the national government and conducted by local propaganda officials, some animation and cartoon companies with creative ambitions look to joint ventures with offshore distribution markets. Creatworld is a cartoon company located in an animation base in Binhai, a special export development zone close to the city of Tianjin. In 2001 the company was unable to obtain development finance in China. Their output was a highly stylised rendering of China's classic stories, well known to Asian readers: *Romance of the Three Kingdoms*, *The Dream of Red Mansions*, *The Journey to the West*, and *Outlaws of the Marsh* (also known as *The Water Margin*).

Creatworld's comic renditions of the four popular novels generated interest in the Korean and Japanese publishing industries. When the company was facing the prospect of closing down, a South Korean publisher initiated a joint venture deal worth RMB 10 million to act as the international copyright agency for these books. Following this, Japan's Toppan Printing approached Creatworld and both parties signed a deal to publish 10,000 sets of *Water Margin* with 7 per cent of royalties going to Creatworld. In mid-2006, *The Water Margin* was published in Japan. Since then the comic books have entered other international market including Korea, France, Britain and Germany. Since 2006, 540,000 copies have been sold (Ma 2009).

The comic book series entered the international market thanks to its copyright value. This channel represents a different kind of market strategy in China. Usually original works target domestic markets first, before considering international markets. For Creatworld, it was the reverse. Several domestic publishers approached the company after the books' initial success in Japanese market. Overseas success made domestic publishers confident about reception in the domestic market. Then Creatworld struck a deal with Anhui Publishing Group in June 2008. The ensuing sales figures validated the vote of confidence. The complete set of *Romance of the Three Kingdoms*, composed of 20 books, was priced at RMB 480 and 2,700 sets were sold within a month of the launch in April 2009 (Chen and Zhang 2009).

The overseas success generated enough promotion in China to make the company a model example of China's soft power strategy. In 2008, the Ministry of Culture (MoC) launched a project to support original cartoon and animation (MoC 2008). Under the project plan, RMB 7 million was be utilised to develop cartoons, animation works and creative talents. The four Chinese classics comic book series won the first award, gaining financial support for further development.

The animation production market: intangible concerns

Such ventures into overseas markets are rare and investment capital is hard to source with few strong content markets. Jonathan Wang, CEO of the leading Chinese production company GreatDreams, contends that the industry needs 'smart money' (interview Wang, 12 May 2008). Wang was formerly a leader in the retail industry before moving into the animation business. Considering the financial equity required to register as an animation producing company – according to one respondent a balance of RMB 500,000 in the Bank of China – it is understandable why investment often comes from people with capital but without experience in creative industries (interview Wang, Shanghai May 2008). In one sense, this is an advantage. Business acumen and corporate governance introduced from other industries often compensate for the lack of managerial knowledge among animators and technicians.

For the time being the industry is locked into low-value circular flow of product and ideas. Despite market size in terms of channels and viewers –

up to 600 channels and over a million potential viewers – the revenue obtained from selling animation within China, even for high-performing production companies, is less than 15 per cent of the production budget (interview Wang, 12 May 2008). To offset this gap, local governments offer incentive bonuses. For instance, like many regions that have invested in animation bases, the Wuxi municipal government in coastal Jiangsu Province provides a range of incentives, including a year's free rent if a company locates to the Wuxi National Animation Base. The attraction of Wuxi according to its publicists is lifestyle. However, Wuxi Animation Base is geographically disadvantaged by being too far from Shanghai and too close to its competitor Suzhou Industrial Park. If a 2D animation made by a company situated within the Wuxi Animation Base is screened on CCTV, the company receives a bonus of RMB 1,800 per minute; a 3D animation attracts a bonus of RMB 3,600 (interview Shi, 7 May 2008). According to another respondent CCTV itself pays on average RMB 800 per minute (interview George Yu, 10 May 2008).

While in theory at least this results-based bonus system might seem like an incentive to produce good quality, the figure does not depend on quality. It is a figure allocated for buying animation by CCTV animation channels. As a senior executive in Wuxi Animation Base explains, companies often use relationships (*guanxi*) to ensure their product is broadcast on CCTV (interview Shi, 6 May 2008). This model does not provide much hope for the thousands of new operators currently moving into the industry in response to government policies aimed at boosting quantity. It is the key issue of quality that remains in the background. Moreover, while it is possible to broadcast on multiple channels in China, once an animation product is seen on the national cartoon network other potential buyers have already lost interest. Alternatively, avoiding the CCTV option and pitching to provincial and city stations results in lower rates, as low as RMB 10 per minute (interview Yu, 10 May 2008).

The animation business: the tangible market

While the intangible content market is fragile, the material goods or derivative market is robust, assuming that one's content is broadcast on a leading channel. Compared with animation production – the actual business of creating original content – the animation business operates on a more industrial basis and incorporates a range of endeavours that include retail networks, logistics, product placement, franchising and licensing. The case of Sunchime Cartoon Company is a good illustration (see Donald 2005). Until 2008, Sunchime (Sanchen) was widely regarded as China's most successful animation company. It had seemingly risen from relative obscurity in Hunan Province to prove to both central and provincial governments the potential of home-grown animation. Yet

Sanchen's rise, and its eventual demise, highlights weaknesses in China's immature market system. The story began in the mid-1990s when the Sanchen Cultural Development Company was formed in response to central government policy aimed at developing youth programming in the face of perceived threats to the Chinese industry from Disney and Japanese animation. Quotas were set in place to fast-track appropriate content and limit the amount of non-Chinese animation. By 2006, these policies had extended to banning 'foreign' animation from Chinese peak-hour programming slots, originally between 6 pm and 8 pm. In February 2008 these bans were extended to 6 to 9 pm (Chung 2008).

In 2000, Sanchen and Hunan Eastern Cartoon Cultural Company established the Hunan Sunchime Cartoon Archive Development Limited Company and entered into the animated cartoon production business. Their product was *The 3000 Whys of Blue Cat and Naughty Mouse* (*Lanmao Taoji 3000 wen*). The creative director was Wang Hong. Functioning as educational content, this product had the approval of the government ministries and was used as a teaching aid in primary schools. With television stations on the lookout for content approved by the national government, the 'blue cat' soon became a household name.

In the case of Sunchime, their content was the 'blue cat' and the 'buyers' were the hundreds of TV stations in China. The end users were initially the consumers of the programme – the children of China. However, Sunchime ran into resistance when trying to monetise its content. Having used China's television stations to build a fan base for the cartoon character, Sunchime subsequently experienced difficulty forcing stations to pay licence fees to broadcast. Production costs were between RMB 6,000 and 8,000 per minute while the average fee paid by stations was between RMB 5 and RMB 10 per minute (Zhou 2005). There were claims that Chinese TV stations were willing to pay licence fees and observe legitimate industry practices with international animation companies while under-cutting the value of Chinese champions such as the Blue Cat franchise.

The alternative revenue source is advertising and merchandising, using the broadcast channel as the platform for a range of derivative products. This is not uncommon in animation worldwide. Lash and Lury (2007) use the example of Pixar's *Toy Story* to describe how the world of manufacturing is moving closer to the world of ideas: in their words, a collapsing of superstructure into base. In China, moreover, integrating *Made in China* products with *Created in China* content is a means of survival in an ecology in which intellectual protection assumes low priority in terms of trade. Stations allowed Sunchime to promote Blue Cat merchandise in the programme. This proved a much more lucrative model and the Blue Cat logo was quickly patented. However, an inability on the part of Sunchime to control the practice known as 'zapping' – replacing the company's product advertising with local advertisements – led to recriminations. Having advertising spots (*suipian guanggao*) in lieu of programme licence fees was beneficial in so far as it promoted ancillary product lines. The company expanded their merchandising operations, extending the brand from audio-visual products to books, stationery, toys, clothing, shoes, hats, food products, beverages, cosmetics, bicycles, and household electronic goods (Zhou 2005).

This success established a new financial model for China's cartoon and animation industry. By February 2003, the company had earned **RMB 60 million**, but this success brought with it imitation of its brand and numerous fake 'blue cat' products. The company's business plan of diversifying without necessarily differentiating further reduced their brand equity and focus. In May 2008, Sunchime's content business was absorbed by GreatDreams (Hongmeng), also a Hunan company. GreatDreams was able to leverage on venture capital from the US company Sequoia and in the process establish a more sustainable management structure by bringing in personnel from the financial management services and retailing.

In China the dominant logic of the communications system has been *channel before content*. In other words, the Chinese leadership ensured there is enough infrastructure to carry propaganda messages. This development model still prevails but might be rephrased as *base before superstructure*. In the past two years, coinciding with a push to increase animation output, there has been a massive expansion of animation companies. Many of the current 5,473 registered animation companies in China are located in animation bases and parks. In 2006, moreover, only 11 companies produced over 2,000 minutes of content (interview Wang, 12 May 2008). As I have pointed out, there is no real market for content and currently no sustainable market mechanism for stimulating original content. Most will fall back on OEM (original equipment manufacturing), a term which refers to manufacturing to specifications. It is likely that many animation bases across the country will finish up as real estate parks.

Animation parks

In May 2008 I witnessed an X|Media|Lab industry forum in Suzhou, 100 kilometres west of Shanghai. More than 20 Chinese animation companies paid a substantial registration fee (by Chinese standards) to attend the three-day event in Suzhou Industrial Park, which included presentations by representatives of Hollywood's elite followed by two days of business matching and mentoring. This industry format is well known in the international business community but for most of the Chinese participants it was an unprecedented opportunity to learn. Among the Chinese there was great interest in how the 'creative elite' conceive, incubate and pitch ideas. The technical expertise of the Chinese companies was on display in the work shown. One of the Los Angeles-based mentors was heard to comment that if people walked into his studio and displayed similar portfolios, they would be hired on the spot.

Since 2005, Suzhou has participated in the development of China's cultural and creative industries, most notably by turning parts of its huge Suzhou Industrial Park (SIP) over to media and digital content production. The SIP was inaugurated in 1994 with substantial investment and co-management from the Singaporean government. The construction of creative content bases, or 'clusters', within existing industrial zones is most notable in the field of animation. Since 2005, China has established nearly 30 national animation bases. The question of why there need to be so many national animation bases would seem to be a valid one for an outside observer. However, in China, the conferral of national status is much sought after as it allows local governments to more freely dispense with red tape, in turn encouraging new enterprises. In 2011, the problem of oversupply of bases and undersupply of creative output became an issue, with the Ministry of Culture putting existing bases 'under review'.

The main centres, often situated within an existing industrial or free trade zone area, are in Shanghai, Beijing, Hunan, Hangzhou, Guangzhou,

Table 7.2 National Animation bases accredited by SARFT

First batch of nine national animation bases. Approved by SARFT 6 December 2004	The Shanghai Animation Film Studio China Central Television China International TV Corporation Sunchime Cartoon Group China Film Group Corporation Hunan Golden Eagle Limited cartoons Hangzhou Hi-tech Development Zone Animation Industry Park Changzhou Film and Television Animation Co. Ltd Shanghai ToonMax Cartoon Satellite TV Media and Entertainment Limited Guangzhou Conghua Southern Animation Co-production Centre
Second batch of a total of six national animation industry bases. Approved by SARFT 27 May 2005	Shenzhen Animation Production Centre Dalian High-Tech Industrial Park Animation Industry Park Suzhou Industrial Park Animation Industry Park Wuxi Taihu Lake Digital Animation, Film and Television Creative Business Park Changcun Film Group Jiang Tong Animation Co. Ltd
Third batch of national animation industry bases. Approved by SARFT 15 August 2007	Chongqing Nan'an District Tea Garden New District Animation Industry Base Industry Base Nanjing Software Park

Suzhou, Shenzhen, Dalian, Nanjing, Changzhou and Wuxi. Local governments also offer a range of industry sweeteners, such as preferential policies enabling start-up firms to enjoy tax holidays, to obtain housing and educational services for employees and their children, as well as financial incentives if content is successful. In the main this entails content being purchased by China Central Television (CCTV).

The Suzhou national animation base is enfolded within the Suzhou Creative Industry Park, which is referred to as the Phase 5 development of the Suzhou Industrial Science Park (SISPARK), itself within the larger Suzhou Industrial Park. The Creative Industry Park occupies 720,000 square metres to the south of Dushu Lake higher-education district and the aptly named Idea Pumping Station in Jijihu Road, a kind of convention and enterprise development complex. Software outsourcing is the main source of revenue, which together with animation outsourcing has established the area as a market leader, competing primarily with Dalian, Shenzhen and Hangzhou. National animation base status was conferred by the State Administration of Radio Film and TV (SARFT) in June 2005; the base occupies 40,000 square metres and houses about 30 companies.

According to Nelson Chu, vice-president of Sandman Animation, a company established in 2007 and now employing more than 80 staff, both fees for service work and co-production are beneficial to the animation industry in China in terms of nurturing competence and knowledge transfer. Although outsourcing, the bottom level of the innovation ecology, does not produce any direct profit from copyright and market access, it does provide opportunities to learn about quality standards and management. In addition, Chu says that having international contracts will attract and maintain higher-talented staff because greater revenue is associated with the overseas animation industry. In terms of knowledge transfer, he believes co-production is even more beneficial as the Chinese participants can be involved in the whole operation from beginning to end. Chu takes a long-term development view: he says that the animation industry in China is currently very young. Companies undertake service and production work while learning through co-operation; in time they will seek to shift the focus to creativity (Chu, interview 23 October 2008). Xu Shian, a developer from Suzhou Shiao Animation Company, believes that Suzhou International Science Park's policy support provides an edge, compared with other bases in China. He says that the key reason for basing their company at Suzhou was policy support. It has quickly grown from three to more than 70 employees and now has the ability to focus on original creative work. In Shiao, he says, each department has a person responsible for maintaining links in the creative process (Xu, interview 23 October 2008).

George Yu of Hongying, a large Taiwan-owned company which is a subsidiary of the Suzhou-based Wang Films, believes that the next generation of animators will be very good. However, he says that the key problem is that buyers of animation, the television channels in China, are state-owned and they all follow a pattern of paying minimal fees for animation.

Subsequently, the goal of all animation companies is to get their product screened on CCTV, which pays a premium, an average of RMB 800 per minute regardless of quality. If CCTV accepts, the strategy is to follow hard with product merchandising such as toys, stationery and DVDs. Other stations pay considerably less, ranging from RMB 20 to RMB 100 per minute. Because of this rights payment dilemma, investors are more inclined to put their funds into TV drama. Yu believes that foreign investment is a double-edged sword. Foreign investment can mean that an animation project is regarded by the State Administration of Radio, Film and TV (SARFT) as a co-production, and because of the preferential policy towards local animation content on CCTV, some foreign invested projects have not been screened. (Yu, interview 12 May 2008).

Concluding remarks: desperately seeking spillovers

Knowledge 'spillovers' do occur in media industry bases but less so among Chinese domestic companies who are often disinclined to share resources. Transfer of ideas occurs most successfully through mergers, co-productions and joint ventures. The defining logic is therefore not globalisation as much as regionalisation. The Beijing International Media Cluster is potentially a powerful engine to raise the level of China's media. The difficulty to date has been reconciling a need to produce national content with the aspiration to internationalise. Chinese domestic companies have been locked into a non-competitive institutional environment with little reward for originality and creativity. The tendency to recycle and appropriate is therefore not surprising. The introduction of international players, and especially entrepreneurs from East Asia, into the ecology is generating change, however measured. As the case of animation shows, international companies need to work in China, often for bottom-line reasons, as much as Chinese players need to learn from international experience.

The X|Media|Lab event in the Suzhou Industrial Park in May 2008 witnessed the coming together of Western expertise and knowledge with Chinese know-how and ideas. The Suzhou Animation Base has adopted a 'learning environment' model, one in which accepted ways of operating (routines) are challenged. An inevitable consequence of this process is *creative destruction*. The replacement of old ways of operating means that many businesses will die out and their productive resources will be absorbed by other contenders. In this transformation many bases will fail. Those that find a way of connecting with the dynamic world of ideas and international capital will provide a way forward; in other words, the tangible and the intangible will come together.

8 Culture, creativity, innovation, imagination

> Dao gave birth to the one
> The one gave birth to the two,
> The two gave birth to the three,
> The three gave birth to all the myriad things.
> (*The Laozi* 42)[1]

> All the species of things transform into one another by the process of variation in form. Their beginning and their ending is time an unbroken ring, of which it is impossible to find the principle.
> (*The Zhuangzi.* 9.7)[2]

In this final chapter I present some further thoughts about the relationship between culture, creativity and innovation. My concern here is to reflect in a somewhat different mode on the outbreak of creative clusters and *inter alia* the unprecedented interest in creativity in China and East Asia. Several key questions remain unanswered. Is creativity, however construed, an appropriate solution to China's economic development problems? Does the focus on economic creativity override individual creativity, the touchstone of Western pluralism? Is commercial culture lessening the ideological straightjacket that many say has suppressed creative imagination? Is recombination a better description of the creative process than originality and if so, is China defining a new paradigm?

In attempting to answer these questions I want to foreground the elasticity of creativity. There is no gold standard; likewise, in creativity there is no east or west – but there are I believe different ways of understanding the creative process. In looking to history to provide clues I am cognisant of the fact that my observations are conjecture. Evidently, we are programmed by the past, by cultural legacies and pedagogic practices. On the other hand, we respond to cues from popular culture and international flows of knowledge. Increasingly peer communities and social networks determine our responses to events. However, if we accept research conducted by psychologists and educationalists on capacities of

Asian students to engage critically with knowledge and question authority, together with historical accounts of the primacy of learning in China, we might be led to construe that creativity in China is diminished by the weight of tradition, particularly the emphasis on harmony and respect for the knowledge of elders (Baark 2007; Puett 2001; Elvin 1975; Lloyd and Sivin 2002; Munro 1996; Needham 1969; Nisbett 2003; Lloyd 2007). Undoubtedly, institutions of the past exert an influence. Equally, we need to be cognisant of the weight of political conformity – the fear on the part of China's leaders, often irrational, that new knowledge might undermine social stability.

My observations in this chapter are intended to stimulate debate about epistemological foundations underpinning the contemporary discourse of creative industries in China. While much of the following discussion is exploratory, it is informed by the research I have done over the past several years. In summarising the main findings of this study, I believe that the practice of clustering, which is illustrated by the hundreds of parks, bases, zones, precincts and incubators, is an expedient response to cultural insecurity. The dawn of the cultural economy in China – as I mentioned in the introduction, this term provides a more useful description of events – precipitated an inordinate interest in creativity. Whereas creativity has been central to the institutions of democratic societies, some would even say the key fabric of civil society, in China it is manifest in the interplay between formal and informal institutions. Formal institutions – official organs of cultural policy such as government study groups and academic think-tanks – seek out the status and prestige associated with creativity and innovation but they lack an intuitive understanding of creative processes. Informal and grassroots institutions are quick to make the connections between ideas but the expression of new ideas is intimately constrained by censorship. I will return to this point in the final section.

The definition of creativity that I have found most applicable to the research of creative clusters is:

> The fitting of new ideas and alternative visions to existing norms, values and patterns, where such 'fitting' encompasses invention, differentiation, adaptation, learning and diffusion.

Clusters are by definition agglomerations. In China the emphasis is on exploitation more so than discovery, what Wang Jici calls, 'taking the low road' (Wang Jici 2007a). However, this does not suggest that variations and adaptations are necessarily a degraded form of innovation. Ideas are accumulated in nodes of intellectual networking. Intellectual property is 'discovered' in clustering activities and in communities of practice (Amin and Roberts 2008): in Silicon Valley, Hollywood, Bollywood, Soho, Chinawood and thousands of communities worldwide. Furthermore, there are many different kinds of ideational communities. Some ideas are of a paradigmatic nature, inducing change slowly, mainly through a process of continuous confirmation and falsification; for instance, modernism in Europe or economic gradualism in China during the 1980s.

Ideas can also be critical or non-critical. Critical ideas interconnect with large subsets of the total network of ideas, in turn generating an expanded infrastructure for further theoretical or critical development, in this way expanding intellectual and creative fields. The field is then forced to adapt in order to accommodate a fast-moving, self-generating process of change. In this critical process, infinitesimal change in one variable can produce substantive change in networks of ideas and interactions (Andersson and Andersson 2006). Non-critical ideas, moreover, support the status quo. The point to note in this exercise is the role China's state-owned media, particularly information media, have played, and continue to play in this process. Do they produce critical knowledge, or are they uncritical of systemic change, locked into government-prescribed propaganda boxes, and tied to a static vision of autonomous innovation?

Chinese policy advisors have identified clustering as a means of turning the intangible and the mysterious attributes of creativity into material forms (paintings, artefacts, sculptures) – in other words, 'things' with which they are familiar. Cluster master plans have circulated as factories are turned over to developers and investors seeking to take advantage of the government's advocacy of the cultural economy. State-opened enterprises, private business entrepreneurs and university research centres have joined in cultural and creative industries projects thanks to generous incentives from local governments. Setting up a factory, calling it a cluster and producing contracted products is an obvious business model. International animation companies, design firms, movie production companies and international fashion houses have played a part by outsourcing work to low cost China. Artists have joined in the great cluster movement. As Bert de Muynck (2010: 107) wrote prophetically:

> In Beijing, a group of artists accidentally discovered a new urban program, a way of living between art and economy. A couple of years ago, they transformed an old industrial factory into an experimental laboratory. Eager to capitalize on their creativity, they failed to foresee how their act of innovation would destroy the source of this creativity: the place itself. The art factory soon turned into an art market. Art was produced in another part of town, but still consumed in the factory. In the end, it was all about place-making, branding and imposing international policies upon a local context. Today it doesn't matter what is on display, as it is about a brand – in the Beijing case 798 – and the creative industries. Once that formula was understood, tested and controlled, it served as a model radiating from Beijing outwards. This led to a formulation of the future of the

Chinese city, a city where creative business districts (CBDs) and special creative zones (SCZs) are an indispensable part of urban planning. These areas offer everything between creativity and consumption, folk cultures and foreign intrigue, coffee and cultural critique.

Being and becoming

In 1989, the cognitive psychologist Howard Gardner, author of a number of books and essays on education, spent a short period in China. Gardner relates an incident that seemed to him to define Chinese social conformity, that is, measured against the American focus on the individual. Whenever Gardner and his wife left their Beijing hotel for an outing they were required to place their room key in a receptacle. Excited, his young son would take the key and try to push it in the narrow rectangular slot, banging it, sometimes dropping it. While the parents played along with these efforts, the Chinese room maids at the hotel, seeing the boy struggling to make the key drop, would invariably offer assistance by carefully directing how this action should be done properly: by placing the key carefully and guiding it slowly.

Gardner's reaction to these incidents is interesting: he suggests the good-natured assistance of the maids is akin to interference in the natural process of childlike curiosity. Gardner's interpretation reflects how most Western cultures like to think of childhood, as a state of playful learning, of carefree experimentation, of self-discovery. As young children we learn to walk and talk, and to know our way around the world by constantly discovering new things and processing new information. As we grow we receive praise and condemnation; we are asked to conform to a rule-bound system of society. The need to conform, to pass exams, and the fear of making mistakes induces a more conservative mindset. Trying something to see 'what happens' becomes less of an option. The focus shifts from 'becoming' (experimenting, testing, challenging) to 'being' (fitting in, being moulded, being normal).

In an account of the hotel incident and his time in Beijing, Gardner proposed five interconnecting points of 'relative difference' between Chinese and American society, which 'fuse into a greater, one might almost say, Confucian, whole'. First, Gardner suggests that life in Chinese society is analogous to a performance with carefully delineated roles. He contends it is therefore important to know where one's position is relative to persons of authority and influence. His second point concerns art. Gardner contends that the function of art is to inculcate good behaviour and in doing so the prevailing view is that art should be 'beautiful and good'. His third point emphasis the requirement of control and hierarchy. Gardner says: 'In China traditionally "the people" must look in two directions: upward, toward those who have authority, and backward, to the traditions of the past' (Gardner 2006: 123). The fourth proposition is that education takes place by careful shaping. Gardner remarks that child rearing in China follows a behaviourist model, with good conduct and performance highly rewarded. The corollary is that education is broken down into the smallest possible units to be mastered and 'performed' with relatively little attention to ideas, abstract thinking. Finally, whereas American society emphasises creativity and innovation, and therefore risk-taking, the Chinese approach is about moderation and mastery of the basic elements, while allowing 'minor modifications'.

While most of his observations are supported by research on Chinese tradition, society and politics, it is worth setting out Gardner's conclusion in relation to creativity, a topic on which he is acknowledged as an expert commentator:

> Indeed, this toleration of minor modifications comes close to my own notion of how 'creativity' is understood in China – as neither a massive dislocation nor a radical re-conceptualization but rather as a modest, continuous, and cumulative alteration of existing schemes or practices.
>
> (Gardner 2006: 127)

These are interesting observations made at the point of socialisation. Is creativity therefore qualitatively different in China than in the West? How is creativity, or lack of creativity, related to our upbringing, to the function of art, to the notion of performance, to the problematic of control? Indeed, how far should we look back to find the answers? The search for traditional explanations often leads to charges of essentialism. While it is fairly non-controversial to impute that most persons of Chinese heritage are socially conditioned in various degrees by Confucian values inherited through generations, it is somewhat more problematic to assert that the mentalities of contemporary Europeans or citizens of the US are shaped by the ancient Greeks. Are the East Asian cultural foundations deeper or did the European Enlightenment's faith in scientific knowledge forever change the Western psyche? In the latter case, the conventional standpoint is to emphasise the consequences of the rise of Western humanism leading to the liberation of the individual, democracy, universal rights, and by the twentieth century particularly, widespread affluence and consumerist lifestyles (Carroll 2004; Van Doren 1991). Investigating deeper, however, we might find other solid foundations: the idea of a Hebrew god creating order from chaos, a god that always was, being, not becoming.

The idea of continuous transformation or what scholars of Chinese philosophy call 'becoming', goes against the grain of Western European thought, which according to scholars has privileged equilibrium and permanence; this is a legacy dating to the ancient Greeks (Hall and Ames

1995). With the intensification of the scientific method during the European Enlightenment, thinkers identified causes and effects by applying processes of rational investigation. Natural causality was superior; the shifting of power towards nature, and the natural sciences, meant that its opposite – culture – became the subject of laws or norms that sought to differentiate humans from other animals. These norms varied according to which interest group was in power.

Tradition is a long bow. At best it can offer partial understandings of cross-cultural creative capacities. We might infer that Chinese people are more likely to co-operate and less likely to seek authorial status than their Western counterparts, an explanation sometimes proffered to rationalise high levels of imitation in the cultural sectors. Cultural generalisations such as this invariably rub up against the fact that values are continually in flux and that economic pressures produce their own behavioural norms. The sharing of creative ideas is far more prevalent among international companies in China than it is among Chinese businesses. Local businesses situated in environments designed to maximise knowledge spillovers seem to distrust their neighbours. Of course, it is possible to advance a cultural explanation for this: why would you trust an outsider? But then again why would international companies share knowledge more freely when they know it may be used to undermine their business. The answers are not simple. The social sharing model or 'creative commons' has developed against the grain of international intellectual property wisdom (Montgomery 2010).

I believe the underlying source code of Chinese-style innovation (and creativity) hinges on where one places emphasis: for instance, on novelty, utility, experimentation, self-expression or spontaneity. The tendency to seek minor modifications may well be part of the cultural DNA of Chinese people but we need to be mindful of 'blaming' Confucius and his followers for diminishing a Chinese capacity for creative expression. The scenario sketched out by Howard Gardner is perhaps likely to be influenced more by recent events than those occurring 2,000 years ago. Moreover, creative expression in a Western register may not be 'the sole criteria of truth', to paraphrase the former Chinese leader Deng Xiaoping.

Reprise: Creativity in question

The relationship between culture, creativity and innovation is opaque, perhaps more so in China where these terms are invested with national significance. One of the most cited descriptions of the term 'culture' comes from the British cultural scholar Raymond Williams' *Keywords*, in which he begins: 'Culture is one of the two or three most complicated words in the English language.' As I noted in the introduction, Williams' depiction of creativity in the same publication is less well known: 'no word in

English carries a more consistently positive reference than "creative" ...yet the very width of the reference involved not only difficulties of meaning, but also through habit, a kind of unthinking repetition which at times makes the word seem useless' (Williams 1988: 19). Williams believed 'an obvious difficulty' exists because the term 'creative' places a necessary stress on originality and innovation. The difficulty exists because of overuse of the term for practices that are not creative.

The noun form 'creativity' conjures up a range of associations: some are banal; others are specific and useful. It is applied loosely to products and processes produced by businesses that involve negligible amounts of novelty. More specifically to this study, the uptake of the term 'creative industries' by national, regional and district governments is based on a faith in its capacity to transform non-productive culture into value-added enterprise. One of my research colleagues in China who publishes an annual 'creative industries report' told me that it is necessary to use the term 'creative industries' as much and as widely as possible because important policy advisors will see its usefulness. Hence in China we find the following terms: creative agriculture, creative manufacturing and creative tourism. But this definitional largesse towards creativity is not confined to China. Currently, a number of reports, including UNCTAD's *Creative Economy Global Report*, itemise a range of creative activities ranging from carpet making to creative R&D (UNCTAD 2008, 2010).

Of course, one can always 'fit' more and more pursuits into the cultural and creative industries family by designating core and non-core activities. The 'problem' here is that many core activities listed in such reports simply don't involve novelty; furthermore, many show little evidence of originality. Of course, they can still be regarded as creative as long as we downgrade the emphasis on newness and originality, as I believe has been the case in China. Indeed, considering all products and services available for consumption in the economy, we can observe a continuum: at one end there are those made to a certain preconceived specification; for instance, most people would concur that assembly line manufacturing is an uncreative activity. We might choose to include carpet making, garment manufacture and the outsourcing of animation here. At the other end of the continuum is originality, the much vaunted breakthroughs in style and paradigm; for instance Picasso's cube, Einstein's theory of relativity, and the Tang poetry of Dufu. In the middle and taking up a lot of the territory is 'proficiency' in various forms (which is useful but not so novel) and 'eccentricity' (which is novel but not so useful) (Moran 2009).

Likewise, the term 'innovation' often reflects expediency. Steve Fuller calls it 'the first global policy craze of the twenty-first century' (2006: 103). He notes how the tightness of fit between innovation and capitalism in turn reflects a desire to turn non-capital into capital. Moreover, the 'economic definition' of innovation differs from invention or creativity in that it implies diffusion: 'an invention is an innovation only after it has been adopted by a community of users' (Hermann-Pillath 2010: 36). Whether innovation is new, or just a recombination of what already exists, is often decided in patent offices and law courts. Helga Nowotny writes that depending on how one draws the boundaries between old and new, 'the new can appear as something whose contours are already known or as a radical break with the given' (2008: 11). Yet as scholars of innovation note, innovation is most often associated with technological progress. The rapid industrialisation of Europe in the eighteenth and nineteenth centuries was the result of a long series of cumulative innovations that can be traced back to the Middle Ages (Nowotny 2008).

In *The Nature of Technology* Brian Arthur has coined the term 'combinatorial evolution': he says: 'Early technologies form using existing primitive technologies as components. These new technologies in time become possible components – building blocks – for the construction of new technologies. Some of these in turn go on to become possible building blocks for the creation of newer technologies' (Arthur 2009: 21). Taking the argument further, Stephen Johnson refers to the 'adjacent possible', the idea that new combinations of technologies, of ideas, open doors: 'the history of cultural progress is, almost without exception, a story of one door leading to another' (Johnson 2010: 36).

Likewise, quantum physicists tell us that the world is always renewing: that even 'elementary particles' need to be understood 'as abstractions from a stream of events or a flow of process, in which every object is regarded as in essence a relatively invariant form of such abstraction' (Bohm 1996: 92). Similarly, the French philosopher Henri Bergson believed that what we see as reality is nothing more than an abstraction from constant movement, likening reality to a cinematographic image: there is constant movement but we seek to isolate the frames (Bergson 1998). Paraphrasing Bergson, the isolation of the particular from the flux (the becoming) can produce an illusion that innovations are new.

The ten thousand things

This conundrum has a parallel in Chinese philosophy. In the traditional Chinese worldview *wanwu* referred to 'the ten thousand things'. This metaphor described a world in flux, in comparison to a Western equilibrium model (Hall and Ames 1998; Ledderose 2000). In the Chinese traditional view change occurred through a process of efficacious configurations. New models emerged as persons of qualified learning (situated within collective scholarly networks) personalised formal practices, commented on texts and produced variations (Hall and Ames 1998; Collins 1998; Lloyd and Sivin 2002). These text-based learning networks produced 'knowledge about'. Today, as the ethos of recombination, reinvention and reassembling spreads with the use of technology, the 'ten thousand things' have taken on new configurations, new variations and often surprising new uses.

The 'ten thousand things' were regarded as a way of understanding variation according to existing natural patterns. In one of the few studies of innovation in traditional China, Michael Puett (2001) notes how the 'ambivalence of creation' contrasted with the scientific model of innovation taken up by the West during the Enlightenment. In traditional China innovation was about the efficacious use of resources; in making the most of circumstances. Chinese artists and artisans did not privilege originality but rather believed that variations, mutations, and adaptations over time would eventually bring further change. They emphasised reproduction over creativity. As a text from the Song Dynasty tells us: 'The ten thousand things are produced and reproduced, so that variation and transformation have no end' (Zhou Dunyi, in Ledderose 2000).

This approach to creativity therefore hangs on the interplay of 'similar differences' and 'different similarities' (Bohm 1996). If they are identical or just mechanical copies then there is obviously no creativity. Perception identifies differences; it gathers differences and then sorts these into similarities and correlations. According to Hall and Ames (1995) the Chinese metaphysical world is based on correlative thinking, as opposed to the Western approach which is founded on causal thinking; for instance in the Chinese world there are correlations between heaven (*tian*) and humanity (*ren*), between change (*bian*) and continuity (*tong*), between stuff (*ti*) and function (*yong*). Hall and Ames note that according to this worldview the well-known phrase 'as different as night and day' would be 'as different as night-becoming-day from day-becoming-night' (Hall and Ames 1998: 127).

Many accounts have advanced the view that the separation of nature and culture resulted in the superiority of Western science and philosophy; it led to a consequent downgrading of the achievements of the 'East', whose philosophers, Confucius, Mencius and Laozi and Zhuangzi, had no need for a separate concept of nature (Mokyr 2002). For others, the suggestion that causal thinking should serve as a universal norm is a case of 'transcendental pretence'. According to Hall and Ames, 'causal thinking' comes to be associated with the essential, the universal, and the permanent rather than the idiosyncratic, the particular, and the transitory character of things and events', which they identify with Chinese thought (Hall and Ames 1995: 18). Causal thinking, at least in the Anglo-European philosophical tradition, is associated with the concept of freedom, placing an emphasis on deliberative action more so than process. In the Chinese view a yin/yang conceptualisation evokes rhythmic interaction, a balancing of passive and active moments (Hall 1982).

The ten thousand things and the interplay between difference and similarity can be illustrated in a number of ways but perhaps the most instructive is the written language. The Chinese language has some 50,000 characters and these are composed by rearranging modules taken from a repertoire of some 200 parts. The language teaches how to build units through combination of elements. The visual mode also encourages pattern recognition, which itself is the basis of the Chinese system. In discussing Chinese architecture, the tomb of the terracotta warriors, and Chinese bronzes among other things, Ledderose comments: 'The Chinese, professing to take nature as their master, were never coy about producing through reproduction. They did not see the contrast between original and reproduction in such categorical terms as did westerners' (Ledderose 2000: 7).

The salient points are process, adaptation and fitting. Change occurs through efficacious combinations. The interplay between culture and creativity illustrates a tension between similarity and difference, illustrating what the sinologist François Jullien terms 'tendency' or 'propensity' (*shi*): that is, 'mutual attraction between two poles' (Jullien 1995: 229). Drawing on this analogy we might surmise that the nature of culture is *yin*, which 'congeals' or 'concentrates itself', while creativity is its other, the *yang*, 'rising up' and 'dispersing' (Jullien 1995). The dispersing can proceed harmoniously, producing efficacious social benefits, innovations and aesthetic displays; alternatively it can proceed disharmoniously, and destructively, generating systemic and paradigmatic change. It is the former mode of dispersal that the Chinese state recognises as the blueprint for its 'innovation nation' strategy; the latter form is disruptive. For this reason creativity needs to be harmonised.

Adaptation and recombination: pragmatic applications

Epistemological investigations deserve more attention than space permits in this concluding chapter. The point I wish to emphasise is that creativity is more complex than technical proficiency but at the same time it is rarely invention: similarity and difference underpin our perceptions of novelty; re-combinations, or 're-creations', are omnipresent and unacknowledged (Pope 2005). The pragmatic application of creative industries, however, avoids these inconvenient nuances. What policymakers, entrepreneurs and investors are more interested in is *utilitarian creativity*, more akin to innovation. Amabile says that creativity is defined as the production of novel and useful ideas by individuals or small teams of individuals working closely together whereas innovation is the successful implementation of creative ideas by an organisation (Amabile 1996). However, as I have mentioned in relation to some of the creative industries reports, if we hold too dearly to the idea of novelty and originality we condemn much of the creative economy data as nonsensical.

In a thought-provoking account of copyright, piracy and cinema in Asia, Laikwan Pang (2006: 4–8) explores what she calls 'identity-difference dynamics'. Pang argues that consumerism and globalisation are self-reinforcing in generating products where value hinges on an interplay between the familiar and the new; in doing so she contends that 'new' and 'original' are misleading and conditional descriptions: in effect all copyrighted works are constitutive of an endless chain of creativity and copying. Echoing Henri Bergson's cinematographic metaphor mentioned above, 'copyright law attempts to freeze the act of creativity at the moment when the product is introduced, conferring on it the status of intellectual property' (Pang 2006: 7). Pang also writes about 'culture's will to copy', the centrality of 'mimesis' to the worldviews of Plato and Aristotle, and how continuous generation of difference undermines copyright law. However, while the dynamic interplay between identity and difference is unquestionably exacerbated by globalisation and consumerism, my sense is that this duality is a human survival mechanism dating back to our ancient forebears, one borne out in the development of fiction. Stories began as oral traditions; they were both instructive and entertaining; they procreated thanks to the printing press and more recently the modern film and publishing industries. At the same time stories have been constantly 're-created' through non-commercial channels. Stories are templates for more stories, more variations, and ever more adaptations. For that reason both the capitalist inclination to regulate creativity and the Chinese socialist penchant for planning creativity (and creative clusters) ultimately lead into an epistemological cul-de-sac. Further reinforcing the endless chain of 'becoming' (not being) is language, which constantly evolves and changes. Language by this account is an open system. If creativity is the production of novelty then aesthetic events that purport to represent novelty rely on the incompleteness of the product (or the idea) that provided the inspiration: the novel, the film score, the poem, the painting, the musical composition, the blog entry. And so it goes.

How can we then understand creativity in a way that accommodates policy and business while still engendering a sense of change, of variety, of value? The solution might be 'adaptive creativity', a term used by Sheridan Tatsuno in his book *Created in Japan: from Imitators to World Class Innovators*. Tatsuno wrote in relation to Japanese ingenuity: 'in the West, creativity is viewed as an epiphany and only one phase in the creative process – the generation of new ideas that triggers dramatic breakthroughs – is emphasized' (Tatsuno 1990: 49).

He goes on:

> In the broadest sense, creativity reflects a fresh, novel and unorthodox way of thinking and viewing the world. We need to expand our Western notion of creativity to include all forms of creativity, including Japanese creativity.
>
> (Tatsuno 1990: 49–50)

Tatsuno, writing at a time when Japan was breaking new ground in miniature consumer electronics formats, makes some interesting points in comparing East and West. He cites Roger Van Oech's graphic portrayal of the creative process, expressed as *A Kick in the Seat of the Pants* (a later version was *A Whack to the Side of the Head*) (van Oech 1986). Van Oech suggests that people play four different roles in the creative process: explorer (searching for new information), artist (turning this into new ideas), judge (evaluating the merits), and warrior (acting on the idea). To these four, Tastuno adds the 'antique dealer': the practice of recycling old ideas for new applications. In China, the term 'putting new wine in old bottles' was used to describe how the Maoist revolutionaries rewrote Chinese cultural policy. Rather than trying to rewrite the source code, they used old cultural forms and updated these with Marxist content.

It is tempting to think of the Eastern idea of reincarnation here. Tatsuno writes about the mandala of creativity. The mandala was originally a Hindu concept but made its way into Pure Land Buddhism to represent the idea of unending cycles and constant improvement. While nirvana is not exactly what drives the corporate mind, the quest for improvement always figures in considerations. Recycling ideas and imitation is a business model that is shedding its negative image. Oded Shenkar, author of *Copycats: How Smart Companies Use Imitation to Gain a Strategic Edge*, suggests that the age of novel-product innovation is passing. Shenkar's interest in the role played by imitation in business strategy was aroused during 30 years of study on China. While imitation has always been widespread, it has gained a bad name due to the emphasis placed on innovation (and novelty). Due to the forces of globalisation and the codification of knowledge, which facilitate reverse engineering, imitation 'is becoming more feasible for a wide array of products and services, process, and business models, as well as more attractive in costs, benefits and potential return' (Shenkar 2010: 43).

In their seminal study of China's IT industry Breznitz and Murphree (2011) draw attention to what they call 'two myths': first the 'Western techno-fetishism of novelty, which equates innovation only with the creation of new technologies and products' (2011: 2); the second myth is that China's capacity to be innovate must necessarily be measured against an idealised Silicon Valley benchmark. In fact, according to the authors of this study, what China does so effectively is second-level innovation – the mixing of new techniques and technologies in order to come up with new solutions, including solutions in organisation of production, packaging and marketing. This ingenuity allows Chinese businesses to move into new niches that have been made profitable by an innovator elsewhere.

Such modularity allows a different perspective on creativity, one more associated with Lego and IKEA than Picasso and Proust. The interplay between similarity and difference is universal. It's what we do subconsciously when we acknowledge a powerful idea. The 'creative industries' is similar and different to the 'content', 'copyright' and 'cultural' industries. The interplay between similarity and difference is evident in respect to copyright law. International businesses are seemingly at a loss to stop Chinese companies appropriating their images and their business models. In China IKEA competes with a Chinese franchise IJIA, somehow cleverer because JIA signifies 'home'. Coffee shops in China have taken the logo of Starbucks and reworked it, banking on the association of Starbucks and (Western) coffee drinkers. How very unoriginal, how derivative, one might say. We choose to favour the terms 'novelty' and 'originality' over the more generic ideas of similarity and difference.

Phases, evolution and emergence

Is creative clustering a just development process for an immature 'industry'? This is a view expressed by a number of writers: that there is a bigger picture, an evolutionary process leading to a less clustered and more communitarian society. In effect, the cluster model operates a hierarchical form of governance while the governance of 'communities' is situated midway along a continuum between hierarchy and network (Dal Fiore 2007).

In *How Creativity is Changing China*, Li Wuwei (2011) outlines in detail a transformation of China's economy and society. Li explains how China is currently seeking to activate its latent creative resources, building what he calls 'cultural soft power'. In his view important transformations have already taken place in cultural sectors and effects are being felt in other economic sectors; eventually, he says, China will transform into a creative society. Li proposes three such transformations: creative industries–creative economy–creative society. In this millennial vision China's economy will be released from dependence on low-cost manufacturing and processing. Significantly, the negative externalities of this world factory model, in particular problems of polluted environments and the loss of intellectual property earnings to foreign entities, will be alleviated. Indeed, one of the most interesting sections is where Li compares China's innovative capacity with those of foreign companies. He says:

> 'They eat the meat and we eat the bone. They eat the rice and we eat the bran.' This apt description reminds us that the Made in China model is founded on 'sweat industries'. Made in China and 'created by foreign capital' now symbolize competition among nations for China's low cost resources.
>
> (Li 2011: 9)

Li's three-stage transformational model of industry–economy–society is promoted as a 'Creative China plan' in the post-global economic crisis period. Li's is an important and powerful voice. However, the genesis of the vision dates back to Beijing in early 2004 when Liu Shifa, Vice-director of the Market Development section within the Ministry of Culture, wrote an article called 'Implementing the creative century plan; developing the creative China campaign'. In this manifesto Liu wrote:

> We are now focusing our attention on the new century: from creative industries to creative economy then to creative society. We are also focusing attention on China today: from Made in China to 'created in China'. We are advocating the implementation of a creative century plan, and the development of the creative China campaign.
>
> (Liu 2004)

The creative China campaign, the creative century plan, and the slogan 'from made in China to created in China' received an airing at an international cultural industries conference in Shanxi in May 2004. However, the key points of the plan, which included a wholesale shift of attention to enabling creativity and a move away from imitation, were lost among clamours for cultural protection, a theme dear to the hearts of the cultural officials in attendance. The manifesto was taken up by the Creative China Industrial Alliance, a group who subsequently publicised the slogan: from Made in China to Created in China (Keane 2007).

The concern with identifying stages of development in creative industries globally is echoed in recent work by John Hartley (2011). Hartley identifies four phases of the creative industries beginning with 'creative clusters' and culminating in 'creative cities'. In contrast to much of the research in China that seeks to validate creativity as an industrial process by treating culture as 'just another industry', Hartley believes creativity needs to be accounted for at an ever-increasing distance from industry, and government. His first phase, CI1 (creative industries 1), a 'closed expert pipeline', reflects the DCMS industrial categorisation of 13 sectors charged with producing outputs. The outputs in phase one are invariably quantified as intellectual property according to internationally recognised processes, namely copyright, digital rights management and trademarks. These intangibles are often described as the 'weightless economy', although for Hartley weightlessness goes far beyond formal industry sectors and sub-sectors. The description 'closed expert pipeline' implies that debates about creative industries are generally supply side and confined to pursuits identified as cultural and symbolic. Expertise generally emanates from cultural policy professionals and cultural academics.

Reflecting Li Wuwei's position, Hartley's second phase is 'creative economy'. This he calls the 'open expert system' where businesses in all sectors, not just cultural and media, add value through innovation; for instance through business-to business services. An example might be when a marketing consultant engages with an advertising team to promote a campaign. The creative economy here is a broader metaphorical canvas and is not to be conflated with UNCTAD's *Creative Economy* definition, which ascribes to the first phase by identifying and counting outputs based primarily on culturally defined occupations.

Hartley's third phase is an 'open innovation network'. Here Hartley makes a familiar move. It is the creative citizen who is now empowered. Among the terms promoted in the CI3 phase are user-created content, consumer entrepreneurship, open source movement, cloud culture, DIY culture and micro-productivity. These three stages form the core of Hartley's critique of the creative industries. In 2011, however, Hartley added a fourth phase, which was CI4, or creative cities. He says:

> It is not until you reach stages 3 and 4, where creativity reaches cultural dimensions located in cities, rather than being confined to production processes located in firms, that the connections between culture and economy, individual talent and societal scale, can come into focus. Furthermore, it is only at that point that you can take account of the growth of ICTs, digital media and the internet. In other words, if you confine the notion of creative industries to the traditional creative disciplines and their industrial or occupational form, you will never be able to account for the importance – both economic and cultural – of user-created content and the burgeoning scale of computer-based social networks.
>
> (Hartley 2011: 9)

Both Li Wuwei's three stages and Hartley's four phases try to describe what is occurring as society evolves, as grassroots participation in the production of meaning and symbolic capital are enabled by digital technologies. Li is explicitly referring to China. In his description the benefits of the creative industries flow directly to the nation in terms of soft power: the assumption is that the creative society will not be disruptive: creativity is fundamentally harmonious and creative clusters are means to an end. Hartley's version on the other hand is disruptive. In keeping with a Schumpeterian 'creative destruction' perspective, it is both incremental and dynamic. Societies are not harmonious constructs in Hartley's terms: 'The answer is that cumulative or incremental change coexists with "explosion" or what Tom Paine would have called revolution. Cumulative change is co-dependent; disruptive change is random chance. Both require openness to the possibilities of the future' (Hartley 2011: 14).

Formal and informal economies

In conclusion I offer a different perspective on the longevity of the creative industries in China. My perspective is not about stages of development as in the examples mentioned above, nor great social transformation and liberation of thought. I am sanguine about the future of creative industries in China. I suggest that there are three levels of interrelated activity: the first in the realm of state planning; the latter two concern market readjustment and co-creation. While the following model can apply to all societies, I believe the distinctions are more finely drawn in China and are contingent on the legacy of authoritarianism and state intervention into cultural markets.

The first level is political reform: this is self-evident when we reflect on the history of China in the twentieth century. The key platform of statecraft in China is reform [*gaige*]. In effect reform is a process of constantly designing policy to development objectives, although in practice the nature of reform has been contingent on the Marxist-Leninist canon as interpreted by successive Chinese leaders. Reform is also about 'seeking truth from facts', as Deng Xiaoping, the architect of China's reform, put it. At the central level reform symbolises the legitimacy of the Chinese Communist Party (CCP). For the past three decades China's rapid economic growth has been tied to an export-focused model, aided by low-cost labour, special economic zones, and industrial clusters. The role of policy is therefore to provide the right levers to allow the accumulation and the upgrading of the economy, to encourage investments in clusters and in infrastructure. In China the creative economy also illustrates the aspirations of municipal and local governments to generate capital from the cultural market. Cultural policy is therefore closely aligned with economic growth theory, urban regeneration and local entrepreneurship. In this triangular relationship there is a sense that government must shoulder much of the responsibility for planning. As a result, there is recognition of the need for 'informed' top-down planning. Reform is also about trial and error: the evidence from this study of cultural quarters and clusters shows that there are many trials and even more errors. Structured uncertainty persists; and a buffet of development models is provided for policymakers to pick potential winners.

The Eleventh Five Year Plan (2005–2010) introduced new reform ideas; in particular it signalled an attempt to modify China's economic development model, and its self-identity, by looking outward. Terms such as 'soft power' (*ruanshili*), 'going out' (*zou chuqu*), 'autonomous innovation' (*zizhu chuangxin*) and 'creative nation' (*chuangxin guojia*) gradually superseded the rhetoric of modernisation in China's media. Even 'harmonious society' (*hexie shehui*), the Chinese Communist Party's formula for rebalancing society, entailed recognition that the nation was becoming a global power.

The first level represents what some political scientists and economists call formal institutions: 'the rules, regulations, policies, and procedures that are promulgated and meant to be enforced by entities and agents generally recognized as being official' (Tsai 2006: 125). However, institutional reform is confounded by ambiguity and overlapping jurisdictions; this provides opportunities for actors to 'adjust, ignore, or evade discrete portions of formal institutions' (*ibid.*). A well-known maxim in Chinese is *shang you zhengce, xia you duice* ('above there are policies, below there are strategies'). In a book entitled *Informal Rules: The Real Games of Chinese History*, initially published in China in 2000 and subsequently banned, the author Wu Si wrote: 'Outside the formal regulations of every kind of system in Chinese society, and behind every clear statement, there are unwritten rules that are widely recognized' (Wu 2000: preface). He goes on to say that these kind of unwritten rules determine the rhythms of everyday life. In effect, the formal institutions of society are underpinned by informal institutions, which are in the main inherited from culture. In turn, officialdom has its own informal rules and processes. In media content industries for instance, a phone call from a leading official to a television station might be regarded as carrying more weight than a document issued by the respective regulatory bureau.

Whereas the language of reform is ultimately dictated by party officials, the role of thinking about reform is increasingly delegated to epistemic communities. In many instances such communities are informal alliances; for instance, an epistemic community or think-tank that maintains close links to local policymakers; the Creative China Industrial Alliance (CCIA) in Beijing is one such group. Often a bureaucratic entrepreneur will perform the role of cultural intermediary working close to local officials who are looking for ways to monetise creative clusters (the case of Zhang Changcheng in the Fangjia 46 project in Chapter 4). Epistemic communities are therefore keen to promote models, or 'invent models' that appeal to policy officials. Whether this is evidence of traditional Chinese mindsets or strategic manoeuvres predicated on structured uncertainty is a moot point.

From a cultural policy perspective the first level symbolises official culture (*guanfang wenhua*). In the past era of orthodox socialism, cultural policy was prescriptive; ministries and bureaus located in Beijing mandated certain forms of expression and ruled others out of bounds. To some extent the current self-organisation of the market and the emergence of new models of marketing and distribution are eroding the hegemony, and the informal rules of official culture. Wu Si says: 'The market laws of supply and demand are replacing the informal rules of officialdom' (Wu 2000: preface). Nevertheless the state maintains an interventionist role when it comes to cultural expression. Quotas are still applied to the production of 'main melody' television dramas to assure that the Chinese people receive appropriate moral training. Propaganda officials closely monitor programming. Moreover, state funds subsidise a high proportion of cultural output.

The effect of political supervision is most acutely felt on a second level of the creative innovation system. Broadly speaking, this is the realm of commercial popular culture – the tangible manifestation of creative industries. Rigid regulation of media industry sectors constrains innovation and drives agents into informal economies and into clustering activities. The practice of forming clusters, and of opting to be located in a cluster, is frequently a strategy for obviating the risk and uncertainty of the creative industries. While agglomeration ought to engender 'spillovers' and 'increasing returns', in effect we see a widespread tendency to avoid sharing of ideas, a lack of intellectual property generating product and lock-in effects as businesses opt for safe business models. As discussed in Chapter 3, from the perspective of local government cluster development is a process of attracting business and investment (*zhao shang yinzi*). However, concessions are often made available discretely to lure influential tenants that might raise the profile of the cluster. In the case of Shanghai's Old Millfun (see Chapter 6), rent charges were waived for the Reading Club of Harvard University (Zheng 2010).

In other sectors we find a range of informal practices; many are condoned by officials; for instance in publishing the practice whereby the state assigns book numbers (*shuhao*) is intended to regulate the production of printed media. The effect of these constraints compels 'official publishing houses' to outsource their quota to smaller fly-by-night studios. In art clusters such as 798 and Songzhuang (Chapter 5) a high degree of informal brokerage is evident in auctions together with the practice of taking 'short cuts' to market by mass producing images that appeal to tourists (Ulfstjerne 2009). In the Dafencun art cluster in southern Shenzhen the proclivity for mass replication of existing art is regaled by local officials as a successful creative industries business model. In television production overt supervision of content has over time reduced incentives to take risks: TV drama scripts have to be presented to officials beforehand. In the media we see opportunism more than 'novel products'. Producers, directors and scriptwriters search for ideas that can be replicated without too much financial investment and without producing political conflict. New versions of cultural classics and updated tales of revolutionary heroes known as *Red Classics* are common, together with a predilection to adapt in literature, TV drama, online games, visual arts and animation (Qian 2008). Reproductions and adaptations appeal to new market segments.

The market level searches international and regional environments, as well as online communities, for ideas to exploit and commercialise. One of the more interesting phenomena has been an adaptation of the Confucian Analects by Yu Dan, a professor of literature from Beijing Normal University. *Confucius from the Heart* mixes the advice of the venerable sage with Buddhism and Western pop psychology (Yu 2009). The book has been a smash hit, a best seller, earning the ire of many university-based Confucian scholars. *Confucius from the Heart* has also been translated into English. Rather than originate ideas, there is a tendency to refine and recycle: this occurs firstly because many adaptations are themselves imaginative (Henningsen 2010) and secondly because there is a lack of protection of intellectual ideas in the market. Once a format is successful it spreads until its potency is exhausted by repetition. The adaptation of successful formulas is not confined to content industries. The celebrated film-maker Zhang Yimou has recently made a successful move into tourism projects. Zhang's *Impressions Series*, elaborate outdoor spectacles in rural locations, repackages local legends with the techniques of a cinematographer, mixing in elements of New Age music and popular culture. Following Zhang's success a number of similar tourism projects by leading film directors have appeared.

Popular culture of course extends beyond the realm of the market. It concerns the activities of youth, pranksters, amateurs and dissidents. This third level – informal grassroots culture – is probably the most important. It is typified by adaptive activity in non-commercial spheres. Much of the activity currently occurring in online communities is not aimed directly at profiteering, but rather functions as informal and amateur incubation. In other words it is both *re-creation* and *recreation*. The productiveness of this layer is not measured by economic success but by impact. China has more than 420 million netizens and over 600 million registered mobile phone users. The capacity to contribute spontaneously to online communities, whether in banal chatroom conversations or in the viewing of satirical spoofs of Chinese celebrities highlights the potency of user-generated content. In a groundbreaking study of new independent video culture in China, Paola Voci uses the idea of 'lightness' to underscore practitioners' 'resistance to being framed into and validated by either market, art, or political discourses' (Voci 2010: xx).

Whereas levels one (official) and two (popular culture) require navigation of censors, the third level is conspicuous by its risk culture. One particularly interesting example of spoofing culture is a short video made by a team at CCTV headed up by Cui Yongyuan, the host of a serious mainstream current affairs talk show called *Oriental Horizon* (*Dongfang shikong*). Obviously limited by the constraints of CCTV, in 2001 Cui and his colleagues released a video called *Splitting Up in October*, parodying the internal power struggles in CCTV. It soon went viral, with the effect of enhancing Cui's reputation with the 'masses' as more than just an anchor man for the regime. As long as such activities don't undermine social stability they are likely to be tolerated as signs of increased openness.

Networked social communities are sites of rapid experimentation, drawing on the ingenuity of users and the interpretations of communities. A great deal of 'moderately' disruptive activity takes place despite the continual attempts of authorities to rein in unorthodox practices. However, we need to ask: to what extent are these recreational activities, these 'new ten thousand things', transformational? In the current era 'the new ten thousand things' are open to constant interpretation. This 'grassroots soft power' has a potential 'commons' effect, albeit constrained by governmental technologies of power.

The three levels I have mentioned comprise an innovation system with limitations. The layers are enfolded. However, the tendency to date has been for commentators to see these as separate domains. The top level is concerned with truth and doesn't understand creativity; it seeks out advice and tests ideas cautiously. Conversely, the realm of commercial popular culture struggles to understand the market in a restricted content environment; it has one eye on the regulators and one eye on social network markets. It is in the third level, the sphere of *recreation*, that we find the most innovative work and prospects for further social liberalisation. Historically, the third level has always existed and provided ideas for the official level. Deng Xiaoping's famous reform dictum of crossing the river by feeling the stones is often interpreted as grassroots innovation: let the informal sectors take risks; they may succeed and provide new ways forward of they may fall in the water and drown.

Concluding remarks: From the tangible to the intangible

The answer to the question: 'what happens next?' is unclear – indeed like the concept of creative industries and much of the clustering environment already discussed in this book. Introduced into China in 2004, the creative industries met with resistance from central government power bases while engendering support among growth coalitions. Despite a history of Sinicising foreign ideas, often noted by adding the phrase 'with Chinese characteristics', the creative industries idea might be viewed as somewhat incongruous in a cultural system where for more than 2000 years people have been counselled to follow the prescriptions of sages, worthies, and in the case of Chinese Communist Party Chairman Mao Zedong, charismatic leaders. The Confucian view, although modified over history, was that a sage does not create, but merely transmits (Makeham 2003). The education system in China has followed, and continues to follow this pattern. However, while the idea that creativity has its natural home in the West is contested, there is a move within some intellectual and business circles to make China more innovative and creative; this has in turn provided an ideological buffer for the creative industries. The conversion of residential and factory space into clusters, with the assistance of officials, however, means that there is a need to show return on investment. The emphasis falls on activities that generate visible returns, attract tourists and cause minimal disruption. It is probably the model most likely to succeed in the current climate. This model is also stimulated by a flow of scholar-consultants and practitioners from northern Europe, many of whom are 'literate' in the language of the creative industries and willing to engage in co-productions, partnerships and joint ventures.

The language used in China is pragmatic: cultural, creative and cultural/creative. The creative industries discourse in China should not be evaluated through the same ideological lenses as in democratic states where creative expression is a given. Nonetheless, its uptake is shaped by international influences. Many of the scholar-consultants who advise propaganda officials in municipal and local governments present a case for creative communities, greater tolerance and more business transparency. These arguments about tolerance and transparency are more difficult to prosecute to the supporters of the cultural industries in Beijing. Proximity to Tiananmen conjures up memories of Western-influenced democracy supporters. However, the international discourse of creativity is central to the 'creative industries package' in China. The future will tell if creativity is harmonious or destructive.

Appendix 1: Category confusion

Discussing the distinctions of terminology might appear like academic obfuscation for some observers but it is necessary to understand why China operates a cultural rather than a creative economy, and why political considerations override the kind of risk taking associated with entrepreneurs in free market economies. The distinction between institutions and industries and between culture and creativity also allows us to diagnose problems in China's statistics, including its cultural exports.

The UK's DCMS categorisation of creative industries in 1998 comprised 13 segments. Most jurisdictions have followed the UK model, with occasional variations.

- Advertising
- Architecture
- Art and Antiques Market
- Crafts
- Design
- Designer Fashion
- Film and Video
- Interactive Leisure Software
- Music
- Performing Arts
- Publishing
- Software and Computer Services
- Television and Radio.

The compromise terminology of 'cultural and creative industries' (CCI) used in Beijing comprises 9 main sectors, 27 sub-sectors and 88 smaller sectors. The nine sectors are:

- broadcasting, TV and film
- cultural activities and performing arts
- media and publishing
- software, internet and IT services

- advertising and exhibition
- arts and crafts market
- design service
- tourism
- leisure entertainment and associated services.

The inclusion of tourism is understandable as a cultural industry; after all, China has thousands of cultural parks, and more seem to be added each day. The data for tourism are derived from national statistics and show no differentiation among cultural tourism, recreational tourism and national holiday tourism. Competition between Shanghai and Beijing is one explanation for the retention of tourism in Beijing as the latter claims ownership of many cultural 'crown jewels' in China's history.

The alternative Beijing School, which is responsible for the *China Creative Industries Development Report*, offers a more eclectic approach, incorporating the following:

- Film and TV culture
- Telecommunication and software
- Craft and fashion
- Design services
- Exhibition, performance and publication
- Consultation and planning
- Recreation and entertainment
- Scientific research and education.

The divisions here are a mix of the core creative sectors, the resolutely uncreative (telecommunication services) with the sometimes creative (carpet and tapestry manufacture). Tourism services are also included, as are museums and cultural relic sights.

The Shanghai School is championed by Li Wuwei, who is now the Vice-chairman of the Chinese Peoples' Political Consultative Conference and the Director of the Shanghai Creative Industries Association. The author of a number of recent books and articles including *Creativity is Changing China* (Li 2009), Li advocates core creative industries, surrounded by supporting, associated and spin-off industries. Li maintains there are intersections and overlaps between creative and cultural industries, the main difference being that cultural industries emphasize the industrialization of culture, while creative industries stress the importance of human creativity.

The Shanghai School nominates 5 main sectors, 38 sub-sectors and 55 smaller sectors. The five main sectors are:

- R&D Design: include industrial design, arts and crafts design, software design, etc.

- Architectural design: include engineering design services, architectural design services, interior design, etc.
- Culture and media: include performing arts, broadcasting, TV, film production, etc.
- Consulting and creative planning: include market research, stock consulting, exhibition and services, etc.
- Lifestyle and leisure: leisure sport, leisure entertainment, event programming, tourism photography, etc.

Institutions and industries

The terminology of industry was inherited from the success of the Chinese export and processing economy. There has, however, been ongoing debate about the relationships between the terms for industry and enterprise (*chanye* and *qiye* respectively) and the term for public institution (*shiye*).

The Ministry of Culture, along with the Propaganda Department (now referred to in China as the Publicity Department), believes that the overwhelming majority of China's cultural economy is traditional, and is the result of collective endeavour. The latter entity maintains the position that China's cultural sector is split into two categories: public institutions (*shiye*) and commercial industries (*chanye*). Because of its responsibility for maintaining spiritual civilisation the Propaganda Department consistently warns that reformers needed to be careful in distinguishing what is commercial and what is public.

The transformation from institutions to industries has been a long-running theme in Chinese national policy advisory communities, research centres, think-tanks and internal Chinese Communist Party study groups. As early as 2005, the Ministry of Finance, the General Administration of Customs and the State Administration of Tax issued a notice (*tongzhi*) allowing the waiver of tax for publicly supported institutions (*shiye*) who converted to industries (*chanye*).[1] The ruling provided an income tax holiday of three years for all units converting to industries. However, while the new autonomous industries were encouraged through such generous policies, the Publicity Department of the Chinese Communist Party continued to find ways to encourage the longevity of public institutions. In 2006, a policy document was released simultaneously from the Ministry of Finance and the Publicity Department of the CCP Central Committee allowing cultural propaganda institutions to enjoy preferential value added tax policies.[2] Film distribution institutions would enjoy preferential tax policies with 5 per cent of box office revenue be set aside to establish a 'special fund for the development of national film industry' and a 'special fund for good film'.

Notes

Introduction: China's new creative clusters

1 Shi Nian (2010) *The Water Margin: Outlaws of the Marsh*, Translated by J.H. Jackson. Tokyo: Tuttle Publishing, p. 592.

3 Clusters and regional development

1 Bin Jin, 'Ding Lei Hangzhou bianshen 'chuangyi nongmin', zhujin nongju yanjiu taoci' ['Move to farmhouse and research ceramics - Ding Lei became a farmer in Hangzhou'] *China News*, 17 August 2009, available at: http://www.chinanews.com/cj/cj-cjrw/news/2009/08-17/1822295.shtml (accessed 20/03/2011).

4 Beijing: creative capital or state-managed openness?

1 The term 'Long Tail' describes the retailing strategy of selling a large number of unique items in relatively small quantities – usually in addition to selling fewer popular items in large quantities.
2 Jerry Wang in an interview with the author on 20 July 2005 in Beijing.
3 See http://www.beinet.net.cn/enews/200612/t146634.htm
4 *Policies on Promoting the Development of Cultural and Creative Industries in Beijing* (*Beijingshi cujin wenhua chuangyi chanye fazhan de ruogan zhengce*).
5 *The Investment Guidance Catalogue for Beijing Cultural and Creative Industries* (*Beijing shi wenhua chuangyi chanye touzi zhidao mulu*).
6 *Eleventh Five-Year Plan for the Development of Beijing's Cultural and Creative Industry* (*Beijing shi shiyiwu shiqi wenhua chuangyi chanye fazhan guihua*).
7 *Measures on the Administration of Loan Discount for the Beijing Cultural and Creative Industries* (Trial Implementation) (*Beijing shi wenhua chuangyi chanye daikuan tiexi guanli banfa*).

5 Art districts: the pin-up child of the Chinese creative economy

1 Interview with Deputy Party Secretary, Songzhuang, 12 October 2010.
2 For reasons of confidentiality names of interviewees at Songzhuang are not noted in the text.
3 Interview, 12 October 2010.
4 Artist Interview, 12 October 2010.
5 Interview with Deputy Party Secretary, Songzhuang, 12 October 2010.

6   Interview with Deputy Party Secretary, Songzhuang, 12 October 2010.

6 Shanghai's cluster-led creative renaissance
1   KIC Promotional Brochure.

7 Media districts, parks and bases
1   Source: http://bq.chuban.cc/tz/200812/t20081222_42355.html

8 Culture, creativity, innovation, imagination
1   For this translation see Stephen R. Bokenkamp (1997) *Early Daoist Scriptures*. Berkeley: University of California Press, p. 166.
2   Cited in Herrlee G. Creel (1970) *What is Taoism?* Chicago: University of Chicago Press, p. 27.

Appendix 1: Category confusion
1   Notice on Certain Preferential Tax Policies for Cultural Enterprises Converting from Cultural Institutions during the Course of Cultural System Reform (*guanya wenhua tizhi gaige zhong jingyingxing wenhua shiye danwei zhuanzhihou giye de ruogan shuishou zhengce wenti de tongzhi*).
2   Several Economic Policies of the Ministry of Finance and the Ministry of Publicity Department of the CPC Central Committee on Further Supporting the Development of Cultural Undertakings (*caizhengbu zhongxuanbu guanyu jinyibu zhichi wenhua shiye fazhan ruogan jingji zhengce de tongzhi*).

References

Ai, Weiwei (2009) S Village, B Village. In Mangurian, Ray and Ray, Mary-Ann (eds.) *Caochangdi: Beijing Inside Out*. Hong Kong: Timezone 8, pp. 420–1.
Amabile, Teresa (1996) *Creativity in Context*. Boulder, CO.: Westview Press.
Amabile, Teresa M. and Steve J. Kramer (2010) What really motivates workers. *Harvard Business Review* 88 (1), pp. 44–5.
Amin, Ash and Roberts, Joanne (2008) The resurgence of community in economic thought and practice. In Amin, Ash and Roberts, Joanne (eds.) *Community, Economic Creativity and Organization*. Oxford: Oxford University Press, pp11–36.
Andersson, Åke and Andersson, David Emmanuel (2006) *The Economics of Experiences, the Arts and Entertainment*. Cheltenham: Edward Elgar Press.
Arthur, Brian (2009) *The Nature of Technology: What It Is and How It Evolves*. New York: The Free Press.
Baark, Eric (2007) Knowledge and innovation in China: historical legacies and emerging institutions. *Asia Pacific Business Review* 13 (3), pp. 337–56.
Bakhshi, Hasan, McVittie, Eric and Simmie, James (2008) Creating innovation: Do the creative industries support innovation in the wider economy? *NESTA research report* (Feb 2008): London.
Baldwin, Richard (2006) Globalisation: the great unbundling(s). *Economic Council of Finland*, available at www.tinyurl.com/2ol2n8.
Banks, Mark and O'Connor, Justin (2009) After the creative industries. *International Journal of Cultural Policy*, special issue edited by Mark Banks and Justine O'Connor 15 (4) pp. 365–73.
Bassett, K. (1993) Urban cultural strategies and urban regeneration: a case study and critique. *Environment and Planning A* 25 (12), pp. 1773–89.
Becker, Howard (2008/1982) *Art Worlds*. Berkeley: University of California Press.
Beijing City Plan (2004–2020) approved by the State Council in 2005. See http://www.bjghw.gov.cn/ztgh/
Beijing International (2011) Beijing e-government site. http://www.ebeijing.gov.cn/ Accessed 16 May 2011.
Beijing Municipal Planning Commission (2002) *Conservation Planning of 25 Historic Sites in Beijing Old City*. Beijing: Yanshan Publishing (in Chinese).
Belleflamme, Paul, Picard, Pierre M. and Thisse, Jacques-Francois (2000) An economic theory of regional clusters. *Journal of Urban Economics*, 48 (1), pp. 158–84.

Belussi, Fiorenza and Sedita, Silvia (2010) Industrial districts as open learning systems: combining emergent and deliberate knowledge systems. *Regional Studies* 1–20.
Bennett, Tony (1997) Culture, government and the social. *Culture and Policy* 8 (3), pp. 169–76.
Bennett, Tony (2003) *Culture: a Reformer's Science*. Sydney: Allen and Unwin.
Bergson, Henri (1998/1911) *Creative Evolution*, authorized translation by Arthur Mitchell. New York: Dover Publications.
Bernell, Robert (2008) The core of an art district is its artist. In Chang Lei and Zhu Qi (eds.) *Beijing 798 Now*. Beijing: Timezone 8 Books, pp. 146–7.
Bilton, Chris (2007) *Management and Creativity: From Creative Industries to Creative Management*. London: Blackwell.
Black, Daniel, Epstein, Stephen and Tokita, Alison (eds.) (2010) *Complicated Currents: Media Production, the Korean Wave, and Soft Power in East Asia*. Monash: Monash U. E-Press.
Boden, Margaret (2004) *The Creative Mind: Myths and Mechanisms* 2nd edition. London: Routledge.
Bohm, David (1996) *On Creativity*. London: Routledge.
Bokenkamp, Stephen R. (1997) *Early Daoist Scriptures*. Berkeley: University of California Press.
Breznitz, Dan and Murphree, Michael (2011) *Run of the Red Queen: Government, Innovation and Economic Growth in China*. New Haven: Yale University Press.
Callaghan, William A. (2010) *China: the Pessoptimist Nation*. Oxford: Oxford University Press.
Can, Xin (2008) Only chaos allows the creation of new rules. Interview with Can Xin by Zhi Zi. In Chang Lei and Zhu Qi (eds.) *Beijing 798 Now*. Beijing: Timezone 8 Books, pp, 150–1.
Cao, Z. (2005) Artists have moved out and the prosperity remains. *Laodong Daily* (Workers Daily), 2 November, p. 6 (in Chinese).
Carillo, Francisco (ed.) (2006) *Knowledge Cities: Approaches, Experiences and Perspectives*. Burlington, MA: Butterworth-Heinemann.
Carroll, John (2004) *The Wreck of Western Culture: Humanism Revisited*. Melbourne: Scribe.
Caves, Richard (2000) *Creative Industries: Contracts between Art and Commerce*. Cambridge, MA: Harvard UP.
CCPR (2003) *Baseline Study of Hong Kong's Creative Industries*. Centre for Cultural Policy Research., The University of Hong Kong: Hong Kong SAR.
Chang, Shaun (2008) Great expectations: China's cultural industry and case study of a government-sponsored cluster. *Creative Industries Journal* 3 (1), pp. 263–73.
Chen Guanzhong (2004) *You yibai ge liyou bu gai zai Beijing shenghuo wei shenme hai zai zhe?* ('Given a hundred reasons that one should not live in Beijing, why is one still here?'). In Chen Guanzhong, Liao Weitang and Yan Jun (eds.) *Boximiya Zhongguo* (Bohemian China) Guilin: Guanxi University Press, pp. 53–9.
Chen, Weidong and Zhang, Hong (2009) Chen Weidong: innovative model to export comic book series of four Chinese classic novels. Retrieved September 25, 2009, from http://news.xinhuanet.com/zgjx/2009-06/17/content_11555828.htm
Chew, Matthew (2010) Delineating the emergent global cultural dynamic of 'lobalization': The case of pass-off menswear in China. *Continuum* 24 (4), pp. 559–71.

China Daily (2006) 'Cultural Deficit Cause for Concern,' 10 March 2006, http://www.china.org.cn/english/culture/161006.htm (accessed April 28, 2009).

China Publishing Net (2011) (in Chinese) Beijing CBD international media cluster. Available online at http://bq.chuban.cc/tz/200812/t20081222_42355.html Accessed 16 May 2011.

Chua Beng-huat and Iwabuchi, Koichi (2008) (eds.) *East Asian Pop Culture: Analysing the Korean Wave*. Hong Kong: HKU Press.

Chung, Olivia (2008) China's cartoon police not amused. *Asia Times*. Retrieved on 20 May 2008 from http://www.atimes.com/atimes/China/JC04Ad01.html

Ci Jiwei (1994) *Dialectic of the Chinese Revolution*. Stanford: Stanford University Press.

Clunas, Craig (2009) *Art in China*. 2nd edition. Oxford: Oxford University Press.

Collins, Randolph (1998) *The Sociology of Philosophies: a Global Theory of Intellectual Change*. Cambridge: Harvard University Press.

Cowen, Tyler (2003) *Creative Destruction: How Globalization is Changing the World's Cultures*. Princeton: Princeton University Press.

Creativity Brand Lifestyle (2007) Promotional booklet of the 2007 Shanghai Creative Industries Week. Shanghai: Shanghai Creative Industries Centre.

Creel, Herrlee G. (1970) *What is Taoism?* Chicago: University of Chicago Press.

Cui, Baoguo (ed.) (2010) *Blue Book of China's Media 2010*. Beijing: Social Sciences Academic Press.

Cunningham, Stuart (2009) Trojan horse or Rorschach blot? Creative industries discourse around the world. *International Journal of Cultural Policy* 15 (4), pp. 375–86.

Cunningham, Stuart (forthcoming 2012) The creative cities discourse: production and/or consumption? In Anheier, H. K. and Isar, Y. R. (eds.) *Cultural Policy and Governance in a New Metropolitan Age. The Cultures and Globalization Series Volume 5*, London: Sage Publications.

Curtin, Michael (2007) *Playing to the World's Biggest Audience: The Globalization of Chinese Film and TV*. Berkeley: University of California Press.

Czikszentmihályi, Mihaly (1990) The domain of creativity. In Runco, Mark A. and Albert, Robert S. (eds.) *Theories of Creativity*. Newbury Park, CA: Sage Publications, pp. 325–39.

Dal Fiore, Filippo (2007) Communities versus networks: the implications on innovation and social change. *American Behavioural Scientist* 50 (7), pp. 857–66.

Darwent, Charles (2005) Chen Yifei: painter and filmmaker who became the Chinese Martha Stewart. Available at http://www.independent.co.uk/news/obituaries/chen-yifei-489446.html

Davis, Darrell William (2010) Market and marketization in the China film business. *Cinema Journal* 49 (3), pp. 121–5.

De Munyck, Bert (2007) The rise and fall of Beijing's creative business district. *Commercial Real Estate* 4 (April 2007). See http://idash.org/pipermail/my-ci/2007-May/000299.html

De Muynck, Bert (2010) Architecture on the move: Urban and architectural design in Inner Mongolia. In Moran, Albert and Keane, Michael (eds.) *Cultural Adaptation*. London: Routledge, pp. 101–13.

Denton, Kirk A. (ed.) (1996) *Modern Chinese Literary Thought: Writings on Literature 1893–1945*. California: Stanford University Press.

Department for Culture, Media and Sport (DCMS) (2001) Creative Industries Mapping Document 2001. 2nd edition. London, UK: Department of Culture, Media and Sport. Retrieved 16 May 2011.
Diao, Ying (2008) Recession winds chill exporters. *China Daily*, 9 December, p. 13.
Dicken, Peter (2003) *Global Shift: Reshaping the Global Economic Map in the 21st Century*. 4th edition. London: Sage.
Digital 21 (2010) Hong Kong and Shanghai ICT Industries Forge Stronger Bonds with New MoU Press release, available at http://www.info.gov.hk/digital21/eng/press/press_releases_201009142000.htm Accessed 15 May 2011.
Ding Sheng (2008) *The Dragon's Hidden Wings: How China Rises with its Soft Power*. Lanham: Lexington Books.
Donald, Stephanie Hemelryk (2002) Crazy rabbits! Children's media culture. In Donald, Stephanie Hemelryk, Keane, Michael and Yin, H. (eds.) *Media in China: Consumption, Content and Crisis*. Surrey: RoutledgeCurzon, pp. 128–38.
Donald, Stephanie Hemelryk (2005) *Little Friends: Children's Film and Media Culture in China*. Lanham: Rowman and Littlefield.
Dover, Bruce (2008) *Rupert's Adventures in China: How Murdoch Lost a Fortune and Found a Wife*. Sydney: Viking Press.
Dunning, John (ed.) (2000) *Regions, Globalization and the Knowledge-based Economy*. London: Oxford University Press.
Dutton, Michael (1998) *Streetlife China*. Cambridge: Cambridge University Press.
Duxbury, Nancy and Murray, Catherine (2010) Creative spaces. In Anheir, H. and Isar, Y. Raj (eds.) *Cultural Expression, Creativity and Innovation*. Los Angeles: Sage, pp. 200–14.
Elvin, Mark (1975) Skills and resources in late traditional China. In Perkins, D. H. (ed.) *China's Modern Economy in Historical Perspective*. Stanford: Stanford University Press, pp. 85–113.
Ergazakis, Kostas, Metaxiotis, Kosta and Psarras, John (2004) Towards knowledge cities: conceptual analysis and success stories. *Journal of Knowledge Management*, 8 (5), pp. 5–15.
Ergazakis, Kostas, Metaxiotis, Kosta, and Psarras, John (2006) An emerging pattern of successful knowledge cities' main features. In Carillo, Francisco J. (ed.) *Knowledge Cities: Approaches, Experiences and Perspectives*. Burlington, MA: Butterworth-Heinemann.
Evans, Graeme (2001) *Cultural Planning: an Urban Renaissance?* London: Routledge.
Evans, Graeme (2005) Measure for measure: evaluating the evidence of culture's contribution to regeneration. *Urban Studies* 42 (5/6), pp. 959–83.
Evans, Graeme (2009) Creative cities, creative spaces and urban policy. *Urban Studies* 46 (5), pp. 1003–40.
Faure, David (2006) *China and Capitalism: A History of Business Enterprise in Modern China*. Hong Kong: Hong Kong University Press.
Florida, Richard (1995) Toward the learning region. *Futures* 27 (5), pp. 527–36.
Florida, Richard (2002) *The Rise of the Creative Class*. New York: Basic Books.
Florida, Richard (2008) *Who's Your City?* New York: Basic Books.
Florida, Richard, and Tinagli, Irene (2004) Europe in the Creative Age, report funded by Alfred Sloan Foundation, co-published with DEMOS. Available at http://creativeclass.com/rfcgdb/articles/Europe_in_the_Creative_Age_2004.pdf Accessed 15 May 2011.

Foucault, Michel (1988) Technologies of the self. In Martin, L. Gutman, H. and Hutton, P. (eds.) *Technologies of the Self*. London: Tavistock, pp. 16–49.

Friedmann, John (2005) *China's Urban Transition*. Minneapolis: University of Minnesota Press.

Fuller, Steve (2006) *The Intellectual*. Cambridge: Totem Books.

Gardner, Howard (1993) *Creating Minds: an Anatomy of Creativity Seen through the Lives of Freud, Einstein, Picasso, Stravinsky, Eliot, Graham and Ghandi*. New York: Basic Books.

Gardner, Howard (2006) *The Development and Education of the Mind: the Selected Works of Howard Gardner*. London: Routledge.

Gertler, Meric S. (2008) Buzz without being there? Communities of practice in context. In Amin, A. and Roberts, J. (eds.). Oxford: Oxford University Press, pp. 203–26.

Gratton, Lynda (2007) *Hot Spots: Why Some Teams, Workplaces and Organzations Buzz With Energy and Why Some Don't*. San Francisco: Berrett-Koehler Publishers.

Gu Shulin and Lundvall, Bengt-Åke (2006) China's innovation system and the move towards harmonious growth and endogenous innovation. *Innovation, Management, Policy and Practice* 8, pp. 1–26.

Guenzi, Alberto (2009) Early industrial districts. In Beccattini, Giacomo Bellandi, Marco and de Propris, Lisa (eds.) *A Handbook of Industrial Districts*. Cheltenham: Edward Elgar, pp. 3–10.

Gunn, Simon (2008) How Manchester is amused. In Heßler, Martina and Zimmermann, Clemens (eds.) *Creative Urban Milieus: Historical Perspectives on Culture, Economy and the City*. Frankfurt: Campus Verlag, pp. 101–118.

Hall, David L. (1982) *The Uncertain Phoenix: Adventures Towards a Post-Cultural Sensibility*. New York: Fordham University Press.

Hall, David L. and Ames, Roger T. (1995) *Anticipating China: Thinking through the Narratives of Chinese and Western Culture*. Albany: State University of New York Press.

Hall, David L. and Ames, Roger T. (1998) *Thinking from the Han: Self, Truth and Transcendence in Chinese and Western Culture*. Albany: State University of New York Press.

Hangzhou Municipal Bureau of Statistics (2011) News Bulletin of Hangzhou's Economy 2010 (2010 nian Hangzhou jingji yunxing qingkuang xinwen tongbao). Available at: http://www.hzstats.gov.cn/web/ShowNews.aspx?id=-JompSP8oWdE=

Hansen, Mette Halskov and Svarverud, Rune (2010) *iChina: the Rise of the Individual in Modern Chinese Society*. Copenhagen: NIAS Press.

Hartley, John (2011) The urgency of interdisciplinarity: sooner or later we're going to need a cultural science. Presentation at Complexity Seminar Series, Queensland University of Technology, 1 April 2011.

He Dan (2011) 'Extravagant image projects criticizes', *China Daily Online*: http://www.chinadaily.com.cn/china/2011npc/2011-03/11/content_12152743.htm Accessed 16 May 2011.

He, Wenchao (2004) *718 gongchang: 798 yishu: yifen shehui shiyan de baogao* ('718 factory, 798 art: A report on a social experiment'). In Huang Rui (ed.) *Beijing 798: Reflections on art, Architecture and Society in China* (Chinese language section). Hong Kong: Timezone 8.

Hegel, Georg W.F. (1975) *Lectures on the Philosophy of World History: Introduction: Reason in History*. Translated by H.B. Nisbet. Cambridge: Cambridge University Press.

Henningsen, Lina (2010) *Copyright Matters: Imitation, Creativity and Authenticity in Contemporary Chinese Literature*. Belgium: Intersentia N.V.

Hermann-Pillath, Carsten (2010) *The Economics of Identity and Creativity: a Cultural Science Approach*. Brisbane: Queensland University Press.

Hodgson, Geoffrey (1999) *Economics and Utopia: Why the Learning Economy is Not the End of History*. London: Routledge.

Hong Kong General Chamber of Commerce (2003) Developing Hong Kong's creative industries – An action-oriented strategy. *Discussion paper by the Hong Kong General Chamber of Commerce* March 2003. Available online at http://www.chamber.org.hk/memberarea/chamber_view/others/Creative_industries.pdf Accessed 15 May 2011.

Howkins, John (2001) *The Creative Economy: How People Make Money from Ideas*. London: The Penguin Group.

Hu Huilin (2002) *Zai zijin de fazhan zhong baozhang Zhongguo de guoji wenhua anquan* ('While positively developing safeguard China's national cultural security'). *Wenyi bao*. 10 Oct 2002.

Hu Jintao (2007) Hold high the great banner of socialism with Chinese characteristics and strive for new victories in building a moderately prosperous society in all respects. Report to the 17th national Congress of the Communist party of China, October 15, 2007. English version available at http://www.bjreview.co.cn/document/txt/2007-11/20/content_86325.htm Accessed 08-02-08.

Huang, Philip C. C. (2011) The theoretical and practical implications of China's development experience: the role of informal economic practices. *Modern China* 37 (1) pp. 3–43.

Huang Yasheng (2008) *Capitalism with Chinese Characteristics: Entrepreneurship and the State*. Cambridge: Cambridge University Press.

Hui, Desmond (2006) From cultural to creative industries: Strategies for Chaoyang District, Beijing. *International Journal of Cultural Studies* 9(3), pp. 317–33.

Huot, Claire (2000) *China's New Cultural Scene: A Handbook of Changes*. Durham and New York: Duke University Press.

Iwabuchi, Koichi (2002) *Recentring Globalization: Popular Culture and Japanese Transnationalism*. Durham and London: Duke University Press.

Jacobs, Jane (1961) *The Death and Life of Great American Cities*. New York: Vintage Books.

Jiang, Wei (2008) Foshan's ceramics industry cracks up, *China Daily* 10 Nov 2008. Available at http://www.chinadaily.com/cn/bizchina/2008-11/10/content_7190536.htm

Johnson, Steven (2010) *Where Good Ideas Come From: the Natural History of Innovation*. New York: Riverhead Books.

Jullien, François (1995) *The Propensity of Things: Towards a History of Efficacy in China*. Translated by Janet Lloyd. New York: Zone Books.

Keane, Michael (2001) By the way, FUCK YOU! Feng Xiaogang's disturbing television dramas. *Continuum* 15 (1), pp. 57–66.

Keane, Michael (2002) Television drama in China: Engineering souls for the market. In King, Richard and Craig, Timothy (eds.) *Global Goes Local: Popular Culture in Asia.* University of British Colombia Press, pp. 176–202.
Keane, Michael (2007) *Created in China: The Great New Leap Forward.* London: Routledge.
Keane, Michael (2008) From National Preoccupation to Overseas Aspiration. In Zhui, Ying, Keane, Michael and Bai, Ruoyun (eds.), *TV Drama in China.* Hong Kong: Hong Kong University Press, pp. 145–6.
Keane, Michael (2009) Creative industries in China: four perspectives on social transformation. *The International Journal of Cultural Policy*, 15(4), pp. 431–43.
Keane, Michael (2009a) Between the tangible and the intangible: China's new development dilemma. *Chinese Journal of Communication*, 2(1), pp. 77–91.
Keane, Michael (2010) Keeping up with the neighbours: China's soft power ambitions. *Cinema Journal* 49 (3), pp. 130–5.
Keane, Michael and Liu, R. (2009) Independent television production, TV formats and media diversity in China In Moran, Albert (ed.) *TV Formats Worldwide: Global Flows in Television* Chicago: Chicago University Press, pp. 241–54.
Kenney, Martin (2000) (ed.) *Understanding Silicon Valley: The Anatomy of an Entrepreneurial Region.* Stanford: Stanford University Press.
Kenney, Martin and Florida, Richard (2004) Locating global advantage: industry dynamics in the international economy. Stanford: Stanford University Press.
Knight, Nick (2006) Reflecting on the paradox of globalisation: China's search for cultural identity and security. *China: an International Journal* 4 (1), pp. 1–31.
Kong Jianhua (2008) Further research on Beijing's Songzhuang original creation art cluster (*Beijing Songzhuang yuanchuang yishu jijuqu fazhan zai yanjiu*). In Qi Yongfeng (ed.) *China's Cultural Industries Year Book 2008* (*Zhongguo wenhua chanye xueshu nianjian*). Beijing: Culture and Art Publishing House, pp. 1165–9.
Kong, Lily (2009) Beyond networks and relations: towards rethinking cluster theory. In Kong, Lily and O'Connor, Justin (eds.) *Creative Economies: Creative Cities.* Dordrecht: Springer, pp. 61–76.
Kong, Lily, Gibson, Chris, Khoo, L-M. and Semple, A-L. (2006) Knowledges of the creative economy: towards a relational geography of diffusion and adaptation in Asia. *Asia Pacific Viewpoint* 47 (2), pp. 173–94.
Kotkin, Joel (2005) *The City: a Global History.* New York: Random House.
Kraus, Richard (2004) *The Party and the Arty: the New Politics of Culture.* Lanham, Boulder: Rowman and Littlefield.
Knight, Nick (2006) Reflecting on the paradox of globalisation: China's search for cultural identity and security. *China: an International Journal* 4 (1), pp. 1–31.
Krugman, Paul (1991) Increasing returns and economic geography. *Journal of Political Economy* 99, pp. 483–99.
Kuhn, Dieter (2009) *The Age of Confucian Rule: the Song Transformation of China.* Cambridge, MA: Harvard University Press.
Landry, Charles (2000) *The Creative City.* London: Comedia.
Landry, Charles (2006) *The Art of City Making.* London: Earthscan.
Lash, Scott and Lury, Celia (2007) *Global Culture Industry.* Cambridge: Polity Press.
Leadbeater, Charles (2008) *WE-THINK: Mass Innovation Not Mass Production.* London: Profile Books.

Leadbeater, Charles (2010) *Cloud Culture: The Future of Global Cultural Relations*. London: Counterpoint.
Leadbeater, Charles and Oakley, Kate (1999) *The Independents: Britain's New Cultural Entrepreneurs*. London: Demos.
Ledderose, Lothar (2000) *The Ten Thousand Things: Module and Mass Production in Chinese Art*. Princeton: Princeton University Press.
Lee Keehyeung (2008) Mapping out the cultural politics of the 'Korean Wave' in contemporary South Korea. In Chua B-H and Iwabuchi (eds.) *East Asian Pop Culture*. Hong Kong: HKU Press, pp. 175–90.
Lemoine, Francoise and Ünal-Kesenci, Deniz (2004) Assembly trade and technology transfer: The case of China. *World Development* 32(5), pp. 829–50.
Lent, John A. (2001) *Animation in Asia and the Pacific*. Bloomington: Indiana University Press.
Lévy-Bruhl, L. (1923) *Primitive Mentality* [translated by Lilian A. Clare from *La Mentalité Primitive* (Paris, 1922)] London, 1923.
Li Lanqing (2009) *Breaking Through: the Birth of China's Opening Up Policy*. Translated by Ling Yuan and Zhang Siying. New York: Oxford University Press.
Li Lillian, Dray-Novey, Alison and Kong, Haili (2007) *Beijing: From Imperial Capital to Olympic City*. Basingstoke: Palgrave Macmillan.
Li Wuwei (2009) *Chuangyi gaibian Zhongguo [Creativity is Changing China]*. Beijing: Xinhua Publishing.
Li Wuwei (2011) *How Creativity is Changing China*. In Keane, Michael (ed.). Translated by Keane, Michael, Li, Hui and Guo, Meijun. London: Bloomsbury Academic Press.
Li Yilin (2008) Not every product is suitable for launching here. In Chang Lei and Zhu Qi (eds.) *Beijing 798 Now*. Beijing: Timezone 8 Books, p. 168.
Li Zhang (2001) *Strangers in the City: Reconfigurations of Space, Power, and Social Networks*. Stanford: Stanford University Press.
Liang Zai (1999) Foreign investment, economic growth and temporary migration: the case of Shenzhen Special Economic Zone, China. *Development and Society* 28 (1), pp. 115–37.
Liu Chang (2008) Policy sprawl: the internal logic of spatial production. In Mars, Neville and Hornsby, Adrian (eds.) *The Chinese Dream: a Society Under Construction*. Amsterdam: 010 Publishers, pp. 286–338.
Liu Kai (2008) Creative edge of cities: a comparative analysis of the top 500 creative industries businesses in Beijing and Shanghai. *Creative Industries Journal* 3 (1), pp. 227–44.
Liu Shifa (2004) Implementing the creative century plan and promoting the creative China campaign. *The Second International Forum on China Cultural Industries Anthology*. Beijing: People's Daily Press.
Liu Xiaoshi (1997) Liang Szechen's planning scheme for Beijing: A historic proposal. *Ekistics* 64 (385-387): 251–4.
Liu Yan and Chen Xu (2008) Ecstaquarter on Huangpu River: an interview with the director of one of Shanghai's most innovative creative clusters. *Creative Industries Journal* 1 (3), pp. 275–82.
Lloyd, Geoffrey. E. R. (2007) *Cognitive Variations: Reflections on the Unity and Diversity of the Human Mind*. Oxford: Clarendon Press.

Lloyd, Geoffrey and Sivin, Nathan (2002) *The Way and the Word: Science and Medicine in Early China and Greece*. New Haven: Yale University Press.
Lu Di (2005) *Explorations on Private Television in China* (in Chinese). Shanghai: Fudan University Press.
Lundvall, B-A. Johnson, B., Andersen, E. S. and Dalum, B. (2007) National systems of production, innovation, and competence-building. In Polenske, K. (ed.) *The Economic Geography of Innovation*. Cambridge: Cambridge University Press, pp. 213–40.
Ma Gengshen (2009) Tianjin's home-grown comic books venture into the world market. *Jinwan bao*, p. 1. Retrieved 29 September from http://www.jwb.com.cn/jwb/html/2009-09/14/content_378679.htm
Ma Yuezhu (2008) *Fermented in Songzhuang* (*Zhang zai Songzhuang de mao*) (*Lanzhou Shi: Gansu meishu chuban she*, vii (in Chinese).
McAndrew, Clare (2011) Art market report: a new global landscape, available at: http://www.tefaf.com/DesktopDefault.aspx?tabid=78, accessed 20/03/2011.
McGee, T. G., Lin, George, C. S., Marton, Andrew, Mark Y.L. Wang and Wu Jiaping (2007) *China's Urban Space: Development Under Market Socialism*. London: Routledge.
McGray, Douglas (2002) Japan's Gross National Cool. *Foreign Policy Journal*. Retrieved 18 August 2008 from www.foreignpolicy.com/story/files/story178.php
Makeham, John (2003) *Transmitters and Creators: Chinese Commentators and Commentaries on the Analects*. Cambridge, MA: Harvard University Press.
Mangurian, Robert and Ray, Mary-Ann (2009) Urban rural conundrums: Off centre people space in Caochangdi, Beijing. In Mangurian, Robert and Ray, Mary-Ann (eds.) *Caochangdi: Beijing Inside Out*. Hong Kong: Timezone 8, pp. 423–36.
Mao, Isaac (nd) 'Sharism: a Mind Revolution'. Online resource available at http://freesouls.cc/essays/07-isaac-mao-sharism.html Accessed 16 May 2011.
Mao Qizhi and Jin Ying (1997) Development issues and planning strategies in the Beijing metropolitan region. *Ekistics* 64 (385-387), pp. 203–10.
Mao Zedong (1940) *Xin minzhuzhuyi lun* ('On new democracy'), *Zhongguo wenhua* 1, 15 Feb 1940, in Denton, K. (ed.), *Modern Chinese Literary Thought: writings on literature 1893–1945*. Stanford: Stanford University Press.
Mao Zedong (1971) *Selected Readings from the Works of Mao Tse-tung*. Beijing: Foreign Languages Press.
Mars, Neville and Hornsby, Adrian (2008) *The Chinese Dream: a Society Under Construction*. Rotterdam: NAI Publishers.
Marshall, Alfred (1920/1990) *The Principles of Economics* [1920], 8th edition. Philadelphia: Porcupine.
Martin, Ron, and Sunley, Peter (2003) Deconstructing clusters: chaotic concept or policy panacea? *Journal of Economic Geography* 3(1), pp. 5–35.
MoC (2008) *Ministry of Culture launched the project to support original cartoon and animation*. Retrieved 20 September 2009 from http://www.mcprc.gov.cn/xxfb/xwzx/whxw/200810/t20081006_58290.html.
Mockros, Carol and Csikszentmihályi, Mihályi (1999) The social construction of creative lives. In Montuori, Alfonso, and Purser, Ronald, E. (eds.) *Social Creativity Volume 1*. New Jersey: Hampton Press, pp. 175–218.
Mokyr, Joel (2002) *The Gifts of Athena: Historical Origins of the Knowledge Economy*. Princeton: Princeton University Press.

Mommaas, Hans (2004) Cultural clusters and the post-industrial city: Towards the remapping of urban cultural policy. *Urban Studies* 41(3), pp. 507–32.

Mommaas, Hans (2009) Spaces of culture and economy: mapping the cultural-creative landscape. In Kong, Lily and O'Connor, Justin (eds.) *Creative Economies: Creative Cities*. Dordrecht: Springer, pp. 45–60.

Montgomery, John (2003) Cultural quarters as mechanism for urban regeneration. Part 1 Conceptualising cultural quarters. *Planning Practice and Research* 18 (4), pp. 293–306.

Montgomery, John (2010) *The New Wealth of Cities: City Dynamics and the Fifth Wave*. Aldershot: Ashgate.

Montgomery, Lucy (2010) *China's Creative Industries: Copyright, Social Network Markets and the Business of Culture in a Digital Age*. Cheltenham: Edward Elgar.

Montgomery, Lucy and Keane, Michael (2006) Learning to love the market: Copyright, culture and China. In Thomas, Pradip and Servaes, Jan (eds.) *Intellectual Property Rights and Communications in Asia: Conflicting Traditions*. New Delhi: Sage Publications, pp. 130–48.

Moran, Seana (2009) Creativity: a systems perspective. In Rickards Tudor, Runco, Mark and Moger, Susan (eds.) *The Routledge Companion to Creativity*. London: Routledge, pp. 292–301.

Munro, Donald J. (1996) *The Imperial Style of Enquiry in Twentieth Century China*. Anne Arbor, MI: Centre for Chinese Studies.

Napoli, Philip (2003) *Audience Economics: Media Institutions and the Marketplace*. New York: Columbia University Press.

Needham, Joseph (1969) *The Grand Titration: Science and Society in East and West*. London: George Allen and Unwin.

Nisbett, Richard E. (2003) *The Geography of Thought: How Asians and Westerners Think Differently... and Why*. New York: Free Press.

Nooteboom, Bart (2008) Cognitive distance in and between communities of practice and firms: where do exploration and exploitation take place and how are they connected? In Amin, Ash and Roberts, Joanne (eds) *Community, Economic Creativity and Organization*. London: Oxford University Press, pp. 123–47.

Nowotny, Helga (2008) *Insatiable Curiosity: Innovation in a Fragile Future*. Cambridge, MA: MIT Press.

Nye, Joseph (1990) *Bound to Lead: The Changing Nature of American Power*. New York: Basic Books.

Oakley, Kate (2004) Not so cool Britannia: the role of creative industries in economic development. *International Journal of Cultural Studies* 7 (1), pp. 67–77.

Oakley, Kate (2012 forthcoming) In its own image: New Labour and the cultural workforce. *Cultural Trends*, Special Issue *'A Golden Age': Reflecting on New Labour's Cultural Policy and its Post-Recession Legacy*.

Ochs, Alexander (2008) The quality of 798 has improved but it hasn't changed for the better. In Chang Lei and Zhu Qi (eds.) *Beijing 798 Now*. Beijing: Timezone 8 Books, pp. 186–7.

O'Connor, Justin and Gu, Xin (2006) A new modernity: the arrival of creative industries in China. *International Journal of Cultural Studies* 9 (3) pp. 271–84.

O'Mara, Margaret (2005) *Cities of Knowledge: Cold War Science and the Search for the Next Silicon Valley*. Princeton, NJ: Princeton University Press.

Oyama, Shinji (2009) The East Asian brandscape: distribution of Japanese brands in the age of globalization. In Berry, Chris, Liscutin, Nicola and Mackintosh, Jonathan D. (eds.) *Cultural Studies and Cultural Industries in Northeast Asia.* Hong Kong: HKU Press, pp. 135–50.

Pang, Laikwan (2006) *Cultural Control and Globalization in Asia: Copyright, Piracy, and Cinema.* London: Routledge.

Pang, Laikwan (2009) The transgression of sharing and copying: pirating Japanese animation in China. In Berry, Chris, Liscutin, Nicola and Mackintosh, Jonathan D. (eds.) *Cultural Studies and Cultural Industries in North-East Asia.* Hong Kong University Press, pp. 119–34.

Pease, Rowan (2009) Korean pop music in China: nationalism, authenticity and gender. In Berry, Chris, Liscutin, Nicola and Mackintosh, Jonathan D. (eds.) *Cultural Studies and Cultural Industries in Northeast Asia.* Hong Kong: HKP Press, pp. 151–68.

Peck, Jamie (2005) Struggling with the creative class. *International Journal of Urban and Rural Research* 29 (4), pp. 740–70.

People's Daily Online (2006) China's Cultural Trade Deficit on the Rise. 19 April 2006. http://english.people.com.cn/200504/15/print20050415_181119.html (accessed 28 April 2009).

Piccioni, Monica (2008) There's been an influx of inadequately qualified investors. In Chang Lei and Zhu Qi (eds.) *Beijing 798 Now.* Beijing: Timezone 8 Books, pp. 162–5.

Pollack, Barbara (2010) *The Wild, Wild East: An American Art Critic's Adventures in China.* Beijing: Timezone 8 Publishing, p. 12.

Pope, Rob (2005) *Creativity: Theory, History and Practice.* London: Routledge.

Porter, Michael (1996) Competitive advantage, agglomeration economies and regional policy. *International Regional Science Review* 19(1), pp. 85–94.

Porter, Michael (1990) *The Competitive Advantage of Nations.* New York: Free Press.

Porter, Michael (1998) Clusters and the new economics of competition. *Harvard Business Review* Nov-Dec., pp. 77–90.

Potts, Jason (2011) *Creative Industries and Economic Evolution.* Cheltenham: Edward Elgar.

Potts, Jason, Cunningham, Stuart, Hartley, John and Ormerod, Paul (2008) Social network markets: A new definition of creative industries. *Journal of Cultural Economics* 32 (3), pp. 167–85.

Potts, Jason and Cunningham, Stuart (2008) Four models of the creative industries *International Journal of Cultural Policy* 14 (3), pp. 233–48.

Puett, Michael J. (2001) *The Ambivalence of Creation: Debates Concerning Innovation and Artifice in Early China.* Stanford CA: Stanford University Press.

Qian Gong (2008) A trip down memory lane: remaking and rereading the red classics. In Zhu, Ying, Keane, Michael and Bai, Ruoyun (eds.) *TV Drama in China,* Hong Kong: HKU Press, pp. 157–72.

Rehn, Alf and De Cock, Christian (2009) Deconstructing creativity. In Rickards, Tudor, Runco, Mark and Moger, Susan (eds.) *The Routledge Companion to Creativity.* London: Routledge, pp. 222–31.

Renmin (2011) *China Cultural Industry Development Index Research.* Report prepared by Renmin University.

Rifkin, Joel (2000) *The Age of Access: How the Shift from Ownership to Access is Transforming Work.* London: Penguin.

Rodríguez-Clare, A. (2007) Clusters and comparative advantage: Implications for industrial policy. *Journal of Development Economics*, 82 (1), pp. 43–57.

Roodhouse, Simon (2006) *Cultural Quarters: Principles and Practice.* Chicago: University of Chicago Press.

Ruiz, Christine (2011) For Guy Ullens, the dream of a Chinese art museum 'is over', *The Art Newspaper* online. Available at http://www.theartnewspaper.com/articles/For+Guy+Ullens,+the+dream+of+a+Chinese+art+museum+%E2%80%9Cis+over%E2%80%9D/23179 Accessed 15 May 2011.

SARFT (2010) *Report on Development of China's Radio, Film and Television.* Beijing: Xin Hua Press (China).

Schell, Orville (1995) *Mandate of Heaven: A New Generation of Entrepreneurs, Dissidents, Bohemians and Technocrats Lays Claim to China's Future.* New York: Simon & Schuster.

Scott, Allan J. (2004) The other Hollywood: the organizational and geographical bases of television-program production. *Media Culture and Society* 26 (2), pp. 183–205.

Sennett, Richard (2008) *The Craftsman*, London: Penguin Books.

Shang, Dan and Doulet, Jean-Francois and Keane, Michael (2009) Urban informatics in China: exploring the emergence of the Chinese City 2.0. In Foth, Marcus (ed.) *Handbook of Research on Urban Informatics: The Practice and Promise of the Real-Time City.* Hershey, PA: Information Science Reference, IGI Global, pp. 379–90.

Shenkar, Oded (2010) *Copycats: How Smart Companies Use Imitation to Gain a Strategic Edge.* Boston, MA: Harvard Business School.

Shim, Doobo (2006) Hybridity and the rise of Korean popular culture in Asia. *Media, Culture and Society* 28(1), pp. 25–44.

Shim, Doobo (2008) The growth of Korean cultural industries and the Korean Wave. In Chua Beng-Huat and Iwabuchi, Koichi (eds.) *East Asian Pop Culture.* Hong Kong: HKU Press, pp.15–32.

Shin, Hyun Bang (2010) 'Urban conservation and revalorisation of dilapidated historic quarters' the case of nanluoguxiang in Beijing. *Cities* 27: S43–S54.

Shinohara, Hiroyuki (2009) Mutation of Tianzifang: Taikang Road, Shanghai. Paper presented at the 4th International Conference of the International Forum on Urbanism (IFoU), 26–28 November 2009 Amsterdam/Delft.

Shu Yang (2008) An art district is not a cultural industrial park. In Chang Lei and Zhu Qi (eds.) *Beijing 798 Now.* Beijing: Timezone 8 Books, p. 136–7.

Smith, Karen (2008) The heart of the art. In Pearson, Alexandra and Cavender, Lucy (eds.) *Beijing:Portrait of a City.* Hong Hong: The Middle Kingdom Bookworm, pp. 106–21.

Storper, Michael (1997) *The Regional World: Territorial Development in a Global Economy.* New York: Guilford.

Storper, Michael and Venables, Anthony J. (2004) Buzz: face to face contact and the urban economy. *Journal of Economic Geography* 4, pp. 351–70.

Sugden, Roger, Wei Ping and Wilson, James (2006) Clusters, governance and the development of local economies: a framework for case studies. In Pitelis, Christos, Sugden, Roger and Wilson, James R. (eds.) *Clusters and Globalisation: the Development of Urban and Regional Economies.* Cheltenham: Edward Elgar, pp. 82–95.

Sun Wanning (2010) Mission impossible? Soft power, communication capacity, and the globalization of Chinese media. *International Journal of Communication* 4, pp. 54–72.

Swedberg, Richard (2006) The cultural entrepreneur and the creative industries: beginning in Vienna. *Journal of Cultural Economics* 30, pp. 243–61.

Tang, S. and B. Li (2005) *The Research on Reforming the Production System and Developing Television Industry*. Beijing: China Communication University Press.

Tatsuno, Sheridan (1990) *Created in Japan: From Imitators to World-class Innovators*. New York: Harper and Row.

Taub-Pervizpour, Lora (2004) Independent production companies. In Newcomb, Horace (ed.) *Encyclopaedia of Television*. 2nd edition. New York: Fitzroy Dearbourn.

Teng Ssu-yü and Fairbank, J. K. (1979) *China's Response to the West: a Documentary Survey*. Cambridge, MA: Harvard University Press.

Throsby, David (2010) *The Economics of Cultural Policy*. Cambridge: Cambridge UP.

Tsai, Kellee, S. (2006) Adaptive informal institutions and endogenous institutional change in China. *World Politics* (October), pp. 116–41.

Ulfstjerne, Michael (2009) *Originality and Imitation: The Production of Artistic Value in the Songzhuang Artist Community as Ideology and Praxis* (unpublished master's thesis). Copenhagen Business School.

UNCTAD (2008) *Creative Economy Report 2008*. Geneva: United Nations.

UNCTAD (2010) *Creative Economy Report 2010*. Geneva: United Nations.

Van Doren, Charles (1991) *A History of Knowledge: Past, Present and Future*. New York: Random House.

Van Oech, Roger (1986) *A Kick in the Seat of the Pants*: New York: Harper Paperbacks.

Visser, Robin (2004) Space of disappearance: Aesthetic responses to contemporary Beijing city planning. *Journal of Contemporary China* 13 (39), pp. 2777–3310.

Voci, Paola (2010) *China on Video: Smaller Screen Realities*. London: Routledge.

Voltaire (1828) *Oeuvres completes de Voltaire*. Paris: Baudouin Frères.

Wang, Jici (2007) Industrial clusters in China: the low road versus the high road in cluster development. In Scott, Allen and Garofoli, Giacocchino (eds.) *Development on the Ground: Clusters, Networks and Regions in Emerging Economies*. London: Routledge, pp. 145–64.

Wang, Jici (2007a) Incubators for culture and creative industries: clusters vs parks'. (in Chinese). In Zhang Xiaoming, Ying Caolong and Li Ping (eds.) *Blue Book of International Cultural Industry Development Report*. Beijing: Social Sciences Academic Press, pp. 361–66.

Wang, Jici, Zhang, Chun, Wang, Ching-Ning and Chen, Ping (2010) Local milieu in developing China's cultural and creative industry: the case of Nanluoguxiang in Beijing. *International Journal of Asian Business and Information Management* 1 (1), pp. 10–22.

Wang, Jici and Mei, Lixia (2009) Trajectories and prospects of industrial districts in China. In Becattini, Giacomo, Bellandi, Marco, and de Propris, Lisa (eds.), *A Handbook of Industrial Districts*. Cheltenham: Edward Elgar Press, pp. 598–612.

Wang Jing (2004) The global reach of new discourses: How far can creative industries travel? *International Journal of Cultural Studies*, 7 (1), pp. 9–19.

Wang Jun (2006) City lost. *Volume Special Issue Ubiquitous China*, 2: pp. 72–7.
Wang Ning (2008) Rethinking modern Chinese literature in a global context. *Modern Language Quarterly* 69 (1), pp. 1–11.
Wang Yingyao (2006) Visible top, invisible home: *ke jian de dingceng he bu ke jian de jia*, Cultural Studies). *Wenhua yanjiu* (in Chinese) 4 (90), pp. 107–12.
Wang Yongzhang (2007) An exploratory analysis of 'cultural' and 'creative' industry (*wenhua chanye yu chuangyi chanye tanxi*). In Zhang, Xiaoming, Hu, Huilin and Jiangang, Zhou (eds.) *The Blue Book of China's Culture: Report on Developments of China's Cultural Industry*. Beijing: Social Science Academic Press.
Williams, Raymond (1988) *Key Words: a Vocabulary of Culture and Society*. London: Fontana Press.
Wong, Isabel K. F. (2002) The incantation of Shanghai: singing a city into existence. In Craig, Timothy and King, Richard (eds.) *Global Goes Local: Popular Culture in Asia*. Vancouver: UBC Press, pp. 246–64.
Wu, Fulong, Xu, Jiang and Yeh, Anthony Gar-on (2007) *Urban Development in Post-Reform China: State, Market and Place*. London: Routledge.
Wu, Liangyong (1999) *Rehabilitating the Old City of Beijing: a Project in the Ju'er Hutong Neighbourhood*. Vanvouver: UBC Press.
Wu Si (2000) *Qian guize: Zhongguo lishi zhong de zhenshi youxi* ('The Real Games of Chinese History'). Kunming: Yunnan People's Publishing.
Wu Zhenhuan (2007) I try to explain but words escape me. Preface to Wu Zhenhuan (ed.), *Songzhuang Original Creative*. Beijing: Songzhuang Publications, p. 2.
Wu Weiping (2005) Dynamic cities and creative clusters. World Bank Policy Research Working Paper Series #3509.
Xinhua (2000) 'China's culture sector goes to market', *China Daily*, Nov 27, 2000, p. 4.
Yu Dan (2009) *Confucius from the Heart: Ancient Wisdom for Today's World*. English version translated by Esther Tyldesley, London: Macmillan, originally published 2006 by Zhonghua Book Company.
Yúdice, George (2003) *The Expediency of Culture: Uses of Culture in the Global Era*. Durham and London: Duke University Press.
Yue, Xiaodong and Radowicz, Elizabeth (2002) Perceptions of the most creative Chinese people by undergraduates in Beijing, Guangzhou, Hong Kong and Taipei. *Journal of Creative Behaviour* 36 (2), pp. 88–104.
Zha, Jianying (1995) *China Pop: How Soap Operas, Tabloids, and Bestsellers are Transforming a Culture*. New York: The New Press.
Zhang, Hongxing (2008) Shenzhen: frontier city. In Zhang Hongxing and Lauren Parker (eds.) *China Design Now*. London: V&A Publishing, pp. 42–52.
Zhang, Jingcheng (ed.) (2009) *The Blue Book of China's Creative Industry Development Report*. Beijing: China Economic Press.
Zhang, Xiaoming (2006) From institution to industry: reforms in cultural institutions in China. In Keane, Michael and Hartley, John (eds.) *International Journal of Cultural Studies*. Special Issue: Creative Industries and Innovation in China 9 (3), pp. 297–306.
Zhang, Xiaoming (2008) China's cultural products and 'going out' strategy. In Zhang Xiaoming, Hu Huilin and Zhou Jiangang (eds.) *Bluebook of China's Cultural Industries* (in Chinese). Beijing: CASS.

Zhang, Xiaoming, Hu, Huilin and Zhou, Jiangang (eds.) (2006) *The Blue Book of China's Cultural Industries*. Beijing: Social Sciences Academic Press.
Zhao, Yanrong (2009) Bar, restaurant restrictions for Nannlouguxiang. *China Daily*, available online http://www.chinadaily.com.cn/metro/2009-11/26/content_9054984.htm
Zheng, Jane (2010) The 'Entrepreneurial state' in 'creative industry cluster' development in Shanghai, *Journal of Urban Affairs* 32 (2), pp. 143–70.
Zhou, Yanping (2005) An analysis of the Sanchen Cartoon Company. In Zhang Xiaoming, Hu Huilin and Zhou Jiangang (eds.) *The Blue Book of China's Culture 2005*. Beijing: Beijing Social Sciences Press, pp. 300–6.
Zhou, Rong (2006) Upon the ruins of utopia. *Volume* Special Issue Ubiquitous China 2, pp. 43–7.
Zhou, Yu (2005) An analysis of the Sanchen Cartoon Company. In Zhang, Xiaoming, Hu, Huilin and Zhou, Jiangang (eds.) *The Blue Book of China's Culture 2005* Beijing: Beijing Social Sciences Press (in Chinese), pp. 300–6.
Zhou Yu (2008) *The Inside Story of China's High-Tech Industry: Making Silicon Valley in Beijing*. Lanham: Rowman and Littlefield.
Zhu Jianfei (2003) *Chinese Spatial Strategies: Imperial Beijing 1420–1911*. London: RoutledgeCurzon.
Zimmermann, Clemens (2008) The productivity of the city in the early modern era: the book and art trade in Venice and London. In Heßler, Martina and Zimmermann, Clemens (eds.) *Creative Urban Milieus: Historical Perspectives on Culture, Economy and the City*. Frankfurt: Campus Verlag, pp. 41–77.
Zukin, Sharon (2010) *Naked City: The Death and Life of Authentic Urban Places*. Oxford: Oxford University Press.

Interviews

Artist, anon: Songzhuang October 2010
Chang, Shaun, IFA (InFocusAsia, Beijing), March 2011
Xu, Chen (Xindanwei), Shanghai, March 2011
Du Yubo LOFT49, Hangzhou, September 2010
Lee, Roger, Acewood, Beijing March 2011
Li Huailiang, Director of China National Cultural Trade Research Centre, Beijing March 2011
Liu, Yan (Xindanwei) Shanghai, October 2009, March 2011
Christopher Mahoney, Elevation Workshop, Beijing, March 2011
Qiu Dailun CEO Foshan Creative Industries Park: May 2009, October 2010
Shi Wen, President Hollywood (China) Digital Arts Research and Development Centre, Wuxi Animation Park, May 2008
Song Bo, IINShanghai, Shanghai, October 2010
Wei Na, Elevation Workshop, Beijing, March 2011
Wang, Carol, Shangtex, Shanghai, September 2010
Wang, Jonathan CEO GreatDreams Cartoon Group, May 2008
Wang, Tom CEO Digital Hollywood, Beijing, May 2008; October 2010
Yu, George Suzhou Hong Yang Cartoon Company Ltd., Suzhou, May 2008
Zhang Xiaoming, Chinese Academy of Social Sciences, March 2011

Index

798 Art Zone 7, 40, 52–3, 58, 67, 71–3, 81, 86, 96, 98, 105–7, 109, 111–12, 115, 148, 161, 176

aaajiao 130, 131
Ai Weiwei 9, 112–13, 116–17
adaptation 7, 33, 35, 160, 167–9, 176–7
adaptive creativity 169
Ames, Roger 167
Anderrson, Åke 39
Angremy, Bernice 106
animation 18, 21, 26, 31, 51–4, 59–60, 64, 68, 71, 86–7, 96, 139–40, 142–6, 149–57, 161, 165, 176
anime 18, 21, 149–50
art worlds 98–101, 107
Arthur, Brian 166

Banks, Mark 21
Becker, Howard 99–100
Beijing CBD International Media Industry Cluster (also Capital Media District) 12, 139, 146–7
Beijing Cultural and Creative Industries Promotion Centre 87–8
Beijing Olympics 14, 16, 86, 94, 106, 113
Beijingers in New York (*Beijing ren zai Niuyue*) 81
Bergson, Henri 166, 169
Bernell, Robert 105, 107
black market (piracy) 18, 129, 166
bohemians 42, 45, 52, 135
BOP Consulting 28, 131
Breznitz, Dan 8, 145, 148, 170
Bridge 8 12, 118, 126

Can, Xin 106
Caochangdi 11, 80, 98, 112–13, 116
Cattle Depot Art Village 27
CCTV Towers 85, 147
celebrities 19, 74, 76, 94, 126, 177
chanye 26, 34, 55, 144, 182
Chaoyang district 64, 67, 71, 81, 82, 93, 96, 97, 104, 106, 112, 130, 139, 146–8
Chen, Guanzhong 80
Chen, Xu 130–4
Chen, Yifei 8, 104, 120, 123, 127
Chongqing 22, 54, 56, 119, 155
Ci, Jiwei 24
cloud culture 130, 173
cluster: definition 10, 32, 37–40, 48; industrial clusters 3–5, 32, 49–51, 68, 77, 135, 143, 174
competitive advantage 2, 38, 45, 48, 60–1, 138, 148
Confucius, Confucian 16, 24, 34, 62, 67, 89, 101, 129, 162–4, 167, 176, 178
copyright 6, 26, 87, 142–3, 151, 156, 168–9, 171–2
co-working 12, 119, 129–34
creative: cities 38–9, 41–4; class 3, 35, 44, 47, 59, 67, 79, 98, 116, 123, 125, 135; community 91–2, 95, 132; destruction 66, 145, 157, 173; economy 6–7, 10, 17, 20–2, 35, 46–7, 119, 165, 168, 171–4; human capital 4, 45, 50, 57, 59, 64, 70, 123, 145, 148
Creative Shanghai Riverside 12, 72, 118
creativity, definition 7–9
Csikszentmihályi, Mihaly 9

Cui, Yongyuan 177
cultural: diversity 1, 3, 139; economy 6, 7, 10, 15, 29, 32, 38, 43, 50, 61, 64, 86, 97, 160–1, 182; exports 26, 115, 143, 145; industries 5, 21, 23, 27–30, 33–4, 47, 50, 55, 59, 65, 79–82, 85, 100, 108, 113, 128, 171–2; infrastructure 38–9, 44, 67; innovation ecology 31; insecurity 19, 160; quarters 39–40, 46–7, 52, 57–8, 60, 70, 76–7, 96, 121, 174; regeneration 38–9; security 23, 141
Cunningham, Stuart 29, 43–5
Curtin, Michael 139, 145
Cyberport 42, 123

Dafen village 113–15
Dalian 33, 155–6, 52–4, 56
DCMS (Department for Media Culture and Sport) 21, 34, 82, 172, 180
Deng, Kunyan 72
Deng Xiaoping 1, 4, 25, 112, 114, 140, 164, 174, 178
Du, Yubo 71–2, 74
Durkheim, Emile 41, 45
Duxbury, Nancy 49

entrepreneurs, entrepreneurship 8, 20, 42, 49, 51, 53, 61, 64, 66–8, 70, 79, 81, 98, 112, 114, 126, 130, 132, 134–5, 142, 145, 157, 161, 168, 173–4
epistemic communities 11, 35, 57, 61, 79, 96, 175
Evans, Graeme 43–4

FAKE (Ai Weiwei) 112, 116
Fangjia 46, 78–9, 89–96, 175
farmers 76, 101, 109–12
Feng, Xiaogang 81
floating populations 80, 102
Florida, Richard 3, 44–5, 47, 123
Foshan Creative Industries Park 57, 68–70
Fuller, Steve 165

Gardner, Howard 41, 162–4
Gehua Cultural Development Group 88
gentrification 30, 56, 59, 76, 89, 123, 125
'going out' (*zou chuqu*) 62, 143, 174
governmentality 101
global (economic) financial crisis 16, 21, 68, 70, 89, 171
grassroots culture 30, 132, 160, 173, 177–8
Greenwich Village 5, 53
growth coalitions 11, 21, 51, 53, 57, 61, 78–9, 135, 178
guanxi 94, 135, 146, 152
Guenzi, Alberto 47
Gu, Xin 135–6
Gunn, Simon 43

Hall, David 167
Hall, Peter 45
Hangzhou 53–4, 56, 64, 70–7, 83, 108, 155–6
harmony, harmonisation, harmonious 2, 14–15, 17, 22, 24, 34, 35, 97, 110, 160, 168, 173, 179
harmonious society 17, 62, 111, 174
Hartley, John 172–3
Hengdian World Studios (Chinawood) 52, 54, 138, 145
Hollywood 23, 38, 54, 120, 126, 138–9, 141, 154, 160
Hong Kong 19, 27–8, 31, 42, 44, 56, 58, 67–8, 72, 79, 89, 92, 94, 98, 102, 113–15, 120–3, 139–40, 145
Houhai 81, 89, 95, 105
Howkins, John 6, 21, 46, 74, 125, 131
Hu, Jintao 17
Huang, Philip 62–3
Huang, Rui 105
Huang, Yasheng 12, 135
Huashan 1914 Creative Park 58
hukou 85, 128
hutong 11, 78, 82, 89–91, 94–5

imitation 7, 9, 26, 32, 113, 146, 154, 164, 170, 172, 178
incubators, incubation 3, 10, 30, 32–3, 40, 49, 52, 54, 96, 160, 177
independent, independents 6, 12, 17, 20, 25–6, 32, 62, 90, 92–3, 119, 138, 140, 143–5, 177
individualism 1, 17, 30
informal economies, institutions 11, 160, 173, 175–6
innovation 1–10, 15, 17, 21, 25, 30, 33–5, 55–62, 67–70, 73, 75–7, 78, 81, 82, 86, 90, 116, 119, 123, 130, 140–3, 146, 150, 156, 160–1, 164–79; endogenous 8, 73; independent 17, 22, 86; second generation 55
innovative milieu 3, 11, 122; nation 1,

22, 46, 62, 99
intellectual property (IP) 9, 21, 26, 32–3, 35, 60, 69, 86, 133, 142, 160, 164, 169, 171–2, 176
interactive learning 49, 58, 60
International Creative Industries Alliance (ICIA) 79, 87–8, 91

Jacobs, Jane 45–7
Johnson, Stephen 166
Jullien, Francois 168

KIC (Knowledge Innovation Community) 12, 52, 54, 123, 125
Koolhaas, Rem 85
Korea 18, 19, 32, 53, 79, 139–40, 141–5, 149–51
Korean Wave 19, 32, 142–3
Kotkin, Joel 43
Kraus, Richard 21, 63, 100, 103
Kuhn, Dieter 41

Landry, Charles 39, 43–4
land speculation 60
land use regulations 35, 43, 61, 63–4, 92, 112, 116
Leadbeater, Charlie 20, 129–30
learning regions 3, 38, 44
Ledderose, Luther 48, 166–8
Li, Hongzhang 24
Li, Huailiang 115, 141
Li, Lanqing 24
Liang, Sicheng 83
Li Wuwei 17, 22, 35, 62, 121, 133, 171–3, 181
Li, Xianting 103
Li, Yilin 107
Liu, Shifa 172
Liu, Yan 130–4
local government 1, 2, 4, 7, 10–12, 25, 35, 40, 47, 55, 57, 62–6, 68, 71, 76, 80, 91–2, 96, 98, 105–8, 116, 119, 127, 132, 152, 155–6, 161, 174, 176, 179
localised external economies 10, 39, 48
lock-in effects 2, 176
LOFT 49 52, 70–4
low-cost production 138
Lu Xun 8, 24
Lundvall, Bengt-Åke 38
Luo, Xuan 148

M50 12, 72, 118, 126–9
Made in China 7, 16–17, 26–7, 69, 88, 153, 171–2
Mao, Isaac (Social Brain Foundation) 129
Mao Zedong 1, 4, 17, 84, 102, 107, 115, 120, 126, 178
manga 18
Mangurian, Robert 84, 112
Marshall, Alfred 3, 10, 39
Martin, Ron 37
Marxism 24, 27
Mommaas, Hans 37
Montgomery, J. 46
Multimedia Super Corridor 42
Mumford, Lewis 45
Murdoch, Rupert 141
Murphree, Michael 8, 55, 145–6, 148, 170
Murray, Catherine 49

Nanluoguxiang 11, 52, 59, 78, 89–91, 95
Napoli, Philip 140
New socialist countryside 62, 111
novelty 6, 49, 51, 68, 164–5, 168–71
Nowotny, Helga 166

Oakley, Kate 20
Ochs, Alexander 107
O'Connor, Justin 21, 135–6
Old Millfun (1933) 12, 118, 125–6
Open Door Policy 30
Opium Wars 10, 15, 24
originality 6, 9, 13, 47, 99, 101, 157, 165, 167–8, 171
outsourcing 9, 19, 26, 40, 54, 138, 156, 161

Pang, Laikwan 168–9
Peng, Yang 148
People's Commune Movement 84
Piccioni, Monica 107
pluralism 2, 13, 159
Pollack, Barbara 105
Porter, Michael 3, 37–8, 48
Potts, Jason 48–9
propaganda 16, 25, 31, 35, 61, 81, 103, 140–1, 150, 154, 161, 175, 179, 182
Puett, Michael 167

Qipanshan District (Shenyang) 67
Qingdao 22, 33, 53
Qingdao Creative 100 33, 52–3
Qiu, Dailun 57, 68–70
Qufu 67

Ray, Mary-Ann 112
real estate 1, 2, 16, 32–3, 35, 40, 52, 56, 58, 65–8, 73, 76–7, 81–2, 89, 92, 97, 111, 116, 119, 122, 127, 133, 135, 154
renaissance 11, 41, 43, 47, 98
recombination 13, 34, 48, 159, 166–8
regional innovation systems 3
risk, risk-taking 2, 6, 31–2, 34, 60, 64, 104, 119, 135, 138, 142, 146, 163, 176–8, 180
Rokkaku, Kijyo 74

Sanlitun 67, 81
science and technology parks 50, 54
Scott, Allan 138
Sennett, Richard 47, 99
Schumpeter, Joseph 41, 173
Shanghai Academy of Social Sciences 22, 28
Shanghai Creative Industry Centre 55, 121
Shanghai Textile Group, Shangtex 12, 118, 127–8
shanzhai 32–3, 114, 134
sharism 129, 133
Shenkar, Oled 170
Shenzhen 7, 22, 44, 53, 56, 58, 65, 67, 80, 95, 98, 113–14, 142, 156, 176
shiye 25–6, 31, 34, 88, 140, 144, 182
Shu, Yang 107
Silicon Valley 38, 41, 42, 56, 123, 160, 170
Smith, Karen 103–4
soft infrastructure 39, 68, 133
soft power 2, 15, 16–18, 22, 35, 62, 141, 143, 147, 151, 171, 173, 178
Soho 5, 53, 75, 109, 160
Song, Bo 132–3
Songzhuang 7, 11, 52, 55–6, 59, 80–1, 96, 98, 107–15, 148, 176
spillover effects 60
sticky knowledge 45
Storper, Michael 48
structured uncertainty 145–6, 174–5
Su, Tong 88, 91
Sunley, Martin 37
Suzhou 31, 53, 56, 152, 154–6
Suzhou National Animation base 139, 156–7

tacit knowledge 47, 58
Taiwan 19, 31, 53, 72, 74, 79, 89, 140, 145, 156

Tatsuno, Sheridan 169–70
telecommunications 82, 108
Throsby, David 43–4
Tiananmen Square 9, 81, 83, 86
Tianjin 54, 56, 85, 119, 150
Tianzifang 12, 52, 118, 123–5
theme parks 3, 30, 38, 55, 60, 97, 113
Tiyong 24–5, 29
tourism 6, 16, 29, 53, 67, 71–2, 74, 76, 82, 85–7, 91, 97, 108, 113, 117, 121, 165, 177, 181–2
Tsai, Chih-Chung 74
TVE (Town and Village Enterprise) 4–5, 50
TV serials (drama) 16, 19, 26, 54, 157, 176

Ulfstjerne, Michael 105, 115
Ullens Centre for Contemporary Art 106
uncertainty 33, 40, 145–6, 175–6
urban regimes 51
urban regeneration 8, 47, 122, 174

Van Oech, Roger 170
Voci, Paola 177

Wang, Jici 54, 160
Wang, Jing 30
Wang, Jun 82–3
Wang, Shuo 81, 103
Wang, Yingyao 81
Wang, Yongzhang 28, 34
West Kowloon Cultural District 27
White Horse Lake Creative Eco-City 74–5
Williams, Raymond 6, 164–5
Wong, Isabel 119–20
World Trade Organisation 5, 10, 15, 23, 32, 141–2
Wu, Meisen 123
Wu, Si 175
Wu, Zhenhuan 108
Wushipu Oil Painting Village 67

Xiaobao 110–11
Xi'an Qujiang New District 64, 66–7
Xixi Wetlands Cultural Creative Industries Park 73, 76
Xindanwei (New Work Unit) 12, 118, 129–34
Xinghai Creative Island 53
Xintiandi 72, 122, 127

Yang, Lan 74
Ye, Lang 23
Yu, Dan 176
Yuanmingyuan 103, 105, 109, 112
Yúdice, George 20

Zeng, Guofan 24
Zhang, Hongxing 114
Zhang, Xiaoming 25, 27, 50, 64–6

Zhang Yimou 15, 76, 177
Zhejiang Village 80
Zheng, Jane 2, 10, 119, 121
Zhongguancun 38, 52, 54–6, 89, 91, 96, 104
Zhou, Yu 55
Zhou, Rong 83
Zhu, Deyong 74